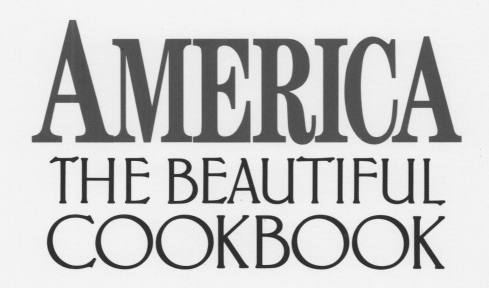

AMERICA
THE BEAUTIFUL
COOKBOOK

AUTHENTIC RECIPES FROM ACROSS AMERICA

NEW YORK CHEESECAKE (recipe page 212)

AUTHENTIC RECIPES FROM ACROSS AMERICA

AMERICA
THE BEAUTIFUL
COOKBOOK

TEXT AND RECIPES
PHILLIP STEPHEN SCHULZ

FOOD PHOTOGRAPHY
ALLAN ROSENBERG

ASSOCIATE FOOD PHOTOGRAPHER: ALLEN V. LOTT
FOOD STYLIST: SUE WHITE
ASSOCIATE FOOD STYLIST: HEIDI GINTNER
PROP STYLIST: AMY GLENN

STONEHENGE

Created and produced by Weldon Owen Pty Limited
43 Victoria Street, McMahons Point,
Sydney, NSW 2060, Australia
Telex AA23038 Fax (02) 929 8352
A member of the Weldon International
    Group of Companies
Sydney • San Francisco • Paris • London

Weldon Owen
President: John Owen
General Manager: Stuart Laurence
Co-Editions Director: Derek Barton
Managing Editor: Jane Fraser
Editor: Virginia Croft
Editorial Assistant: Ruth Jacobson
Production: Mick Bagnato
Design and Art Direction: John Bull,
    The Book Design Company
Map: Mike Gorman
Illustrations: Yolande Bull

Typeset by Letter Perfect, Sydney, Australia
Production by Mandarin Offset, Hong Kong
Printed in Hong Kong

ISBN 0-86706-612-1

This series is published in association with
STONEHENGE PRESS, Alexandria, Va.

President: Mary N. Davis
Publisher: Robert H. Smith
Associate Publisher: Trevor Lunn
Marketing Director: Regina Hall
Editorial Director: Donia Ann Steele

Stonehenge Press is a division of Time-Life Inc. For
more information on and a full description of any of
the Time-Life series, please call 1-800-621-7026 or write:
Reader Information
Time-Life Customer Service
P.O. Box C-32068
Richmond, Virginia 23261-2068

A Weldon Owen ◆ Production

PAGES 2-3: ABOUT A CENTURY AGO, MORE THAN HALF OF THE LAND IN NEW ENGLAND WAS CLEARED OF VEGETATION. TODAY MOST OF THE REGION HAS BEEN REFORESTED, AND RURAL NEW ENGLAND IS AS TYPICALLY PICTURESQUE AS THIS EARLY AUTUMN SCENE IN VERMONT.
BRUCE HANDS

RIGHT: FARM WORKERS PICKING AND PACKING BEANS IN A FIELD NEAR HOMESTEAD, SOUTHERN FLORIDA.

PAGES 8-9: NEW ENGLAND CLAMBAKE (recipe page 74)

PAGES 12-13: LAS VEGAS, NEVADA, WHERE NEON SIGNS ADVERTISE THE BEST SHOWS AND FOOD IN TOWN.
EDDIE HIRONAKA/THE IMAGE BANK

ENDPAPERS: OLD GRATING UTENSILS FOR SALE IN A PENNSYLVANIA JUNK SHOP.
CATHERINE KARNOW

BRUCE HANDS

GREEN BEAN PICKLES (right, recipe page 198), DILL PICKLES (left, recipe page 197) AND SWEET ZUCCHINI CAPS (center, recipe page 198)

CONTENTS

NEAR INTERCOURSE, PENNSYLVANIA, AN AMISH BOY CLEARS A FIELD USING A HORSE-DRAWN PLOW, THE SAME METHOD OF FARMING HIS FOREFATHERS USED IN THE EIGHTEENTH CENTURY.

INTRODUCTION

The simple phrase "America, the Beautiful" conjures up images of the rich and varied landscapes for which our country is renowned—rustic fishing villages hugging the New England coastline, historic colonial hamlets nestled throughout the Northeast, the shimmering inlets and waterways of the Chesapeake Bay, magnificent columned plantations sprawling under live oaks in the South, verdant dairy farms dotting the rolling hills of Wisconsin, rustling cornfields covering the gentle slopes of Iowa, long stretches of waving grain on the sky-filled Great Plains, the restored mining towns of the dramatic Rockies, the pueblos and missions of the stark Southwest, the rain forests of the Northwest and the geographical incongruities of California. And there is beauty in our cities as well—from historic New York, Philadelphia and Boston to architecturally rich Washington, Savannah, New Orleans and San Francisco.

More than any physical attribute, however, what gives this country its unique character is the people who have come here from all parts of the world. It has been said that the very strength of America lies in its diverse ethnic population, a population that, from the earliest Spanish, English, Dutch and French explorers through the African slaves and the German, Scotch-Irish, Swedish, Norwegian, Danish, Mexican and recent Asian immigrants, has left a mark on what we call American cuisine. Each group brought its own ethnic repertoire to the New World, but as recipes changed to accommodate indigenous American ingredients and were adapted to suit the general public taste, the original dishes became barely distinguishable. For this reason America has a cooking style difficult to define. Unlike classic French or Chinese cuisine, for example, American cookery is simple and free-form. Food scholars are hard put to present a recipe for a given dish as the *only* authentic rendering. Apple pie, for example, while English in origin, was first made in a shallow dish by the colonists. Native regional ingredients played just as important a role as ethnic background in the development of recipes. Vermonters sweetened their apple pies with maple syrup; the Pennsylvania Dutch added raisins; and Midwesterners threw in nuts, which flourished in their area.

Any discussion of the roots of our culinary heritage must begin with the peoples who were the original inhabitants, the American Indians. As history has shown, the early colonists were far from self-sufficient and would not have survived without the Indians' help and their knowledge of local ingredients. When the first settlers arrived, the Indians were already stirring up fish stews, corn chowders and pumpkin soups; baking beans and succotash; smoking salmon and other fish; steaming clams on hot rocks buried with seaweed; barbecuing fish and game over open fires; turning corn into meal for breads and cakes, and hominy into grits for porridge; using nut oils and sweetening dishes of all kinds with honey and maple syrup. They had also discovered one of today's favorite snack foods—popcorn. The Indians of the East, Midwest and Southwest were agricultural. On the plains and farther west, they tended to be hunters and gatherers. They lived, for the most part, in well-established societies.

It was an amazingly lush country with fewer than one million native inhabitants that awaited the first explorers. Leif Eriksson may have been the first to see the North American continent around A.D. 1000, but he made no attempt to colonize the land. It was not until Columbus discovered the West Indies, almost five hundred years

CABBAGES GROW IN THE FERTILE PLAINS OF THE SKAGIT VALLEY, AT THE FOOT OF MOUNT BAKER IN WASHINGTON.

later, that the quest for the New World began. Columbus, of course, was searching for a westerly route to the Orient. Little did he know the vastness of the lands he stumbled upon or the lasting effects his discoveries, and those of explorers who followed, would have on the world's foodways.

While much credit is given to the English for settling colonial America, it was the Spanish who first explored the southern section of this land from coast to coast, leaving behind a lasting influence on our cuisine from Florida to California. Juan Ponce de León discovered "La Florida" in 1513, and Hernando de Soto landed at the present site of Tampa Bay in 1539, exploring much of the South east of the Mississippi River. Spanish settlers soon followed, establishing St. Augustine on the Florida coast by 1565. (The British did not settle Jamestown until 1607.) St. Augustine, however, was not a proper settlement but more of a fortress used to keep the French from gaining a foothold in the region. As the Spanish pushed westward, they traded their provisions of pork, cattle, vegetables and fruits to the Indians in exchange for corn, beans and squash. The Creeks and Seminoles of the South were especially quick to take to these new foods. It has been reported that by the time William Penn explored Pennsylvania, peaches, originally brought to the South by the Spanish, were already in full bloom.

Francisco Vásquez de Coronado, searching for the Seven Cities of Cibola, supposedly rich in gold and other treasures, explored much of the Southwest from Mexico to the Great Plains. Missionaries and settlers moved into the region, which includes Texas, New Mexico, southern Colorado and Arizona, and established Santa Fe in 1610, three years after Jamestown. A century later California fell under Spanish influence. In the end, however, Spanish efforts were scattered, mainly because Spain was more

A CHEERFUL AND TRUSTING KANSAS FARMER CHECKS ON THE SALES OF HIS WATERMELONS AND PUMPKINS.

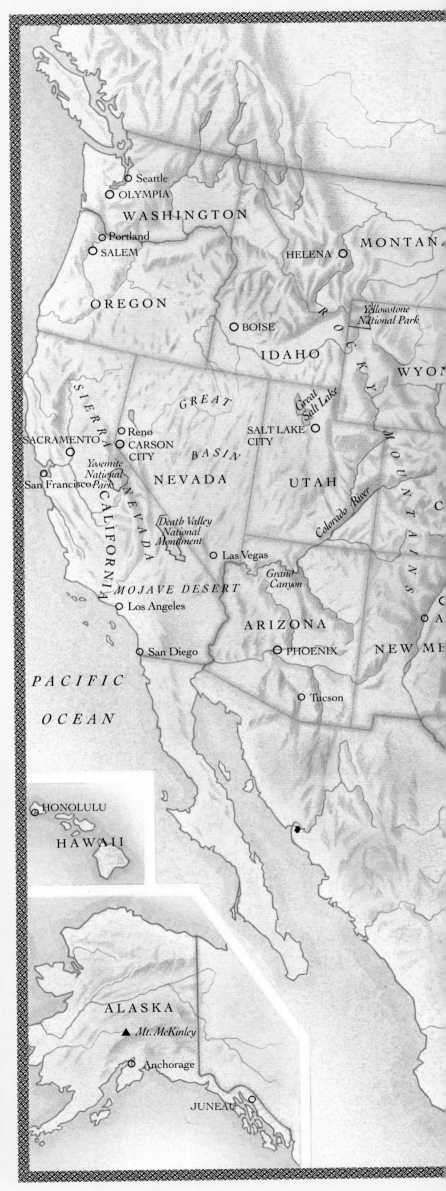

16

OVER THREE HUNDRED VARIETIES OF FISH ABOUND IN THE
CLEAR TROPICAL WATERS OFF THE FLORIDA KEYS.

involved farther south, where the lands were indeed rich and the natives more docile. There remains, however, an everlasting Spanish influence on America. Spanish names abound from Florida throughout the West. And the Spanish, being diligent missionaries, not only brought their Christian beliefs with them but more importantly, at least from a culinary point of view, introduced citrus fruits, figs, olives, sugar, cotton, cattle, sheep, horses, hogs and mules.

Nevertheless, it was the English, even though their early exploratory efforts were minor in comparison with those of the Spanish, who had the most influence on our cuisine. After all, the original colonies that became the United States of America were founded by England and were quickly populated by Englishmen seeking not only religious and political freedoms but also economic freedom from dreary working conditions and low wages. Even today, with the exception of some southwestern states, Americans of all or partial English ancestry dominate nearly every continental state (although German descendants are not far behind).

When the English landed to establish Jamestown, they were not totally unfamiliar with the Indians. The Cabots had set sail for what is now Newfoundland in 1496 and discovered the great cod-fishing banks off that coast. The English had also touched the shores of New England in the 1500s and, like Columbus, brought a few natives back to England for others to marvel at. In the 1600s Sir Walter Raleigh tried, and failed three times, to colonize Roanoke Island off the coast of North Carolina. It is generally believed that the Carolina Croatans massacred the entire colony, although no one is certain because the Croatans were considered "friendly Indians." What happened to those earliest settlers remains a mystery to this day. The Powhatans that the Jamestown settlers met upon their arrival in 1607 were indeed friendly, but amazingly the first arrivals came totally unprepared for the world they encountered. Worse yet, they were an argumentative bunch and reluctant to work, even if they had been equipped with the tools to do the work. Times were tough, but Jamestown survived. Barely. For one thing, the town was established in the low-lying swamplands of the James River. Besides not having enough to eat, the settlers were plagued with diseases. The situation became so extreme that in the terrible winter of 1609 – 10, four out of five died. Even so, none would have made it without Indian assistance.

The Indians taught them how to grow corn, beans and squash and how to catch fish, which ran in such massive schools that Captain John Smith, on an exploration of Chesapeake Bay, wrote that the fish were "lying so thicke with their heads above water" that he tried to catch them with a frying pan. With no success, it might be noted. The women brought traditional English recipes with them and eventually adapted them to the ingredients at hand. During those early years, however, many courageous young Jamestown women actually camped among Indian squaws to observe their cooking rituals firsthand. They learned how to pound corn into meal for use in breads and porridge, how to make hominy out of ashes and water, and how to make stews of game, corn and beans. They were taught how to grub for edible roots, including the sweet potato, and were totally astounded at the Indian method of eating "green" (fresh) corn. Chomping back and forth on the corn cobs may have appeared somewhat "savage" to the colonists, but to this day there is no better way to eat this remarkable vegetable. Wild fruits, berries and grapes were eventually transplanted to garden plots, and in time gardens bloomed. Tobacco, native to Virginia, became a major cultivated crop early on, and by the 1630s Virginians were housed and prospering. The colonists planted artichokes, asparagus, beets, broccoli, cauliflower, cress, cucumbers, mustard and other greens, and imported livestock and poultry to round out their diet of game and wild fowl.

Farther north the Pilgrims had an equally hard time. Fewer than half of the original 102 passengers of the *Mayflower* survived the first winter. And not because of hostile Indians. In fact, they met no Indians when they landed, the local tribes having been wiped out by smallpox. Although the land was rich with game, edible plants, fish and seafood, these settlers also were unprepared for a life of hunting and fishing. Landing in a cold climate just before winter did nothing to improve their chances for survival. (Actually, they had planned to land farther south.) As bad as the winter seemed to them, however, records show that it was comparatively mild that year for the area.

The Pilgrims were totally the opposite of the Jamestown settlers. As soon as they landed on Cape Cod, they formulated a system of government and decided on Plymouth as a good place to begin life in the New World. They worked hard together for the common good, but during that first winter, responsibility fell to the few in good health to take care of the many who fell ill. As had happened in Jamestown, Indians stepped in to save the day—that is, one Indian named Squanto. By circumstance Squanto had been among those natives taken to England and consequently spoke the English language. He had escaped on a journey back, only to find most of his tribe devastated by disease. Although he took up with another tribe and should have resented the English, he stayed with the Pilgrims. Not only did he prove indispensable for communication between Indians and Pilgrims, but he taught the settlers how to sow corn using fish heads as fertilizer and how to plant beans that grew up the cornstalks. He also helped them build weirs and traps of

ERIK LEIGH SIMMONS/THE IMAGE BANK

THE PURPLE HUES OF SUNSET ON THE SNOWCLAD ROOFTOPS OF PORTSMOUTH, NEW HAMPSHIRE,
CREATE A FAIRY-TALE IMAGE TYPICAL OF MANY NEW ENGLAND COASTAL TOWNS.

vines to catch fish. Little by little the colonists became adept at farming, hunting and fishing.

America's heritage is not just an English one. Almost every nation on earth has touched our culture, and one that made a major contribution was the Netherlands. The Dutch who came to North America in the early 1600s were merchants, traders and seamen drawn by the rich fur trade. They were soon followed by wealthy landowners who brought farm laborers, equipment and livestock with them. They quickly settled the fertile Hudson River valley and surrounding area. By 1624 the Dutch had established New Netherlands, with New Amsterdam (Manhattan) as the capital. In the 1800s mass immigration to the United States was sparked by religious conflicts, a potato blight and low income. Many Dutch people settled in rural areas of Michigan, Illinois, Wisconsin and Iowa and in urban New Jersey and New York. They also headed west to Washington, Oregon and California.

Africans also contributed enormously to the development of American culture. The first Africans actually arrived in Virginia in 1619 via a pirated Portuguese ship, one year before the *Mayflower* landed. Like countless Europeans at the time, all twenty of them were sold as indentured servants, and when they worked off their six- or seven-year hitch, they became free men. The majority of Africans, however, were captured up and down the coast of their homelands and sold into slavery. Most of the slaves did not come directly to America but were shipped first to the West Indies for three months of "training" time. Slaves had no rights; legally they were not even considered human. Eventually the question of slavery led to political battles over the admission of new states to the Union and finally to the secession of the southern states from the Union when Abraham Lincoln abolished slavery.

The first permanent French settlements were established along the banks of the St. Lawrence River, in Acadia (now Nova Scotia), and in parts of Maine and Canada, including Quebec. In the late 1600s the great French explorer La Salle set off to descend the Mississippi River and claimed for France the Louisiana Territory,

which included much of the central region of what became the United States. The French settlers were Huguenots, or Protestants, who were persecuted at home. The largely Protestant Dutch settlements also attracted the Huguenots, and many settled in the other colonies as well. In 1755 the British took control of French settlements in Canada and deported all who refused loyalty to the crown. A mass emigration to Louisiana followed. A mispronunciation of *Acadians* led to their being called Cajuns, as their descendants are still known today. Other French people settled parts of Alabama. Many emigrated during the French Revolution, and thousands more came to seek gold in California.

The majority of the first German settlers also fled their country because of religious persecution. Many who left Germany lived in Holland before they made the crossing to America. In colonial times most settled in Pennsylvania and became known as the Pennsylvania Dutch, a misinterpretation. More Germans fled Europe in the nineteenth century as Bismarck came to power. In the 1830s they settled in large numbers in Missouri and southern Illinois. In the 1840s they headed to Texas, and in the 1850s to Wisconsin. Michigan, Missouri and Iowa also had large German communities. These nineteenth-century immigrants, with their brewing and butchering skills, played a significant role in the growth of the Midwest.

The Scandinavian countries are also well represented in the American medley. Although the Swedes had settled Delaware in colonial times and, incidentally, brought the "log cabin" with them, the Dutch quickly ousted them, thus ending any attempts by Sweden to colonize America. The first major large-scale immigration occurred in the 1840s. At that time Sweden was enduring economic hardships, and most farmers had been forced to become sharecroppers for wealthy landlords. A propaganda blitz by American companies seeking laborers sent lecturers to Sweden to recruit settlers. One of the biggest motives for Swedish immigration, however, was the Homestead Act of 1862, which awarded 160 acres of American land to anyone who would farm it for five

NEW ENGLANDERS MARVEL AT THEIR FOUR DISTINCT SEASONS. SPRING IS WARM AND SCENTED, SUMMERS ARE HOT AND HUMID, FALL IS CRISP, CLEAR AND COLORFUL, AND WINTERS ARE COLD AND SNOWY WITH OCCASIONAL BLIZZARDS.

years. The move was on, and Chicago, rather than New York, became the center for Swedish immigrants. The first settlers headed for Illinois, Wisconsin and Iowa. As more and more Swedes arrived, they pushed west into Minnesota, Nebraska, Kansas and the Dakotas. They also settled in large numbers in Washington on the Puget Sound. After the nineteenth century many moved to the urban areas of the Northeast.

Leif Eriksson or not, the first large group of permanent Norwegian settlers also arrived in the nineteenth century, settling in the rural areas of Illinois, Wisconsin, Iowa, Minnesota and the Dakotas. Later immigrants traveled to the West Coast. A few had accompanied the Dutch colonists in the seventeenth century and lived in New Amsterdam when it was founded. It was a Dane named Jonas Bronck who bought and settled the neighboring piece of land, now the Bronx. But the vast majority arrived later, in the nineteenth century, and settled in the Midwest and Nebraska. Also in the late 1800s and early 1900s, a wave of Finnish immigrants traveled to the upper Midwest and Northeast looking to escape economic gloom in Finland. Gold fever attracted many to California and Alaska as well.

The first Irish arrived before 1800 and settled in the South, then pushed westward into the Appalachians with Daniel Boone. After 1830, and particularly when the potato blight hit Ireland in 1845, Irish immigration reached almost one hundred thousand a year. Most settled in the Northeast and the Chicago area and became powerful participants in local politics. The Scots who came to the British colonies settled in the rural areas of North Carolina, New York and Georgia. Economic factors drove many Scots to immigrate in the late 1800s and early 1900s. Most settled along the Atlantic seaboard in urban areas; the rest went to the Midwest. These settlers are often called Scotch-Irish, as Scotland and Northern Ireland made up a distinctly separate constituency of Great Britain.

Although a scattering of Portuguese settled in colonial Pennsylvania, Georgia and South Carolina, most of them came to work on whaling vessels in the nineteenth century and settled in Massachusetts, Rhode Island, California and Hawaii. The Italians settled mainly in New York and a few other major cities. Most of these immigrants were poor and, upon arriving in the 1800s, did not find conditions much better in the States than at home. Hardship united the families into close-knit communities. There was much prejudice against Italian Americans, who were associated in popular misconception with Mafia crime.

Prior to 1890 most immigrants came from northern and western Europe. After that date the majority came from southern and eastern Europe, Latin America, the Middle East and Asia. Hungarians, Yugoslavs, Poles, Russians, Latvians, Romanians, Ukrainians, Lithuanians, Armenians —all are here and in goodly numbers. More than a third of all Puerto Ricans live in the States. Being American citizens since 1917, they are free to move north, and many have left the island because of overcrowding and economic hardship. Cubans, Haitians and Central Americans have mostly migrated as political refugees and settled in Florida and the Southwest. Mexicans continue to come in droves, most illegally, and settle in the Southwest. Many immigrants from the Middle East were Christian Arabs who arrived in the 1900s.

The Chinese came over in the mid-1800s to look for gold and to work for the railroads. The stories of their abuse are well chronicled. The Chinese were instrumental in building the West Coast's fishing, garment, shoe and cigar industries. The Japanese, many of whom first settled in Hawaii until immigration was halted by the government, did not fare much better at first. Organized labor was against cheap labor, including both Chinese and Japanese. California barred the first immigrants from owning land, so most Japanese registered their land in their children's names because those who were born here were automatically citizens. The Japanese, employing farming techniques learned in Japan, had a large effect on California agriculture. Their detention during World War II is something most Americans would rather forget. It took until 1976 for the U.S. government to issue an official apology, and reimbursement for confiscated properties is a long way from being a reality. Some Japanese—Americans have chosen to return to the land and are among the leading suppliers of top-quality produce to the markets. Most, however, have chosen to live in urban areas.

Koreans, Thais, Vietnamese and the many other more recent immigrants have all brought their cuisines with them, opening restaurants featuring their specialties in almost every American city. And due to the increase of interest in this style of cooking, Asian specialty stores are opening everywhere. In addition, Asians, particularly Koreans, have opened small vegetable markets all over.

American cuisine has grown up regionally. New England specialties such as pumpkin soup, baked beans, succotash and the clam bake evolved directly from native Indian dishes. Others, like codfish balls, clam and fish chowders, lobster dinners and steamed clams, evolved from a closeness to the sea. Still others—Yankee pot roast and New England boiled dinner, for instance—grew out of the necessity for hearty, soul-satisfying foods needed to fortify the body against long, cold winters. In the Middle Atlantic states, the Dutch influence was felt early on. Dutch specialties such as pancakes, waffles and cookies were accepted into the colonists' daily fare almost immediately. The Germans brought *Sauerbraten*, potato salad, *Schnitz und Knepp* and funeral pie. English recipes were adapted for use with the blue crabs and turtles that the Chesapeake area became renowned for. Southern cookery was first influenced by the Indians, whose techniques with cornmeal and grits were adapted by the English settlers. Africans played a major role in the cooking of the South too. They used okra in soups and gumbos, and black-eyed peas (cowpeas) in hopping John.

They were expert at making beaten biscuits and developed the South's love of spices. The Spanish first cooked fish with the oranges they introduced into Florida, and much of their influence is still evident in the Caribbean cooking of that state. Both Spanish and French techniques are combined in the Creole cooking of New Orleans. Cajun specialties like peppery jambalayas, crawfish pies and gumbos have roots in French cuisine but have evolved into a totally different style of cooking.

The Midwest, Great Plains and mountain states truly make up the melting pot of this country. New England, Middle Atlantic and southern cooking styles were transplanted as the population moved west, with Scandinavian touches added along the way. Recipes like meatballs, chicken-fried steak, wild rice pilaf, chow-chow, the hamburger and hot dog, not to mention Sloppy Joes and macaroni and cheese, came into being on their own. The Southwest, land of hominy, tortillas, frijoles, barbecue and chuckwagon beans, has its culinary roots in early Spanish and "cowboy" cooking. The Pacific Coast is known for the freshness of its ingredients and a multitude of fish dishes like baked salmon, cioppino and sautéed abalone steaks.

If Americans seem impatient and hurried (running from fad to fad) in comparison with the rest of the world, it is, good or bad, inherent in our makeup. After all, this country was settled by people who were always looking for greener pastures. That outlook was the force behind the Revolution and the force of expansionism that drove the pioneers farther and farther west. It was also the force that took us from the swamps of Jamestown to the valleys of the moon in only 362 years. So it is with food. We are always on the lookout for something better in our lives, and at the moment things are looking up for American cuisine.

Most Americans *do* appreciate good food, even if in this time of two-income households we do not always have time to prepare it ourselves on a daily basis. When we do cook, we cook well. When we do not, we have superb restaurants to feed us, fostered recently by a new pride in regional American specialties. More importantly, talented young chefs, often accorded "superstar" status these days, are demanding top-quality ingredients for their kitchens. Consequently, small farmers, livestock producers, game ranchers, herb growers, wild plant specialists and cheese makers have all been given new life. Furthermore, with all the attention and publicity surrounding chefs and their restaurants, the desire for "the best" has crossed over to the public at large. Gourmet grocers thrive in virtually every major town, and inner-city green markets, set up so that local farmers can sell their wares directly to the people, are becoming commonplace.

To be sure, there are those who poke fun at the United States for such dubious innovations as McDonald's, Kentucky Fried Chicken, Taco Bell and other fast food emporiums, as well as giant supermarkets filled with frozen foods, but convenience foods evolved out of an astonishingly vast supply of resources mixed with a rather large dose of American ingenuity. Fast food is relatively inexpensive, thanks to mass preparation, and mass preparation depends on a network of quick transport—via rail, highway or air—that was only realized through the efforts of such men as G. H. Hammond, who developed the refrigerator rail car, Clarence Birdseye, who revolutionized the food industry with deep-freezing techniques, and Luther Burbank, whose research led to new uses for agricultural products. They made of American resources a cuisine as remarkable in its abundance as it is in its varied cultural roots.

OREGON'S COAST OFFERS SOME OF THE FINEST SCENERY ON THE WESTERN SEABOARD. THE RUGGED COASTLINE IS BROKEN BY BEACHES AND HISTORIC FISHING VILLAGES THAT LINE THE MOUTHS OF RIVERS FEEDING INTO THE PACIFIC.

JOE WILKINS III

NEW ENGLAND

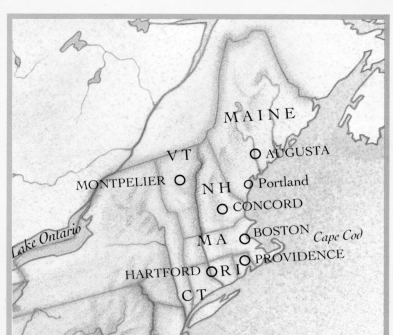

MAINE

VT   AUGUSTA

MONTPELIER   NH   Portland

CONCORD

Lake Ontario   MA   BOSTON   Cape Cod

PROVIDENCE

HARTFORD   R I

CT

NEW ENGLAND

Long before the Pilgrims landed at Cape Cod, the Indian tribes of the Algonquian family in the Northeast were living very well off elk, moose, deer, bear, wild turkey, ducks, geese, partridges, passenger pigeons and quail, among other game. The rivers, lakes and seacoast afforded them a wide variety of fish and shellfish. Wild plants like beach plums, cranberries, crab apples, grapes, berries, wild onions and leeks, lily bulbs, Jerusalem artichokes (sunflower roots), herbs and sunflower seeds were put to good use. These tribes also cultivated what is known as the "Indian triad" or the "three sisters" in Indian lore: corn, beans and squash.

The Indians planted corn and beans in small hillocks fertilized with fish heads. The stalks of corn, growing in rows, became bean poles for the climbing legumes. The corn was ground into cornmeal and used in such everyday foods as samp, a cornmeal porridge. In addition to pumpkin, which was grown virtually throughout the land, the Northeast Indians grew several varieties of yellow summer squash, crookneck and acorn squash. Usually they cooked squash in embers until soft and then seasoned it with bear grease. Pine sap, nut oils, bear grease and fish oils provided extra flavor, and maple syrup and sugar sweetened the pot. The Indians also dried foods and stored them in underground burrows lined with birch tree bark for use in the winter months. The Algonquians, which included the Algonquin, Narragansett, Mohegan and Penobscot tribes, lived in small villages. Farming the rocky, heavily forested land of the New England states was not an easy task with the tools they had at hand. So once a village grew beyond its normal food supply, families moved on to start new communities.

About ten years after the Pilgrims established Plymouth in 1620, a trading company was organized to settle the bay area around present-day Boston. Thousands of other Puritans soon flocked to the fledgling colony. Oddly

A QUINTESSENTIAL NEW ENGLAND COUNTRY STORE IN RIPTON, VERMONT, SELLS SUCH RURAL DELIGHTS AS GENUINE VERMONT SHARP CHEDDAR CHEESE AND MAPLE SYRUP.

PREVIOUS PAGES: THE CHARMS OF VERMONT—LEAFY BACK ROADS, GREEN PASTURES AND THE RURAL TRANQUILITY OF DAIRY FARMS.

LOBSTER BOATS IN ROCKPORT HARBOR, MASSACHUSETTS, SIGNIFY A BUSY INDUSTRY. OTHER HARBORS ON THE NEW ENGLAND COAST HAVE SUCCUMBED TO THE DECLINE IN THE FISHING TRADE.

enough, although the majority of the colonists had left England because of the political oppression of the established church, the Puritans practiced their own oppression by forming a state church with political freedom dependent on membership. This did not sit well with a lot of folks, and the disgruntled left Massachussetts and settled Connecticut, Rhode Island, New Hampshire and Maine, although Maine was to remain under Massachussetts rule for some time to come. Neither Maine nor Vermont were granted "legal" status and thus were not part of the original thirteen colonies. Vermont joined the Union in 1791; Maine, not until 1820.

The New England climate was not a friendly one, and agriculture came slowly. Since the soil and weather were not suited to a cash crop like tobacco, small farms sprang up around the towns and hamlets, but most were family affairs rather than commercial enterprises. The colonists learned their lessons well from the Indians and adapted native corn, squash, bean, fish and game recipes to their own tastes. The kitchen became the center of New England colonial life; virtually every activity took place around the centrally located fireplace. Whereas in the South the kitchen was removed from the living quarters because of the hot summer weather, in the Northeast the kitchen was the "common room." Women became adept at cooking all manner of foods over hot embers. The first "chimneys" were large enough to walk into and used an extravagant amount of fuel. As time went by, they were reduced in size. Long-legged cast-iron skillets were placed over the coals and served as a cooking griddle. Black iron pots were hung on stout pot chains over the fire for boiled dishes. Dutch ovens, boxlike kettles with a lid, stood on legs over the coals, with more coals heaped on top. They were used mainly for baking. Eventually baking ovens were built directly into the brick or stone chimneys. This style of cooking was not to change until the mid-nineteenth century, when the first stove was introduced. Even so, it was almost the turn of the next century before the stove became a common household item.

Surprisingly, the stodgy Puritans started off every day with ale or beer. They had brought barley seeds with them for just that purpose. By law, however, they were not allowed to drink more than *five quarts* a day. When apples took hold, apple cider became the popular drink, which, from all accounts, was most likely "hard," or alcoholic, cider. In Rhode Island rum was distilled from molasses imported from the West Indies. Although consumed with gusto, rum was not considered suitable for everyday "family" drinking. But homemade fruit cordials, spruce beer, elderberry wine and even dandelion wine were allowed at table, and New Englanders had a reputation for being able to put more than a few glassfuls away.

Many New England foods were cooked by boiling for hours on end. In fact, one of the most famous American dishes is the New England boiled dinner of corned beef and vegetables, but boiled fish dinners were also common. Since the New England housewife was responsible for far more than just cooking and did not have the luxury of slave help as in the South, boiling or stewing foods freed her to do other things. Pounding dried corn into meal, for example, was an almost endless chore. There is a story that illustrates the plight of pioneer women in the New England wilds, whose husbands would be gone for days at a time, hunting for game. As they pounded their meal for samp, the women worked out a code to communicate with one another from one valley to the next. In this way, when a baby was on the way, the message could be sent out and help summoned. Life, in fact, was very difficult in those early years and much depended on women. When Jean de Crèvecoeur, the noted French agriculturist and author, spent time in the colonies in the late eighteenth century, he noted: "What a useful requisition a good wife is to an American farmer. How small his chances of prosperity if he draws a blank in that lottery." Many a midwestern farmer would agree with that somewhat underhanded compliment to this day.

The clambake, clam chowder, baked beans, succotash, red flannel hash, codfish balls, boiled dinners, brown bread, Indian pudding and pumpkin pie—all became

ONE OF THE SMALL CITIES SURROUNDING BOSTON, SOMERVILLE WAS ONCE FARMLAND AND A SUMMER RETREAT FOR WEALTHY BOSTONIANS IN THE SEVENTEENTH AND EIGHTEENTH CENTURIES.

THE MORNING SUN'S RAYS SHINE ON A SIMPLE WOOD-FRAME HOUSE ON LAKE EDEN, VERMONT, AFTER THE FIRST SNOWFALL OF THE SEASON.

widely known as New England specialties. These recipes reflect both the Indian culture and the English background of the settlers. The colonists originally learned to cook beans the Indian way—baked in a hole in the ground that was lined with hot rocks. As time progressed, the beans were moved indoors and cooked in large iron pots hung over hot coals. Baked beans with brown bread became the colonial Saturday night supper and is still popular today. The tradition has Puritanical origins. The Puritans were not allowed to do unnecessary labor on the Sabbath, which began at sundown on Saturday and ended at sundown Sunday. Some wives cooked their beans for Saturday night supper and served them reheated not only for Sunday supper but for Sunday breakfast as well. Other not-so-bean-crazy women started their beans on Saturday and left them to cook over low embers until they were perfect for Sunday supper. In any case, Boston became "bean town" and the name stuck.

Just what went into the first American pot of beans has long been debated. Some food pundits claim that Indian cooks used maple syrup and chunks of juicy bear fat to flavor their beans. Others say there was no sweetening at all, that it was the English, with their penchant for sweet meat and vegetable dishes, who first sweetened baked beans. Molasses did become an integral part of Boston baked beans, but it was not until the middle of the nineteenth century that the addition of molasses appeared in printed recipes. Molasses, of course, was much cheaper and easier to come by than sugar in those days. In the

northernmost regions of New England, maple syrup was used extensively. Baked bean suppers traditionally ended with Indian pudding, which was the colonists' version of British steamed pudding but made with cornmeal, the only readily available grain in early America.

Fish have always played an important role in the survival and well-being of New England. As the colonies grew, huge fishing fleets were assembled in the major ports. Daily fishing trips yielded cod, haddock, halibut and mackerel. Whaling became a large part of the fishing industry as well, prompting an influx of Portuguese fishermen. The cod fishing was so good that the colonists were trading dried salt cod with the southern colonies and the West Indies by 1650. They also had a booming trade with Portugal and Spain in exchange for dried fruits, wines and, most importantly, salt and spices. The colonists used ginger and pepper in their cooking, as well as cloves, mace, cinnamon and allspice. Shellfish, too, were important to the region. Lobsters were often steamed in sea water and made into stews for breakfast. The slatted wooden trap, or lobster pot, that New Englanders devised remains unchanged to this day.

New Englanders were, and are, a hardy bunch. Even though this area of the country is now as cosmopolitan as any other region, it still is associated with such hearty fare as the colonial specialties mentioned above. These and later inventions like Parker House rolls, Boston cream pie, brownies, fudge and, of course, the chocolate chip cookie have entered the mainstream of American cookery and become classics in their own right.

SOUPS, CHOWDERS
AND STEWS

IN THE FRENCH QUARTER OF NEW ORLEANS, REGIONAL CREOLE SPECIALTIES SUCH AS GUMBO—A SPICY SOUP MADE WITH OKRA, HERBS AND SEAFOOD OR CHICKEN—ARE SURE TO BE ON EVERY RESTAURANT MENU.

SOUPS, CHOWDERS AND STEWS

It has been said that the soup or stew pot, more than any other food, reflects the personality of a nation.

Most American soups, though based on recipes from other lands, developed around the ingredients on hand at the time the pot was being stirred up. They were influenced as well by the practices of the American Indians who, for instance, taught the colonists how to make stews in pumpkins nestled in hot coals. When sea biscuits, the hard crackers used to thicken early chowders, were not available to the Pilgrims, they followed the Indian method of incorporating ground roots or cornmeal into their chowders. The Pilgrims, of course, were not unfamiliar with fish chowders and stews, but never did they have the inclination, or foresight, to live on the easily available clam until they followed the Indian ways. They learned to make tasty stews of beans, corn and game just as the natives did. In time, ingredients from Europe were brought over and added to the soup pot. Pork, chicken and beef eventually took the place of game, and many vegetables and grains introduced into the New World went into soups as well.

Almost every meal included soup. Farmers, in fact, started the day with a hot bowlful. And pioneers pushing west developed a homemade version of bouillon cubes that could be dried and carried with them. They simply added hot water, and the first "instant" soup was born. The mixture was, appropriately, called "pocket soup."

A chowder is a thickened soup devised of fish, seafood or vegetables. It should be slurpable but not watery, thick but not stewlike. Optimally, a chowder should have a smooth texture. The word itself is a corruption of the French name for a huge copper vessel known as a *chaudière* in which communal thick fish farragos were made. The tradition of chowders seems to have been started by the wives of French fishermen as a thanksgiving offering to God for the safe return of their husbands and sons from the sea. Each homecoming fisherman threw a share of his catch into the bubbling pot, and everyone joined in the feast. Likewise in the farm communities a portion of each man's harvest was shared to celebrate another fruitful season. This practice was common throughout Europe long before America was settled, but it must be pointed out that the American Indians were doing much the same thing.

The most famous of all such American concoctions is New England clam chowder, originally made with nothing but clams, wild onions and herbs, sea biscuits (hard crackers) and spring water. After cattle were imported, milk took the place of water in most chowders. Milk, in fact, became so plentiful that it was often remarked that "milk and ministers were the only things cheap in New England." All early American chowders used crackers as thickening, but today a chowder is most often thickened with a *beurre manié*: equal parts butter and flour mixed into a smooth paste.

DURING THE MONTH OF OCTOBER, PUMPKINS ARE BOUGHT NOT ONLY FOR MAKING RICH AUTUMN SOUPS BUT FOR CARVING OR PAINTING AS HALLOWEEN DECORATIONS.

FROM THE PENNSYLVANIA DUTCH COUNTRY COME HEARTY AND WHOLESOME DISHES SUCH AS CHICKEN "POTPIE".

A stew is based on the technique for braising but requires more liquid added to the pot. The ingredients in a stew, unlike a chowder or soup, are the focal point of the dish. Stews are generally thickened by cooking. A stew by its very nature requires long, slow cooking, with fish stews the exception today. Old recipes did stipulate that even fish be cooked for at least two hours, but now cooks depend on a strong fish stock for the stew, and fresh fish, just barely cooked, for the final flourishes. Stews are generally classified as brown or white. White stews are light in color, as the name implies, and feature veal or fish. In brown stews the meat or poultry is sautéed first, giving the broth not only color but flavor. As with braising, tougher cuts of beef, such as chuck, should be used in brown stews because the cooking is long and these meats will soften without drying out in the process.

In all soups the stock is perhaps the most important ingredient. Although canned broth may be used in long-cooking recipes, fish and vegetable dishes are best made with homemade stock. Leftover gravies, soup stocks and fish poaching liquids should always be frozen for later use. Because of the importance of basic stocks, recipes for chicken, beef and fish are included in the glossary. Stocks should be made well in advance of using, and refrigerated so that all fat can easily be removed from the surface. Although some trace of fat is not harmful to hot soups, it can be cloying to the tongue when incorporated into soups served cold.

SALMON CHOWDER

Washington

SALMON CHOWDER

From the Northwest, where salmon is indeed "king," comes the following chowder cooked with tomatoes and potatoes and enhanced with fresh dill. If the chowder is too thin, simply puree some of the cooked mixture and stir it back into the pot before adding the salmon.

2 tablespoons (1 oz/30 g) unsalted butter
1 large onion, finely chopped
1 garlic clove, minced
3 cups (24 fl oz/750 ml) fish stock (see glossary)
1 cup (8 fl oz/250 ml) chicken stock (see glossary)
1 can (14 oz/440 g) tomatoes, crushed
½ teaspoon sugar
pinch of dried thyme
1 large potato, peeled, cubed and rinsed in cold water
1 teaspoon lemon juice
salt and freshly ground pepper
10 oz (315 g) salmon steak, cut into ½-in (1-cm) pieces
3 tablespoons chopped fresh dill

❧ Melt the butter in a large heavy saucepan over medium-low heat. Add the onion; cook for 1 minute. Add the garlic; cook, covered, 5 minutes longer. Stir in the fish stock, chicken stock, tomatoes, sugar and thyme. Heat to boiling, reduce the heat and simmer, uncovered, for 5 minutes. Add the potato, lemon juice, and salt and pepper to taste. Cook, covered, until the potato is tender, about 12 minutes.
❧ Stir the salmon into the chowder and cook until the fish flakes easily, 3 to 4 minutes. Sprinkle with dill.

SERVES 4

New Hampshire

PUMPKIN SOUP

The northeastern Indians were adept at making soups of pumpkin and other squashes. After cattle were brought over from England, the colonists added dairy products to these soups to make them somewhat more sophisticated.

2 cups (1 lb/500 g) pumpkin puree*
3 tablespoons (1½ oz/50 g) unsalted butter
1 tablespoon brown sugar
¼ teaspoon ground mace
¼ teaspoon freshly grated nutmeg
⅛ teaspoon ground cloves
3 cups (24 fl oz/750 ml) hot milk
2 egg yolks (optional)

❧ Combine the pumpkin, butter, sugar, mace, nutmeg and cloves in a saucepan. Heat to boiling, reduce the heat and cook over low heat for 10 minutes. Whisk in the hot milk and cook without boiling 2 minutes longer.
❧ If using the egg enrichment, whisk the yolks with 1 cup (8 fl oz/250 ml) of the hot soup in a bowl. Whisk back into the soup and cook without boiling until the soup is slightly thickened.

To make fresh pumpkin puree, cut a small (3 lb/1.5 kg) pumpkin in half and scoop out the seeds and strings. Place shell side up on a greased baking sheet and bake in a 325°F (165°C) oven until tender, about 1 hour. Scrape out the pulp and place in a food processor. Process until smooth.

SERVES 4   *Photograph pages 28 – 29*

New Jersey

COLD CREAM OF TOMATO SOUP

Tomatoes, introduced to America via Europe in the 1700s, were not in popular demand until the end of that century. Even so, they were not held in the esteem they are today. Creamy tomato soups are particularly suited for the summer months when tomatoes are at their peak. The following is from New Jersey, where the soil produces some of the best tomatoes grown in the country.

2 tablespoons vegetable oil
1 onion, chopped
1 garlic clove, minced
¼ teaspoon ground mace
2 tablespoons all-purpose (plain) flour
3 cups (24 fl oz/750 ml) hot chicken stock (see glossary)
2 lb (1 kg) ripe tomatoes, coarsely chopped
½ teaspoon sugar
½ cup (4 fl oz/125 ml) sour cream
salt and freshly ground white pepper
chopped fresh chives

❧ Heat the oil in a heavy saucepan over medium-low heat. Add the onion, garlic and mace. Cook, covered, for 5 minutes. Do not let brown.
❧ Sprinkle the onion mixture with the flour and cook, stirring constantly, for 2 minutes. Whisk in the hot stock and add the tomatoes and sugar. Heat to boiling, reduce the heat and simmer, uncovered, for 20 minutes. Let cool to room temperature.
❧ Transfer the soup in batches to a blender or food processor. Blend until smooth, then pour through a sieve into a bowl. Whisk in the sour cream and add salt and pepper to taste. Chill thoroughly and sprinkle with chopped chives before serving.

SERVES 6

MANHATTAN CLAM CHOWDER (top) AND
NEW ENGLAND CLAM CHOWDER (bottom)

New York

MANHATTAN CLAM CHOWDER

*Some say that the tomato version of chowder was invented on Long
Island, where farmers and fishermen live in harmony. Others claim it is
a take-off on the hearty Neapolitan specialty* zuppe di vongole *that
was popular in the early 1900s. This version, too, has its loyal fans.*

1½ to 2 qt (1.5 to 2 l) quahogs or chowder (venus) clams
1 tablespoon cornstarch (cornflour)
1 cup (8 fl oz/250 ml) bottled clam juice
4 oz (125 g) salt pork or bacon, finely chopped
1 large onion, chopped
1 celery stalk, chopped
½ green bell pepper (capsicum), seeded and chopped
1 large carrot, chopped
1 can (16 oz/500 g) plum (egg) tomatoes, chopped, with juices
¼ teaspoon dried thyme
salt and freshly ground pepper
1 potato, peeled and diced
dash of hot red pepper (Tabasco) sauce

❧ Scrub the clams and soak for 30 minutes in a large bowl of
cold water to which you have added the cornstarch. Rinse
well.
❧ Place the clams in a large saucepan with the clam juice. Heat
to boiling, cover and reduce the heat. Simmer until the clams
open, 4 to 5 minutes. Remove the clams from their shells,
adding any liquor to the pot. Chop the clams and set aside.
Strain the liquid. Add water if necessary to make 3 cups (24 fl
oz/750 ml).
❧ Sauté the salt pork in a heavy saucepan over medium heat
until very crisp and rendered of all fat, about 8 minutes.
Transfer with a slotted spoon to a bowl.

❧ Discard all but 1 tablespoon drippings and add the onion.
Cook, scraping the bottom and sides of the pan, until the
onion is lightly browned, about 5 minutes. Add the celery, bell
pepper, carrot, tomatoes, thyme, ½ teaspoon salt and ¼
teaspoon pepper. Heat to boiling, reduce the heat and simmer,
covered, for 30 minutes. Add the potato and continue to cook,
covered, for 20 minutes. Stir in the clams and add the hot
pepper sauce and more salt and pepper to taste.

SERVES 6 TO 8

Massachusetts

NEW ENGLAND CLAM CHOWDER

*One of the greatest American food debates centers on clam chowder, or
rather whether to use tomato in the recipe. New Englanders, for the most
part, are highly offended at the idea and have, in fact, proposed laws
banning the fruit from the dish. A typical New England recipe follows.*

1½ to 2 qt (1.5 to 2 l) quahogs or chowder (venus) clams
1 tablespoon cornstarch (cornflour)
1½ cups (12 fl oz/375 ml) water (or 1 cup/250 ml bottled
    clam juice and ½ cup/125 ml water)
3 lb (1.5 kg) potatoes (about 6 medium), peeled and diced
4 oz (125 g) salt pork or bacon, diced
1 large onion, finely chopped
2 cups (16 fl oz/500 ml) milk, scalded
2 tablespoons (1 oz/30 g) unsalted butter, softened
2 tablespoons all-purpose (plain) flour
2 cups (16 fl oz/500 ml) cream
pinch of dried thyme
salt and freshly ground pepper
chopped fresh parsley

❧ Scrub the clams and soak for 30 minutes in a large bowl of
cold water to which you have added the cornstarch. Rinse
well.
❧ Place the clams with the water (or clam juice and water) in a
large saucepan. Heat to boiling, cover and reduce the heat.
Simmer until the clams open, 4 or 5 minutes. Remove the
clams from their shells, adding any liquor to the pot. Chop the
clams and set aside. Strain the liquid.
❧ Cook the potatoes in boiling salted water for 3 minutes.
Drain.
❧ Sauté the salt pork in a large heavy saucepan over medium-
low heat until golden and rendered of fat. Remove all but 1
tablespoon fat from the pan and add the onion. Cook for 5
minutes. Stir in the milk, scraping the sides and bottom of the
pan. Add the potatoes and strained clam liquid. Heat to boiling,
reduce the heat and simmer for 5 minutes.
❧ Combine the butter with the flour until smooth and stir into
the chowder. Add the cream and thyme. Heat to boiling,
reduce the heat and simmer until thickened, 5 to 10 minutes
longer. Stir in the clams and cook 2 minutes longer. Add salt
and pepper to taste. Sprinkle with parsley.

SERVES 6

South Carolina

SHE-CRAB SOUP

*She-crab soup is said to have originated in Charleston, although
Savannah, Georgia, lays claim to it as well. In the original version, crab
roe was added at the last minute, but laws against harvesting female
crabs have become so strict that roe is a rarity these days. Southern
cooks use crumbled hard-cooked (hard-boiled) egg yolks as a substitute.*

TIFFANY & CO

SHE-CRAB SOUP (left) AND OYSTER AND SPINACH SOUP (right)

3 tablespoons (1½ oz/50 g) unsalted butter
3 tablespoons all-purpose (plain) flour
3 cups (24 fl oz/750 ml) milk
1 cup (8 fl oz/250 ml) cream
1 small onion, grated
½ lb (250 g) crabmeat, picked over
¼ cup (2 fl oz/60 ml) dry sherry
1 teaspoon Worcestershire sauce
¼ teaspoon ground mace
salt and freshly ground white pepper
4 hard-cooked (hard-boiled) egg yolks, crumbled

❦ Melt the butter in a saucepan over medium-low heat. Stir in the flour and cook, stirring constantly, for 2 minutes. Whisk in the milk and cream. Heat to boiling, then reduce the heat. Add the onion, crabmeat, sherry, Worcestershire sauce and mace.

❦ Cook, uncovered, over medium-low heat for 30 minutes. Add salt and pepper to taste. Serve sprinkled with crumbled egg yolks.

SERVES 4 TO 6

Virginia

OYSTER AND SPINACH SOUP

This elegant soup is served at Christmas dinner in virtually all the taverns in historic Colonial Williamsburg. Although rice was called for in many early British recipes, the colonists used it sparingly until the industry flourished in the Carolinas. Oysters, however, were abundant, and spinach grew in almost every garden. The Worcestershire sauce is a more recent amendment.

1 lb (500 g) shucked (opened) oysters (about 1¼ pt), with juices
1 cup (8 fl oz/250 ml) dry white wine
2 cups (16 fl oz/500 ml) chicken stock (see glossary)
2 tablespoons (1 oz/30 g) unsalted butter
1 small onion, finely chopped
1 small garlic clove, minced
1 large celery stalk, finely chopped
1 tablespoon all-purpose (plain) flour
¼ cup (1½ oz/45 g) long-grain rice
¼ teaspoon ground mace
1 teaspoon Worcestershire sauce
2 cups (16 fl oz/500 ml) cream
1½ cups (2½ oz/75 g) chopped fresh spinach
salt and freshly ground pepper

❦ Strain the oysters, reserving the juices, which should measure about ½ cup (4 oz/125 ml). Combine the juices with the wine and stock in a saucepan and heat to boiling. Reduce the heat, add the oysters and poach for 4 minutes. Do not let boil. Strain the oysters, saving the cooking liquid.

❦ Melt the butter in another saucepan over medium-low heat. Add the onion; cook for 1 minute. Add the garlic; cook for 2 minutes. Add the celery; cook 3 minutes longer. Sprinkle with the flour and cook, stirring constantly, for 2 minutes. Whisk in the reserved poaching liquid. Heat to boiling, stir in the rice and reduce the heat. Add the mace and Worcestershire sauce. Simmer, uncovered, for 15 minutes.

❦ Meanwhile, cut the oysters crosswise into strips, if desired.

❦ When the rice is tender, add the cream to the soup and heat to just below boiling. Cook, uncovered, for 5 minutes. Stir in the spinach and cook 4 minutes longer. Add salt and pepper to taste. Stir in the oysters and serve immediately.

SERVES 6

KENTUCKY BURGOO

Kentucky

KENTUCKY BURGOO

Burgoo, a stew of meat and vegetables, is associated with Kentucky but served all over the South. The etymology of the name is fuzzy. It might be a mispronunciation of "barbecue" or even a misunderstanding of "bird stew." What is known is that as early as 1740 British sailors used the term for a porridge of oatmeal, which, of course, has nothing at all to do with Derby Day's most popular dish.

3 thick bacon strips, chopped
1 lb (500 g) beef bones with meat
1 lb (500 g) veal or lamb bones with meat
2 qt (2 l) water
1 chicken, 3½ to 4 lb (1.75 to 2 kg), quartered
1 large onion, chopped
1 large garlic clove, minced
3 celery stalks with leaves, chopped
3 carrots, chopped
3 large tomatoes, seeded and chopped
1 green bell pepper (capsicum), seeded and chopped
2 potatoes, peeled and cubed
2 teaspoons curry powder
1 teaspoon salt
¼ teaspoon freshly ground pepper
¼ teaspoon dried red (chili) pepper flakes
2 tablespoons (1 oz/30 g) unsalted butter, room temperature
2 tablespoons all-purpose (plain) flour
2 cups (8 oz/250 g) fresh butter or lima beans (or 10 oz/315 g frozen, thawed)
1 cup (4 oz/125 g) corn kernels, from 2 large ears (cobs)
2 cups (8 oz/250 g) sliced fresh okra (or 10 oz/315 g frozen, thawed)
4 tablespoons chopped fresh parsley

❦ Sauté the bacon in a large heavy pot or Dutch oven over medium heat until crisp. Push the bacon aside and lightly brown the beef and veal bones. Stir in 1 cup (8 fl oz/250 ml) water, scraping the bottom and sides of the pot. Add the remaining water and heat to boiling. Reduce the heat. Simmer, covered, for 1 hour, skimming the surface as needed.

❦ Transfer the veal bones to a bowl and add the chicken pieces to the pot. Continue to simmer, covered, skimming as needed, until the chicken is tender, about 45 minutes. Transfer the beef bones and chicken to the bowl with the veal bones. Skim the surface of the stock to remove any grease.

❦ Add the onion to the stock, along with the garlic, celery, carrots, tomatoes and bell pepper. Heat to boiling, reduce the heat and simmer, uncovered, for 30 minutes. Add the potatoes, curry powder, salt, ground pepper and red pepper flakes. Simmer, uncovered, for 20 minutes.

❦ Meanwhile, remove the meat from the bones in bite-size pieces.

❦ Mix the butter with the flour until smooth. Stir into the burgoo and add the beans and corn. Simmer, uncovered, for 15 minutes. Stir in the okra and meat and cook 5 minutes longer. Stir in the parsley and serve.

SERVES 6 TO 8

California

CIOPPINO

Cioppino, a fish stew, was created by Italian fishermen in California. Rarely are the ingredients the same from one pot to the next, because the dish depends on the day's catch. There is, however, one basic difference between the northern, San Francisco version and the southern, San Pedro rendering: in the north, red wine is used; in the south, white.

24 clams or mussels or combination of both
1 tablespoon cornstarch (cornflour)
3 live Dungeness (or sand or spanner) crabs
½ cup (4 fl oz/125 ml) olive oil
2 onions, finely chopped (about 1 cup)
1 large green (spring) onion with top, finely chopped
2 garlic cloves, finely chopped
3 cups (24 fl oz/750 ml) fish stock (see glossary)
2 lb (1 kg) ripe tomatoes, peeled, seeded and chopped (about 2 cups)
1 can (17 oz/530 g) plum (egg) tomatoes
2 cups (16 fl oz/500 ml) dry red or white wine
2 celery stalks, finely chopped
1 green bell pepper (capsicum), finely chopped
4 tablespoons chopped fresh parsley
1 teaspoon chopped fresh thyme or ½ teaspoon dried thyme
1 teaspoon fennel seed, crushed
¼ teaspoon crushed saffron
1 garlic clove, mashed
1 teaspoon anchovy paste (essence)
salt and freshly ground pepper
1 lb (500 g) shrimp (green prawns), shelled and deveined
2 lb (1 kg) fish fillets, cut into 2-in (5-cm) pieces

❦ Scrub the clams or mussels and remove the beards from mussels. Soak for 30 minutes in a large bowl of cold water to which you have added the cornstarch. Rinse well. Refrigerate until ready to use.

❦ Place each crab on its back. Position a large heavy knife or cleaver along the line down the center of the underside. Hit the top of knife or cleaver with a mallet to kill the crab instantly; do not cut through its shell. Twist off the claws and legs and set aside. Pry off the shells and scrape out and discard the spongy gills. Cut the crab bodies in half; crack the claws and legs. Refrigerate until ready to use.

❦ Heat the oil in a large heavy pot or Dutch oven over medium heat. Add the onions, green onion and chopped garlic. Reduce the heat to low and cook for 5 minutes. Stir in the fish stock, fresh and canned tomatoes, wine, celery, bell pepper, parsley, thyme, fennel seed and saffron. Slowly heat to boiling, reduce the heat and simmer, uncovered, for 30 minutes.

❦ Place the mashed garlic clove in a bowl. Mix in the anchovy paste with the back of a spoon. Stir into the soup mixture and add salt and pepper to taste.

❦ Just before serving, add the crabs to the soup, along with the clams, mussels, shrimp and fish. Cook, covered, for 8 minutes.

SERVES 8

New York

BEEF AND BARLEY SOUP

This soup recipe is a descendant of the ones brought to this country by Russian immigrants, although the good folks in Montana, where barley grows in abundance, stir up a very similar potful.

2 tablespoons vegetable oil
1¼ lb (625 g) stewing beef, cut into 1-in (2.5-cm) cubes
1 garlic clove
5 cups (1¼ qt/1.25 l) water
½ cup (4 fl oz/125 ml) boiling water
½ oz (15 g) dried mushrooms
1 small onion, chopped
1 carrot, chopped
1½ large celery stalks, chopped (about ¾ cup)
1 large tomato, peeled, seeded and chopped (about 1 cup)
½ teaspoon sugar
1 small parsnip, chopped
1 small white turnip, chopped
pinch of dried thyme
¼ cup (1½ oz/45 g) dried pearl barley
4 cups (1 qt/1 l) beef stock (see glossary)
salt and freshly ground pepper
chopped fresh parsley (optional)

❦ Heat the oil in a large heavy pot or Dutch oven over medium-high heat. Sauté the meat until well browned on all sides. Add the garlic and 1 qt (1 l) water, stirring and scraping the bottom and sides of the pot. Heat to boiling, reduce the heat and simmer, partially covered, for 1 hour. Skim the surface of grease as it rises to the top.

❦ Meanwhile, pour the boiling water over the mushrooms in a small bowl. Let stand for 20 minutes.

❦ Add the mushrooms with their liquid to the soup. Add the onion, carrot, celery, tomato, sugar, parsnip, turnip, thyme,

barley, stock and remaining 1 cup (8 fl oz/250 ml) water. Simmer, partially covered, until the meat is very tender, about 1¼ hours. If the soup becomes too thick, add water. Add salt and pepper to taste. Sprinkle with parsley.

SERVES 6 TO 8

Florida

BLACK BEAN SOUP

Black beans are popular throughout the Caribbean and were introduced into Florida by early Spanish settlers. Black bean soup is a specialty of the many Cuban restaurants in the Miami area.

1 lb (500 g) dried black turtle beans (*frijoles negros*)
⅓ cup (2 oz/60 g) diced salt pork or bacon
2 tablespoons olive oil
½ cup (3 oz/90 g) diced smoked ham
2 onions, chopped
2 garlic cloves, minced
8 cups (2 qt/2 l) beef stock (see glossary)
8 cups (2 qt/2 l) water
1 large bay leaf
1 small onion, studded with 2 cloves
1 small oregano sprig or pinch of dried oregano
pinch of cayenne pepper
2 teaspoons red wine vinegar
2 tablespoons dry sherry
salt and freshly ground pepper

FOR GARNISH

¼ cup (2 oz/60 g) finely chopped smoked ham
1 large green (spring) onion, finely chopped
1 hard-cooked (hard-boiled) egg, chopped
1 lime, thinly sliced

BEEF AND BARLEY SOUP

BLACK BEAN SOUP (left) AND WHITE BEAN SOUP (right)

❦ Soak the beans overnight in cold water to cover. Or place in a large saucepan, cover with cold water, heat to boiling and boil for 2 minutes. Remove from the heat and let stand, covered for 1 hour. Drain.

❦ Cook the salt pork in boiling water for 5 minutes. Drain and pat dry with paper towels.

❦ Heat the oil in a large heavy pot or Dutch oven over medium heat. Add the salt pork and diced ham. Cook, stirring frequently, for 8 minutes. Add the onions and garlic and cook 5 minutes longer.

❦ Add the beans to the pot and stir well. Add the stock, 4 cups (1 qt/1 l) water, the bay leaf, onion studded with cloves, and oregano. Heat to boiling, then reduce the heat. Cook, uncovered, over medium heat, stirring occasionally, until the beans are tender, about 1½ hours. Add the remaining water as the liquid begins to cook off.

❦ Discard the whole onion and bay leaf. Remove more than half of the beans with a slotted spoon and place in a food processor or blender. Puree until smooth, adding soup liquid as needed. Stir the pureed beans back into the soup. Add the cayenne pepper, vinegar, sherry and salt and pepper to taste. Continue to cook until the soup becomes quite thick, 20 to 30 minutes. Serve with garnishes on the side.

SERVES 8

Michigan

WHITE BEAN SOUP

Versions of white bean soup abound, and this one comes from Michigan, where beans are big business. White bean soup came into its own about fifty years ago when it was decreed that white bean soup be served every day in the U.S. Senate dining room. One of the sponsors, of course, was from Michigan.

1 lb (500 g) dried white (haricot) beans
2 tablespoons (1 oz/30 g) unsalted butter
¼ cup (2 fl oz/60 ml) olive oil
4 leeks, washed well and chopped (about 1½ cups)
4 large garlic cloves, minced
2 carrots, chopped
2 celery stalks, chopped
1½ to 2 lb (750 g to 1 kg) smoked ham hocks, excess
    fat removed
4 cups (1 qt/1 l) beef stock (see glossary)
2 cups (16 fl oz/500 ml) chicken stock (see glossary)
2 cups (16 fl oz/500 ml) water
½ teaspoon chopped fresh sage or ⅛ teaspoon dried sage
1 bay leaf
chopped fresh parsley (optional)

❦ Soak the beans overnight in cold water to cover. Or place in a large saucepan, cover with cold water, heat to boiling and boil for 2 minutes. Remove from the heat and let stand, covered, for 1 hour. Drain.

❦ Heat the butter with the oil in a large heavy pot or Dutch oven over medium-low heat. Add the leeks and cook for 1 minute. Add the garlic, carrot and celery and cook 5 minutes longer. Add the ham hocks, beef stock, chicken stock, water, sage and bay leaf. Heat to boiling, reduce the heat and simmer, covered, stirring occasionally, over medium-low heat until the beans are tender, about 1½ hours. Remove from the heat and let cool slightly.

❦ Discard the bay leaf. Remove the ham hocks and cut off the meat. Chop into pieces and set aside.

❦ Place 4 cups (1 qt/1 l) of the bean mixture, in 2 batches, in a food processor or blender. Puree until smooth and stir back into the soup. Add the ham pieces and reheat until warmed through. Sprinkle with parsley.

SERVES 6 TO 8

CONCH CHOWDER (top) AND CODFISH CHOWDER (bottom)

Florida

CONCH CHOWDER

Captain Jim's Conch Hut in St. Augustine is famous for this Florida specialty. Conch (pronounced "conk") is a tough, brightly colored mollusk whose meat must be pounded before it is used. Generally, conch meat is ground or minced and used in salads and soups.

2 oz (60 g) salt pork or bacon, finely chopped
2 onions, finely chopped
1 green bell pepper (capsicum), finely chopped
1 or 2 hot red (chili) peppers, seeded, deveined and minced
2 cans (14 oz/440 g each) plum (egg) tomatoes, chopped
1 can (8 oz/250 g) tomato puree
12 oz (375 g) conch (or giant clam or abalone) meat, coarsely
    ground (minced)
2 teaspoons chopped fresh thyme
1 large bay leaf
1 teaspoon salt
½ teaspoon freshly ground pepper
3 potatoes, peeled and cubed

❧ Sauté the salt pork in a large heavy saucepan or Dutch oven until crisp, about 8 minutes. Add the onions and peppers and cook, stirring frequently, over medium-low heat for 10 minutes.

❧ Add the tomatoes, tomato puree, conch meat, thyme, bay leaf, salt and pepper. Heat to boiling, reduce the heat and simmer, covered, for 30 minutes. Add the potatoes and continue to simmer, covered, 30 minutes longer. (If the mixture becomes too thick, add a little water.) Discard the bay leaf before serving.

SERVES 6

New Hampshire

CODFISH CHOWDER

During long, hard New England winters, fish chowders became almost standard table fare. Codfish, being plentiful, was often featured in these amalgams, but haddock, halibut and flounder were used as well.

2 tablespoons (1 oz/30 g) unsalted butter
1 onion, finely chopped
1 garlic clove, minced
⅓ green bell pepper (capsicum), finely chopped
⅓ celery stalk, minced or chopped
1 carrot, peeled and diced or sliced

2 potatoes, peeled and cubed
4 cups (1 qt/1 l) fish stock (see glossary)
2 teaspoons all-purpose (plain) flour
2½ cups (20 fl oz/625 ml) cream
1½ lb (750 g) codfish (or ling or hake) fillets, cut into 1-in
    (2.5-cm) pieces
salt and freshly ground pepper
chopped fresh parsley

❧ Melt 1 tablespoon of the butter in a large heavy saucepan over medium-low heat. Add the onion; cook for 1 minute. Add the garlic; cook 4 minutes longer. Add the bell pepper, celery, carrot and potatoes and stir until well mixed. Stir in the fish stock and heat to boiling. Reduce the heat and cook, covered, until the vegetables are tender, about 20 minutes.

❧ Mix the remaining 1 tablespoon butter with the flour until smooth. Stir into the chowder along with the cream. Heat to boiling, reduce the heat and cook for 2 minutes. Add the fish and cook 4 minutes longer. Add salt and pepper to taste. Sprinkle with parsley.

SERVES 6

Louisiana

SHRIMP AND OKRA GUMBO

Since shrimp are plentiful along the Gulf Coast, it is only natural they would end up in a pot of gumbo. This recipe does indeed use gombo (okra), which thickens the mixture as it cooks.

¼ cup (2 fl oz/60 ml) vegetable oil
¼ cup (1 oz/30 g) all-purpose (plain) flour
5 tablespoons (2½ oz/80 g) unsalted butter
2 large onions, chopped
1 lb (500 g) fresh (or 3 cups frozen) okra, coarsely chopped
3 large tomatoes, seeded and chopped
2 large green bell peppers (capsicums), seeded and chopped
4 garlic cloves, minced
2½ lb (1.25 kg) shrimp (green prawns), shelled and deveined
1½ qt (1.5 l) chicken stock (see glossary)
2 cups (16 fl oz/500 ml) water
2 tablespoons dried red (chili) pepper flakes
2 bay leaves
2 teaspoons Worcestershire sauce
1 teaspoon ground allspice
1 teaspoon chopped fresh thyme or ¼ teaspoon dried thyme
salt and freshly ground pepper
hot cooked rice
filé powder (ground dried sassafras leaves)
hot red pepper (Tabasco) sauce

❧ Whisk the oil and flour together in a small heavy saucepan. Cook over low heat, stirring frequently, until the roux is the color of dark mahogany, about 45 minutes (do not burn). Set aside.

❧ Heat 3 tablespoons of the butter in a large heavy pot or Dutch oven over medium-low heat. Add the onions; cook for 5 minutes. Stir in the okra and tomatoes; cook, uncovered, 30 minutes longer.

❧ Melt the remaining 2 tablespoons butter in a large skillet over medium-low heat. Add the bell peppers and garlic; cook for 8 minutes. Add the shrimp; cook 3 minutes longer. Add to the tomato mixture, along with the stock, water, red pepper flakes, bay leaves, Worcestershire sauce, allspice, thyme and roux. Heat to boiling, reduce the heat and simmer, partially covered, for 1½ hours. Discard the bay leaves and add salt and pepper to taste. Serve with hot rice and pass the filé powder and hot pepper sauce.

SERVES 8

PIGEON SOUP

Virginia

PIGEON SOUP

Passenger pigeons were once so plentiful (and unwary) that all a colonist had to do was walk into the woods where they were roosting and simply club them over the head. Cornish hens or game birds such as quail or squab make fine substitutes.

2 tablespoons (1 oz/30 g) unsalted butter
2 small pigeons or game hens, about 1 lb (500 g) each,
    split down the back
2 large parsnips, chopped
2 large carrots, chopped
2 leeks, trimmed, washed well and chopped
2 celery stalks with leaves, chopped
pinch of dried thyme
6 cups (1½ qt/1.5 l) chicken stock (see glossary)
2 cups (16 fl oz/500 ml) cream
½ cup (1 oz/30 g) fresh breadcrumbs
½ cup (¾ oz/25 g) shredded spinach, rinsed
1 tablespoon chopped fresh parsley
pinch of freshly grated nutmeg
salt and freshly ground pepper

❦ Melt the butter in a large heavy saucepan over medium heat. When the butter foams, add the split pigeons or game hens, skin side down, and brown lightly. Reduce the heat and place the parsnips, carrots, leeks and celery on top of the pigeons. Sprinkle with thyme. Cook, covered, over low heat for 1 hour.

❦ Add the stock to the pan. Heat to boiling, reduce the heat and simmer, covered, for 30 minutes.

❦ Remove the pigeons or hens from the soup and set aside. Strain the soup into another saucepan, pressing the vegetables to extract the juices.

❦ Mix the cream with the breadcrumbs until smooth and stir into the stock. Heat to boiling, reduce the heat and simmer, uncovered, for 5 minutes. Add the spinach and parsley and simmer 5 minutes longer.

❦ Meanwhile, remove the meat from the pigeons or game hens and cut into bite-size pieces. Sprinkle the meat with nutmeg and salt and pepper to taste. Add to the soup; heat 5 minutes to warm through.

SERVES 6

New York

CORN CHOWDER

The Iroquois Indians tell the tale of a mysterious spirit that came down to earth to walk on their lands. Wherever she trod, corn sprouted forth. Just as corn chowders sprout forth to this day.

6 ears (cobs) of corn
6 bacon strips
1 small yellow (brown) onion, finely chopped
1 small green bell pepper (capsicum), seeded and finely chopped
1 red cayenne pepper or hot red chili pepper, seeded, deveined
    and finely chopped
1 small celery stalk, finely chopped
3 tomatoes, peeled, seeded and finely chopped
1 teaspoon salt
1 teaspoon sugar
⅛ teaspoon ground allspice
1 small bay leaf
2 potatoes, peeled and diced
3 cups light (single) cream or half & half (half cream and half
    milk), room temperature
freshly ground pepper
chopped fresh parsley

❦ Cut the kernels from the corn cobs, but only to half their depth. Then, with the back of the knife, scrape the cobs up and down to remove all the "milk." Set aside. The mixture will resemble scrambled eggs.

❦ Sauté the bacon in a large heavy pot or Dutch oven until crisp. Drain on paper towels. Crumble and reserve.

❦ Discard all but 3 tablespoons bacon drippings from the pot. Add the onion and cook over medium heat until golden, 4 to 5 minutes. Add the peppers and celery and cook 2 minutes longer. Add the tomatoes, scraping the bottom and sides of the pot. Add the salt, sugar, allspice, bay leaf, potatoes and corn. Cook over medium heat until the mixture begins to sizzle. Reduce the heat to low and cook, covered, for 30 minutes. Stir occasionally.

❦ Stir the cream into the chowder and heat just to boiling. Remove from the heat and add pepper to taste. Sprinkle with the bacon and parsley.

SERVES 4 TO 6

CORN CHOWDER

SORREL SOUP (top) AND BEET TOP SOUP (bottom)

Michigan

SORREL SOUP

Sorrel grows wild throughout much of America but is generally considered just a pesky weed. Most of the world's cultivated crop, however, derives from American plants. This soup is a Polish invention from Michigan, where a great many Polish Americans reside.

1 lb (500 g) sorrel, washed well and dried
4 oz (125 g) salt pork or bacon, finely chopped
1 large onion, finely chopped
2 tablespoons all-purpose (plain) flour
2 potatoes, peeled and cubed
2 cups (16 fl oz/500 ml) chicken stock (see glossary)
1 cup (8 fl oz/250 ml) water
1 cup (8 fl oz/250 ml) sour cream, room temperature
salt and freshly ground pepper
chopped fresh parsley

❦ Trim the sorrel, discarding the stems. Chop the leaves and set aside.

❦ Sauté the salt pork in a saucepan over medium heat until golden and crisp, about 10 minutes. Stir in the onion and cook until lightly browned, about 5 minutes.

❦ Reduce the heat to low and whisk in the flour. Cook, stirring constantly, for 2 minutes. Stir in the potatoes, stock, water and sorrel. Heat to boiling, reduce the heat and cook, uncovered, until the potatoes are tender, about 12 minutes.

❦ Remove the pan from the heat and slowly stir in the sour cream. Return to low heat and cook (do not let boil) until warmed through. Add salt and pepper to taste. Sprinkle with parsley.

SERVES 4 TO 6

Colorado

BEET TOP SOUP

Beet greens or tops were eaten in Europe even before the root was deemed edible. Consequently beet tops were often added to soups and salads. Here the tops flavor a potato soup. Large, older greens must be parboiled first to remove the bitterness.

tops from 8 beets (beetroot) (about 2½ cups chopped)
1½ lb (750 g) potatoes, peeled and diced
1½ cups (12 fl oz/375 ml) chicken stock (see glossary)
1 cup light (single) cream or half & half (half cream and half milk), room temperature
2 tablespoons (1 oz/30 g) unsalted butter, softened
1 tablespoon cornstarch (cornflour)
⅛ teaspoon ground allspice
dash of hot red pepper (Tabasco) sauce
salt and freshly ground pepper

❦ Wash the beet tops and remove the stems, including the tough veins down the center of the leaves. (If beet tops are not young and tender, boil for 5 minutes and rinse under cold water; drain.) Coarsely chop the leaves.

❦ Place the beet tops and potatoes in a saucepan and add the stock. Heat to boiling, reduce the heat and simmer, covered, until the potatoes are tender, about 12 minutes. Stir in the cream and simmer, uncovered, for 5 minutes.

❦ Mash the butter with the cornstarch and stir into the soup. Cook until slightly thickened, 4 to 5 minutes. Add the allspice, hot pepper sauce and salt and pepper to taste.

SERVES 4

New York

CHICKEN SOUP WITH MATZO BALLS

Chicken soup appears in many cuisines enriched with rice, noodles, dumplings, won tons and the like. Matzo balls are so used in Jewish communities around the world. By dietary law, no leavening may be added to matzo dough, so here, club soda is added.

1 chicken, 3½ to 4 lb (1.75 to 2 kg)
⅓ cup (3 fl oz/80 ml) water
matzo balls (recipe follows)
6 cups (1½ qt/1.5 l) chicken stock (see glossary)
1 whole onion, unpeeled
1 garlic clove
1 carrot, roughly chopped
1 celery stalk with leaves, broken
1 white turnip, chopped
1 parsnip, chopped
4 whole cloves
1 bay leaf
3 parsley sprigs
½ teaspoon freshly ground pepper
1 teaspoon red wine vinegar
chopped fresh dill

❦ With sharp scissors, remove the fat and excess skin from the cavity and neck area of the chicken. Cut off the wing tips. Peel the neck and scrape off the fat. You should have about ⅔ cup (5 oz/155 g) fat. Refrigerate the chicken, covered.

❦ Place the chicken fat, skin and wing tips in a small saucepan and add the water. Simmer slowly over low heat for about 30 minutes. As the water is absorbed, it will be replaced by chicken fat in the pan. When the fat begins to sizzle, it is rendered. Remove 3 tablespoons for use in the matzo ball recipe. Chill for 30 minutes. Make the matzo balls.

❦ To make the soup, place the chicken in a large heavy pot or Dutch oven. Add the stock, onion, garlic, carrot, celery, turnip, parsnip, cloves, bay leaf, parsley and pepper. Add water to cover, heat to boiling and reduce the heat. Simmer the soup over medium-low heat, skimming the surface as needed, until the chicken is very tender, about 1 hour.

❦ Remove the chicken and carefully separate the meat from bones. Save the meat for another use. Return the bones to the soup and add the vinegar. Simmer 15 minutes longer. Let cool and strain into a clean pot.

❦ To serve, heat the soup to boiling. Reduce the heat, add the matzo balls and simmer for 10 minutes. Sprinkle with dill. Ladle soup into bowls and add one matzo ball to each bowl.

SERVES 8 TO 10

MATZO BALLS

3 eggs
6 tablespoons (3 fl oz/80 ml) cold club soda (soda water)
3 tablespoons cold chicken fat (from preceding recipe)
½ teaspoon salt
pinch of ground white pepper
¾ cup (3 oz/90 g) matzo meal (approximately)
3 qt (3 l) water

❦ Lightly beat the eggs in a bowl. Beat in the club soda, fat and salt and pepper. Slowly beat in ¼ cup (1 oz/30 g) of the matzo meal. Add more matzo meal, 2 tablespoons at a time, until the mixture has the texture of soft mashed potatoes. Refrigerate, covered, for 5 hours.

❦ Heat the water to boiling. With wet hands, shape the matzo mixture into balls about 1½ in (4 cm) in diameter. Drop into the water and reduce the heat to medium. Simmer for 25 minutes. Remove the matzo balls with a slotted spoon and let

cool. Refrigerate until ready to use. Remove from the refrigerator 30 minutes before adding to the soup.

MAKES 8 TO 10 MATZO BALLS

Arkansas

CHICKEN FRICASSEE WITH CORNMEAL DUMPLINGS

Chicken fricassee is thought to be the forerunner of fried chicken. Basically, this dish is nothing more than stewed fried chicken—in this case, topped with cornmeal dumplings, traditional in the Ozarks.

3 tablespoons vegetable oil
1 chicken, 3½ to 4 lb (1.75 to 2 kg), cut into serving pieces
1 onion, chopped
6 green (spring) onions, chopped
1 garlic clove, chopped
1 carrot, chopped
1 bay leaf
2 cups (16 fl oz/500 ml) chicken stock (see glossary)
2 cups (16 fl oz/500 ml) water
3 tablespoons (1½ oz/50 g) plus 2 teaspoons butter
4 oz (125 g) small white mushrooms, caps whole, stems sliced
3 tablespoons all-purpose (plain) flour
¼ teaspoon ground mace
⅓ cup (3 fl oz/80 ml) cream
dash of hot red pepper (Tabasco) sauce
salt and freshly ground pepper

CORNMEAL DUMPLING BATTER

¾ cup (5 oz/155 g) yellow cornmeal
¾ cup (3 oz/90 g) all-purpose (plain) flour
1½ teaspoons baking powder
¾ teaspoon salt
1 small egg, lightly beaten
½ cup (4 fl oz/125 ml) milk

❦ Heat the oil in a large heavy pot or Dutch oven over medium heat. Pat the chicken pieces dry with paper towels and sauté, half at a time, in the hot oil until golden brown, about 15 minutes. Transfer to a plate.

❦ Pour off all the fat and add the onion, green onions, garlic, carrot, bay leaf, chicken stock and water to the pot, scraping the bottom and sides. Add the chicken pieces and heat to boiling. Reduce the heat and simmer, covered, until the chicken is tender, about 30 minutes.

❦ Meanwhile, melt the 2 teaspoons butter in a heavy skillet over medium-high heat. Add the mushrooms and cook, stirring constantly, until golden. Remove from the heat.

❦ To make the dumpling batter, combine the cornmeal, flour, baking powder and salt in a bowl. Beat in the egg and milk to form a soft dough. Keep covered until ready to use.

❦ Transfer the chicken to an ovenproof dish and keep warm in a low oven. Raise the heat under the cooking liquid and boil the stock until reduced by one-third. Strain.

❦ Wipe out the pot, add the remaining 3 tablespoons butter and return to medium-low heat. When the butter foams, stir in the flour. Cook, stirring constantly, for 2 minutes. Whisk in 2½ cups (20 fl oz/625 ml) of the chicken stock and heat to boiling. Reduce the heat and simmer until thickened, about 4 minutes. Add the mace, cream, red pepper sauce and salt and pepper to taste. Add the chicken and sprinkle with mushrooms. Drop the cornmeal dumpling batter, by the large spoonful, over the chicken. Simmer, covered, until the dumplings are firm, about 15 minutes.

SERVES 4

Indiana

RIVEL SOUP WITH CORN

This is an old Mennonite recipe. Rivel literally means "lump." The rivels, or lumps, of dough are like small dumplings in the soup pot. The dumplings must be tiny, so do not overwork the dough or it will clump together in large pieces. Rich milk (or half milk and half light cream) is often used instead of chicken stock.

⅔ cup (3 oz/90 g) all-purpose (plain) flour (approximately)
¼ teaspoon salt
1 egg, lightly beaten
8 cups (2 qt/2 l) chicken stock (see glossary)
2 cups (8 oz/250 g) corn kernels, from 4 large ears (cobs)
freshly ground pepper
1 tablespoon chopped fresh chives

❧ To make the rivels, combine the flour with the salt in a bowl. Add the egg and work gently with your fingertips until the mixture is crumbly. Add more flour if necessary.

❧ Heat the stock in a large heavy saucepan to boiling. Reduce the heat and add the corn and rivels. Simmer, uncovered, for 5 minutes. Add salt and pepper to taste. Sprinkle with chives.

SERVES 6   *Photograph page 45*

Pennsylvania

CHICKEN "POTPIE"

"Potpies" in Pennsylvania Dutch country are noodles. In the following chicken and noodle soup, the noodles are layered. In many recipes noodles are placed on top of the soup to form a cover. It was for this reason that the term "potpie" came to stand for the thick, pastry-covered stew that all Americans are familiar with.

1 chicken, 3½ to 4 lb (1.75 to 2 kg)
2 whole onions, peeled
1 garlic clove
1 thyme sprig or pinch of dried thyme
3 parsley sprigs
1 bay leaf
½ teaspoon freshly ground pepper
4 cups (1 qt/1 l) chicken stock (see glossary)
1 large onion, peeled and chopped
2 large celery stalks, chopped
3 carrots, diced
1 large white turnip, diced
1 large parsnip, diced
1 recipe Pennsylvania Dutch egg noodles (page 157)
3 tablespoons chopped fresh parsley

❧ Place the chicken in a large heavy pot or Dutch oven. Add the whole onions, garlic, thyme, parsley, bay leaf and pepper. Add the stock and enough water to cover. Heat to boiling, reduce the heat and simmer, partially covered, until the chicken is tender, about 1 hour. Skim the surface as needed.

❧ Remove the chicken from the pot and let cool. Strain the stock and keep warm. Remove the chicken meat from the bones and cut into bite-size pieces. Set aside.

❧ Place a third each of the vegetables and chicken pieces in a heavy 5-qt (5-l) pot. Mix gently and cover with a layer of noodles. Repeat the procedure until there are 3 layers of chicken mixture and noodles in the pot. Add enough warm chicken stock to cover, tilting the pot to distribute the liquid. Heat slowly to boiling, reduce the heat and simmer, covered, over medium-low heat for 1 hour. Add more stock if the mixture becomes too dry. Ladle into soup bowls and sprinkle with parsley.

SERVES 4 TO 6

Pennsylvania

PHILADELPHIA PEPPERPOT

Legend has it that this soup was invented to feed George Washington and his troops while they were holed up at Valley Forge. The soup was named after the cook's home town and became so legendary that it was sold on the streets of Philadelphia by black women crying, "Peppery pot! Nice and hot! Makes backs strong, makes lives long."

¾ to 1 lb (375 to 500 g) honeycomb tripe, washed well
1 lb (500 g) veal bones or knuckles
4 cups (1 qt/1 l) chicken stock (see glossary)
2 cups (16 fl oz/500 ml) plus 3 tablespoons water
2 onions, finely chopped
1 garlic clove, minced
1 large celery stalk, chopped
1 large carrot, chopped
1 small green and/or red bell pepper (capsicum), seeded and
    chopped
¼ teaspoon dried thyme
1 bay leaf
1 teaspoon freshly ground pepper
6 tablespoons chopped fresh parsley
1 tablespoon cornstarch (cornflour)
2 potatoes, peeled and cubed
½ cup (4 fl oz/125 ml) cream (optional)
salt and freshly ground pepper

❧ Place the tripe in a large saucepan and cover with cold water. Heat to boiling, reduce the heat and simmer for 15 minutes. Drain and cool. Cut into thin strips about 1 in (2.5 cm) long.

❧ Place the veal bones in a large heavy pot or Dutch oven. Add the stock and 2 cups (16 fl oz/500 ml) water. Heat to boiling, skimming the surface as needed. Add the onions, garlic, celery, carrot, bell pepper, thyme, bay leaf, ground

PHILADELPHIA PEPPERPOT (left) AND CHICKEN "POTPIE"

CLAIRE'S ANTIQUE LINEN & GIFTS

VICHYSSOISE (top) AND CHILLED AVOCADO SOUP (bottom)

pepper, 4 tablespoons parsley and the tripe. Reduce the heat and simmer, covered, for 1 hour.

🐿 In a small bowl, mix the cornstarch with the 3 tablespoons water until smooth and stir into the soup. Add the potatoes and the cream if desired. Cook, uncovered, until the potatoes are tender, about 20 minutes.

🐿 Discard the bay leaf and remove the veal bones from the soup. Scrape any meat from the bones and add to the soup. Add salt and pepper to taste. Sprinkle with the remaining parsley.

SERVES 6

New York

VICHYSSOISE

America's most popular summer soup was invented around 1917 at the Ritz-Carlton Hotel by French chef Louis Diat. Basically, he turned his mother's leek and potato soup into creamy bliss and named it after Vichy, the town near where he grew up. This recipe is based on the original from Diat's Cooking à la Ritz *(1941).*

¼ cup (2 oz/60 g) unsalted butter
3 leeks, trimmed of green, washed well and sliced
1 onion, chopped
2½ lb (1.25 kg) potatoes (about 5 medium), peeled and sliced
4 cups (1 qt/1 l) chicken stock (see glossary)
2 cups (16 fl oz/500 ml) milk
2 cups (16 fl oz/500 ml) light (single) cream or half & half (half cream and half milk)
1 cup (8 fl oz/250 ml) heavy (double) cream
salt and freshly ground white pepper
chopped fresh chives

🐿 Melt the butter in a large heavy saucepan over medium-low heat. Add the leeks and onion and cook until lightly browned, about 8 minutes. Stir in the potatoes and stock. Heat to boiling and boil for 30 minutes. Let cool slightly.

🐿 Place the leek-potato mixture in batches in a food processor or blender. Process until smooth and return to the saucepan. Add the milk and light cream and heat to boiling. Remove from the heat and let cool to room temperature.

🐿 Pour the soup through a sieve into a serving bowl. Stir in the heavy cream and salt and pepper to taste. Chill thoroughly and sprinkle with chives before serving.

SERVES 6 TO 8

California

CHILLED AVOCADO SOUP

The Aztecs were eating avocados long before Spanish settlers brought the fruit to the American Southwest. Avocados easily took hold in California and were introduced into Florida in 1833. The following soup is best made with the dark-skinned California variety. Do not serve it ice cold or the delicate balance of flavors will be muted.

3 cups (24 fl oz/750 ml) chicken stock (see glossary)
3 ripe avocados (dark-skinned California, or Haas, variety), peeled and pitted
1 tablespoon lemon juice
2 cups (16 fl oz/500 ml) cream
dash of hot red pepper (Tabasco) sauce
salt and freshly ground white pepper
1 teaspoon chopped fresh chervil

🐿 Place 2 cups (16 fl oz/500 ml) of the stock in a food processor or blender. Cut the avocados directly into the stock, add the lemon juice and process until smooth. Transfer to a bowl and add the remaining 1 cup (8 fl oz/250 ml) stock and the cream. Chill slightly.

🐿 Before serving, add hot pepper sauce and salt and white pepper to taste. Sprinkle with chervil.

SERVES 4 TO 6

North Carolina

FISH MUDDLE

Technically, a "muddle" is a stew, but it is similar in taste to a chowder. In the Carolinas, however, milk is never added to the pot. Even though the dish contains potatoes, a true Carolinian is not averse to serving the mixture over rice.

¼ cup (1½ oz/45 g) diced salt pork or bacon
6 small green (spring) onions, chopped
½ green bell pepper (capsicum), finely chopped
1 carrot, chopped
2 small baking potatoes, peeled and diced
2 cups (16 fl oz/500 ml) fish stock (approximately) (see glossary)
½ lb (250 g) sea scallops, halved
½ lb (250 g) white fish fillets (haddock, rockfish, cod, whiting), cut into scallop-size pieces
⅛ teaspoon freshly grated nutmeg
dash or 2 of hot red pepper (Tabasco) sauce
salt and freshly ground pepper
1 tablespoon chopped fresh parsley
lemon wedges

❦ Sauté the salt pork in an oil-rubbed large heavy saucepan over medium-low heat for 1 minute. Raise the heat slightly and continue to cook, stirring occasionally, until golden, about 4 minutes longer. Stir in the green onions, bell pepper, carrot and one-third of the diced potatoes. Cook, covered, over medium-low heat for 15 minutes; stir occasionally. Gently mash the potatoes with a heavy spoon.

❦ Add the remaining potatoes and the fish stock to the vegetable mixture. Heat to boiling, reduce the heat and cook, covered, for 12 minutes.

❦ Add the scallops and fish to the stew. Sprinkle with nutmeg and continue to cook, covered, until the fish is done, about 4 minutes. Add more stock if the soup is too thick. Season with hot pepper sauce and salt and pepper to taste. Sprinkle with parsley and serve with lemon wedges.

SERVES 4 TO 6

Louisiana

CHICKEN AND OYSTER GUMBO

In Cajun legend there are said to be more gumbos "in ze pot" than fish in the bayou, birds in the sky, or chaoui (raccoons) under the live oaks. Although the name comes from gombo, an African word for okra, not every gumbo has gombo in it. Gumbo can be made from virtually any ingredients, with chicken and oysters a traditional combination. Filé powder (dried sassafras leaves) is used to thicken the stew — a Choctaw Indian touch—but never cook filé in the stew itself or it will turn into a stringy mess. Cooking a roux slowly until deep mahogany in color is the most important procedure in any gumbo. It requires a close watch but makes a big difference in taste.

3 lb (1.5 kg) cut-up chicken
½ teaspoon salt
¾ teaspoon freshly ground pepper
3 tablespoons (1½ oz/50 g) butter
1 tablespoon vegetable oil
3 tablespoons all-purpose (plain) flour
2 large onions, chopped
2 celery stalks, chopped
1 green bell pepper (capsicum), seeded and chopped
3 garlic cloves, minced
3 cups (24 fl oz/750 ml) chicken stock
1 cup (8 fl oz/250 ml) water
1 tablespoon Worcestershire sauce
1 tablespoon dried red (chili) pepper flakes
1 bay leaf

1 teaspoon chopped fresh thyme
¼ teaspoon ground allspice
⅛ teaspoon ground cloves
18 shucked (opened) oysters
4 tablespoons chopped fresh parsley
4 green (spring) onion tops, minced
hot cooked rice
filé powder (ground dried sassafras leaves)
hot red pepper (Tabasco) sauce

❦ Sprinkle the chicken with salt and ¼ teaspoon pepper. Heat the butter and oil in a large heavy pot or Dutch oven over medium heat. Sauté the chicken pieces until dark brown on all sides, about 20 minutes. Remove from the pan and set aside.

❦ Stir the flour into the drippings and reduce the heat to low. Cook, stirring frequently, until the roux turns the color of dark mahogany, about 45 minutes (do not burn).

❦ Add the onions, celery, bell pepper and garlic to the roux. Cook, stirring constantly, for 5 minutes. Stir in the stock, water, Worcestershire sauce, red pepper flakes, bay leaf, thyme, allspice, cloves and remaining ½ teaspoon ground pepper. Heat to boiling, reduce the heat and simmer, uncovered, for 30 minutes. Add the chicken pieces and continue to simmer, uncovered, for 1

1 large garlic clove, minced
2 tablespoons all-purpose (plain) flour
1 cup (8 fl oz/250 ml) beef stock (see glossary)
1½ cups (12 fl oz/375 ml) dark beer
1½ tablespoons dark brown sugar
¼ cup (2 fl oz/60 ml) red wine vinegar
¼ teaspoon chopped fresh thyme or pinch of dried thyme
1 tablespoon chopped fresh parsley (optional)

❦ Preheat the oven to 350°F (180°C). Pat the beef cubes dry with paper towels. Sprinkle well with salt and pepper.
❦ Heat 2 tablespoons butter with the oil in a large heavy pot or Dutch oven over medium-high heat. Sauté the meat, a few pieces at a time, until well browned and transfer to a plate.
❦ Add the remaining 1 tablespoon butter to the pot and reduce the heat to medium-low. Add the onion; cook for 1 minute. Add the garlic; cook 4 minutes longer. Stir in the flour. Cook, stirring constantly, for 2 minutes. Whisk in the stock, scraping the sides and bottom of the pot. Add the beer, sugar, vinegar, thyme and sautéed meat. Heat to boiling.
❦ Cover and bake in the oven for 1½ hours. Let cool.
❦ Reheat, covered, on top of the stove and sprinkle with parsley before serving.

SERVES 6   *Photograph page 50*

Nevada

BAKED LAMB STEW

The Basque homeland straddles the French and Spanish border, and that influence is obvious in the next stew. Basques are skilled sheepherders and to this day are actively recruited by the American sheep industry. For this reason, almost all Basque-Americans have settled in the West.

4 lb (2 kg) lamb (from the leg), cut into 1½-in (4-cm) cubes
salt and freshly ground pepper
½ cup (2 oz/60 g) all-purpose (plain) flour (approximately)
¼ cup (2 fl oz/60 ml) vegetable oil
2 large onions, chopped
2 large garlic cloves, minced
pinch of saffron
½ cup (4 fl oz/125 ml) dry white wine
5 peeled, chopped tomatoes (about 3½ cups)
1 cup (8 fl oz/250 ml) chicken stock (see glossary)
1 tablespoon sugar
1 tablespoon unsalted butter
1 tablespoon very fine julienne strips of orange peel
¼ cup (2 fl oz/60 ml) cognac, heated
1 cup (4 oz/125 g) shelled green peas
chopped fresh parsley (optional)

❦ Preheat the oven to 375°F (180°C). Pat the lamb cubes dry and sprinkle with salt and pepper. Dust lightly with about ¼ cup (1 oz/30 g) flour, shaking off the excess. Heat the oil in a large heavy pot or Dutch oven and brown the meat, a few pieces at a time, until very dark. Transfer to a plate.
❦ Pour off all but 2 tablespoons fat and add the onions and garlic. Cook, scraping the bottom and sides of the pot, until golden, about 5 minutes. Sprinkle the onions with ¼ cup flour and cook, stirring, for 2 minutes. Sprinkle with saffron and stir in the wine, tomatoes and stock. Sprinkle with sugar and heat to boiling. Cover and bake in the oven until tender, about 1 hour.
❦ Melt the butter in a small saucepan. Add the orange peel and stir to coat. Add the cognac and carefully set aflame. When the flame subsides, add to the stew and return to the oven for another 20 minutes. (If the stew seems too thin, remove the cover during the last 20 minutes.) Stir in the peas and cook 5 minutes longer. Sprinkle with parsley.

SERVES 6 TO 8   *Photograph page 50*

FISH MUDDLE (left) AND CHICKEN AND OYSTER GUMBO (right)

hour, skimming the surface as needed. Discard the bay leaf.
❦ Add the oysters, parsley and green onion tops to the gumbo and cook 5 minutes longer. Serve with hot rice and pass the filé powder and hot pepper sauce.

SERVES 6 TO 8

Wisconsin

OLD-TIME BEEF STEW

Many Americans with German roots can trace their immigrant forefathers to Wisconsin. The following stew is made with one of the products the Germans made Wisconsin famous for—beer. The stew is best made a day ahead and served, German-style, with buttered noodles sprinkled with a few poppy seeds.

3 lb (1.5 kg) stewing beef, cut into 1-in (2.5-cm) cubes
salt and freshly ground pepper
3 tablespoons (1½ oz/50 g) unsalted butter
1 tablespoon vegetable oil
1 large onion, chopped

OLD-TIME BEEF STEW (top left, recipe page 49),
BAKED LAMB STEW (right, recipe page 49) AND
BRUNSWICK STEW (bottom left)

Virginia

BRUNSWICK STEW

The invention of Brunswick stew is sometimes attributed to the Indians who helped the early settlers at Jamestown survive. But another theory is that it was invented by a black slave in Brunswick County, Virginia, using only squirrel meat, without beans and corn. Today's versions substitute chicken or rabbit for the squirrel and add beans, generally limas, and tomatoes, corn and potatoes. In certain southern regions like Kentucky, parts of Georgia, Alabama and Louisiana, sliced okra is added as well.

1 chicken, 3½ to 4 lb (1.75 to 2 kg), cut into pieces
1 large onion, halved and sliced
4 cups (1 qt/1 l) strong chicken stock (see glossary)
2 large tomatoes, seeded and chopped
1 teaspoon sugar
2 potatoes, peeled and diced
1 cup (4 oz/125 g) frozen lima or butter beans, thawed
1 cup (4 oz/125 g) fresh corn kernels, from 2 large ears (cobs)
¼ teaspoon cayenne pepper
salt and freshly ground pepper
chopped fresh parsley (optional)

❧ Place the chicken and onion in a large heavy pot or Dutch oven. Cover with chicken stock and heat to boiling. Reduce the heat and cook, covered, until the chicken is tender, about 30 minutes. Remove the chicken pieces and reserve. Boil the stock down to about 2 cups (16 fl oz/500 ml).

❧ Add the tomatoes to the stock and sprinkle with sugar. Cook, covered, for 20 minutes. Meanwhile, remove the chicken meat from the bones and set aside.

❧ Add the potatoes, beans, corn and cayenne pepper to the pot and continue to cook, covered, for 10 minutes. Remove the cover and cook, stirring frequently, until the stew thickens, about 10 minutes longer. Stir in the chicken meat and heat until warmed through. Add salt and pepper to taste. Sprinkle with parsley.

SERVES 6

Georgia

VEAL STEW WITH MUSHROOMS AND PEAS

Outside the South and Midwest, veal has always been underappreciated. The reason might be its expense; for a short time in the 1930s and 1940s, it was cheap enough that Americans consumed almost ten times as much as they do today. The following stew is from Savannah, one of the most beautiful American cities.

5 tablespoons (2½ oz/80 g) unsalted butter
3 lb (1.5 kg) stewing veal, cut into 1-in (2.5-cm) cubes
1½ tablespoons all-purpose (plain) flour
1 onion, finely chopped
½ cup (4 fl oz/125 ml) chicken stock (see glossary)
½ cup (4 fl oz/125 ml) dry white wine
herb bouquet: 1 thyme sprig, 3 parsley sprigs, 1 bay leaf, 1 green (spring) onion, 1 crushed garlic clove tied in cheesecloth
2 teaspoons vegetable oil
½ lb (250 g) mushroom caps
½ cup (2 oz/60 g) shelled green peas
2 egg yolks
¼ cup (2 fl oz/60 ml) cream
⅛ teaspoon freshly grated nutmeg
dash of hot red pepper (Tabasco) sauce
1 tablespoon lemon juice
salt and freshly ground pepper
chopped fresh parsley (optional)

❧ Melt ¼ cup (2 oz/60 g) of the butter in a large saucepan over medium heat. Add the veal and cook, stirring frequently, until lightly browned, about 5 minutes. Sprinkle with the flour. Cook, stirring constantly, for 2 minutes. Add the onion and continue to cook, stirring constantly, 2 minutes longer. Stir in the stock and wine, scraping the bottom and sides of the pan. Heat to boiling; reduce the heat. Add the herb bouquet and cook, covered, over medium-low heat until the meat is tender, about 50 minutes; stir occasionally.

❧ Meanwhile, heat the remaining 1 tablespoon butter with the oil in a large skillet over medium-high heat. Sauté the mushroom caps until golden and transfer to a bowl.

❧ When the meat is tender, discard the herb bouquet and add the mushrooms and peas; cook, uncovered, for 5 minutes. Reduce the heat to low.

❧ Beat the egg yolks with the cream in a small bowl. Slowly whisk in about 2 tablespoons of the liquid from the saucepan, then stir this mixture back into the stew. Cook over low heat until just thick enough to coat a spoon, about 3 minutes. Do not allow to boil. Add the nutmeg, hot pepper sauce, lemon juice and salt and pepper to taste. Sprinkle with parsley.

SERVES 6

THE MIDDLE ATLANTIC STATES

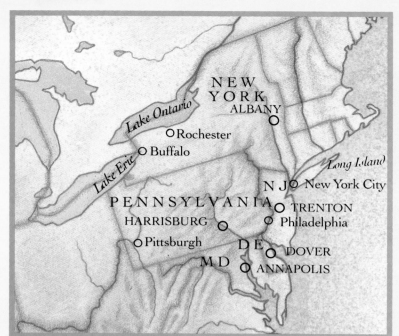

THE MIDDLE ATLANTIC STATES

❧

In the Middle Atlantic region, the Iroquoian Indians dominated the rugged areas of central and northern New York, Pennsylvania and western Maryland. The Algonquians, whose numbers included the Shinnecock, Montauk, Manhattan, Delaware and Nanticoke tribes, lived near the coastal areas, often in fear of the warring Iroquois, Mohawks, Oneidas, Senecas and Eries, to name some of the Iroqouian family. Game was plentiful and many of the same foods were consumed as in the New England area. Fish and shellfish provided ample food for the coastal dwellers. Great sea turtles were abundant and highly prized for their meat. Along the St. Lawrence waterway and elsewhere, eels were cooked with great skill, suspended between two sticks and roasted in front of a roaring fire, stewed or smoked and dried for future use.

Early explorers marveled at the skill of the Iroquoian women at farming the land. Women, in fact, were the landowners in the Iroquoian tribes. Farther west on the plains of the Great Lakes, herds of buffalo grazed on the tall grass and were drawn to the great salt licks. The Iroquois braves became masters of the hunt and made good use of the beasts for food and clothing in that cold climate. The city of Buffalo, New York, now stands on the site. Feasts and ceremonies were common among the Iroquoians, who, like most other Indian families, celebrated the coming of various harvests and seasons throughout the year.

The states that comprise the Middle Atlantic region are, by definition, the ones between New England and Virginia that have a major seaport on the Atlantic Ocean. These include New York, Pennsylvania, New Jersey, Delaware and Maryland. The land in the region varies dramatically, ranging from the rugged Adirondack Mountains to the gentle Chesapeake Bay area. Except in the extreme north, the climate is milder than that of New

EARLY MORNING STORM CLOUDS GATHER OVER THE FARMLANDS IN WESTERN MARYLAND.

PREVIOUS PAGES: PENNSYLVANIA RETAINS MOST OF THE NATURAL CHARMS IT HAD WHEN WILLIAM PENN FIRST SETTLED THERE. THE FARM COUNTRY LANDSCAPE IN BUCKS COUNTY IS AS BEAUTIFUL AND VARIED AS ANY.

THE RED BARN, SUCH AS THIS ONE IN NEW PALTZ, NEW YORK, HAS COME TO SYMBOLIZE RURAL AMERICA. A TOWN FIRST SETTLED BY THE FRENCH HUGUENOTS IN 1678, NEW PALTZ NESTLES IN THE HUDSON RIVER VALLEY.

England, and the first settlers were more prepared than were the Pilgrims, mostly due to the fact that the area had already been briefly explored for fur-trading purposes.

Way back in 1524 an Italian navigator named Giovanni da Verrazano sailed into what is now New York harbor. He did not claim the territory for France, the sponsor of his trip, because, like so many others, he was looking for the elusive route to Asia, and France at that early time was not much interested in the New World. Eighty-five years later Henry Hudson sailed up the fabulous river that now bears his name. Sponsored by the Dutch, he was also looking for the route to the East but found instead a wealth of furs and beaver skins that the native Indians were all too ready to part with for a few trinkets and bottles of gin. The Dutch, quick to take advantage of the situation, set up a trading post at present-day Albany, New York, the gateway to the Iroquois fur trade. Albany was established as a settlement in 1623 along with a sister settlement at Camden, New Jersey. Three years later the Dutch bought the island of Manhattan from the Indians for a value of twenty-four dollars. New Amsterdam, as it was called, became the capital city of the New Netherlands.

The Dutch colonies prospered and soon expanded onto Long Island, up the Hudson River valley, eastward to the Connecticut River, where they ran into British colonists, and southward through New Jersey until they met the Swedes in Delaware. The Swedes, who had founded New Sweden in 1638 when they built Fort Christina near the present site of Wilmington, were no match for the Dutch and were ousted by 1655. Although the first Dutch settlers were not interested in farming, the rich, fertile land beckoned, and it was not long before Dutch farmers with tons of equipment were arriving in large numbers. With them they brought their traditional recipes for porridges and puddings, breads of whole grains, pancakes, waffles, cookies and pastries, including the doughnut (albeit holeless) and crullers. The Dutch loved milk products and brought good dairy stock

with them. They also favored pork, as well as duck and goose. They planted rye, barley, buckwheat and wheat, which grew so well that the area would later become known as "the granary of the Revolution."

Compared to the British colonies, New Netherlands was quite wealthy. It had valuable pelts, lumber and grains to trade for such luxuries as chocolate, sugar, spices, dried fruits, wine and brandy. The English, made increasingly uneasy by the success of the Dutch, sailed into the New Amsterdam harbor one day in 1664 and simply took control. In one fell swoop, New York, New Jersey and Delaware fell under British rule. Although the Dutch reclaimed Manhattan Island ten years later, the effort lasted only fifteen months, and New York was firmly established as English territory.

Until that time the only English foothold in the Middle Atlantic had been on the shores of the Chesapeake Bay, where in 1634 Lord Baltimore was given a grant for the area. The settlers who came to Maryland were mostly well-to-do Catholics and leaned more toward "plantation" living and the gentility of the South. Although the area had plentiful venison and wild turkey, it was the rich supply of seafood that turned it into a gastronomic heaven. The oysters of the bay are legendary, and it was a Maryland specialty to stuff turkey with nothing but oysters. The diamondback terrapin, a saltwater turtle, was so abundant that even the slaves who worked the tobacco fields were allowed their fill. Today it is the Maryland blue crab that is the hallmark of that state. Crab cakes, she-crab soup, crab bakes, crab boils and deviled crab are just a few ways the crab is prepared. Soft-shell crabs, considered a delicacy by most serious diners, are blue crabs that have molted their shells and are harvested before they can grow new ones.

The Quakers settled West New Jersey (there were East and West in those days) in the middle of the seventeenth century. They had originally fled England to Massachusetts but were no more welcome there than they were back home. Then in 1661 a fellow religionist by the name of William Penn was given a grant for what is now Pennsylvania. The Quakers helped settle Philadelphia, and word soon spread that the colony was indeed tolerant of all religious sects. It was the Quakers, some say, who mistakenly labeled the German and Swiss refugees who settled west of Philadelphia "Dutch," a misnomer that resulted either from a mispronunciation of *Deutsch* or from the fact that many had fled to Holland before sailing for the colonies.

Of the first Pennsylvania Dutch who arrived in 1683, most came originally from the Rhine Valley. They were farmers for the most part and chose their land, it has been said, wherever black walnut trees flourished because they knew the soil would be rich in limestone. The foods of the Pennsylvania Dutch are legendary and include such specialties as *Sauerbraten* (sour beef), chicken "potpie" (a stew with noodles), pork and sauerkraut, *Schnitz und Knepp* (sliced dried apples and dumplings), corn fritters, dumplings and noodles, *Fasnachts* (doughnuts), sticky buns, funeral pies and more. Most Pennsylvania Dutch food is on the rich side, meant to satisfy the soul as well as the appetite of the hard-working farmer.

Not just farmers settled in Pennsylvania. Artists, weavers, doctors, teachers—people in every profession came, which allowed the Pennsylvania Dutch to be totally self-sufficient and have very little contact with the outside world. There were different religious sects within the group: Lutherans, Reformed, Moravians, Seventh-Day

Adventists, Schwenkfelders, Mennonites, Dunkards and the Amish. The last three sects were called the "Plain People" because their life was simple, as were their mode of dress and method of worship. The Amish remain the plainest of all and to this day shun modern conveniences such as telephones, radios, television and even electricity. Their horse-and-buggy transportation continues to fascinate twentieth-century America. The other sects were called "Church People." They allowed progress as long as it did not interfere with their religion. The largest group, the Moravians, were early founders of secondary schools, colleges and musical organizations. Nowadays they can be found in the Midwest, South and elsewhere.

The Middle Atlantic states are renowned not only for traditional foods of the region but also for special dishes that developed in the cities. Even though most of these originated at New York's great restaurants in days gone by, they have become standard fare in American homes. New York City can claim vichyssoise, Manhattan clam chowder, eggs Benedict and New York cheesecake. Philadelphia has contributed scrapple (a chilled pork and cornmeal mush served in slices) and Philadelphia pepperpot (a soup of peppers and tripe) as well as a rich style of ice cream that all other ice creams are still judged against. American cities today represent a cross-section of all the immigrants who have come to this country in the last two hundred years. Consequently, ethnic foods such as the Jewish pastrami of New York, the Italian cheesesteak sandwiches of Philadelphia, and the Chinese take-out found everywhere have become a part of the American eating experience.

MARY LOUISE POQUETTE

"LITTLE ITALY" IN LOWER MANHATTAN IS CROWDED WITH TINY RESTAURANTS AND CAFES, MANY OF THEM FAMILY OWNED.

LANCASTER COUNTY, PENNSYLVANIA, IS HOME TO THE AMISH, AN ORTHODOX SECT OF MENNONITES WHOSE SIMPLE RELIGIOUS AND AGRICULTURAL WAYS HAVE NOT CHANGED SINCE THE EIGHTEENTH CENTURY.

JAKE RAJS/THE IMAGE BANK

FISH AND SHELLFISH

FISHING IS AMERICA'S NUMBER-ONE PARTICIPATION SPORT. INLAND FISHERMEN LIKE
THESE IN VERMONT WORK THE LAKES AND STALK THE TROUT IN STREAMS AND RIVERS.

FISH AND SHELLFISH

America's vast coastal areas and numerous rivers and lakes once supplied such an abundance of fish that the waters literally teemed. After the settlers picked up fishing pointers from the Indians, their lives became decidedly easier. In fact, fish was so easy to catch that the colonists soon became tired of it. Even the enormous salmon that swam the Atlantic waters were relegated to no more than once-a-week meals. Herring, flounder, haddock, bass and many other fish were plentiful as well. And the Hudson and Connecticut rivers foamed with shad and sturgeon as they made their annual migratory runs. But it was cod that became the lifeblood of New England. The entire economy, it seems, was built on cod fishing, and, not surprisingly, the cod became the Massachusetts state emblem. New England was world famous for its dried salt cod, virtually the only way to preserve and ship fish in the days before refrigeration.

Americans today have an amazing array of fish to choose from, and fresh fish and shellfish from all areas of the country are available in most large cities. Perch, whitefish, smelt, lake trout, walleyes and coho salmon (introduced in 1966) swim the Great Lakes. Pompano, bluefish, flounder, mackerel, red snapper and swordfish are just a few of the fish that abound in the waters surrounding Florida. Albacore and bluefin tuna, mackerel, flounder, white sea bass, blackfish and, of course, Chinook salmon are the pride of the Pacific. Trout, catfish, sunfish and bass inhabit the myriad freshwater rivers and streams (although only farmed trout and catfish are available in markets).

Reports of American shellfish in colonial days are legendary: forty-pound lobsters, oysters measuring a foot across, clams virtually jumping into pots and on and on. Clams were popular with the coastal Indians ages before the white man set foot on shore. In some areas clam shells were used as money, or *wampum*. Oysters have long been consumed with considerable gusto in this country and were sold by street vendors in the 1800s in every coastal city. Oyster houses serving only oysters on the half shell were common sights as well. Mussels can be found on both coasts clinging to rocks along the surf line, but the largest and sweetest come from the icy waters of Maine. Although mussels are now being successfully "farmed," they do not have the flavor of naturally harvested mussels. Clams, oysters and mussels do require some preparation and must be scrubbed clean with a wire brush before eating or cooking. Mussels require somewhat more work because the "beards" (rock-clinging apparatus) must be pulled from each one. It is best to soak all mollusks in ice-cold water to which a bit of cornstarch (cornflour) has been added. They will then effectively purge themselves of grit. Other mollusks found in the United States include scallops, found on both coasts, conch (pronounced "conk") in Florida, and the famous abalone of the Pacific.

Shrimp (prawns) are, without a doubt, the most popular shellfish in America. There are varieties on all coasts, but the majority come from Atlantic or Gulf waters. They are generally sold frozen, except near the southern coasts, where they are sold fresh. Shrimp are eaten many ways, although the most common perhaps is boiled and served with "cocktail sauce."

Lobsters, *American* lobsters, were so abundant in colonial days that all one had to do was pick them off the beach. Ten-pound lobsters were common in New York harbor before the Revolution, but with progress and increased demand, lobsters have become scarce and expensive and generally weigh in at 1½ to 3 pounds. Although lobsters range along the Atlantic Coast, it is generally agreed that those plucked out of the icy waters off the coast of Maine are the best. The spiny, or rock, lobster of Florida is related to the Pacific variety and is considered inferior to the American lobster by most aficionados.

There are more varieties of crab in America than anywhere else in the world, but the overwhelming majority of crabs eaten in this country are either eastern blue or western Dungeness. The blue crab has made the cuisine of the Chesapeake Bay area famous for its inventive dishes, but it is also found up and down the coast. Soft-shell crabs are actually blue crabs that have shed their shells and are harvested before they can grow new ones. The Pacific Dungeness crabs are rock crabs named after a town in Washington where they were first harvested. They are harvested mainly in the winter months and are controlled by size limit. Also, only the males may be taken. Farther to the north is the giant King crab, or Alaskan crab, which is valued mainly for its long claws and is sold frozen. The stone crab, a delicacy in Florida, is favored for the sweet meat of its claws. By law, only its claws may be harvested; the crab is returned to the ocean, where it will grow new claws in months. Stone crab is most often served ice cold, which subdues the iodine taste inherent to the species.

BRIAN PARKER/TOM STACK & ASSOCIATES

THE PIKE PLACE MARKET IN SEATTLE, WASHINGTON, WAS ESTABLISHED IN 1907 AND IS FAMOUS FOR ITS FRESH LOCAL SEAFOOD AND PRODUCE, NOT TO MENTION AN ATMOSPHERE ALL ITS OWN.

IN THE NINETEENTH CENTURY, NANTUCKET WAS AN IMPORTANT WHALING CENTER. TODAY THE CHARMING COBBLESTONE STREETS AND WEATHERED FISHING SHACKS LURE ONLY TOURISTS, PART-TIME FISHERMEN AND ARTISTS.

and gently toss until mixed. Shape into 10 2½-in (6-cm) patties. Place on a plate in a single layer, cover with wax paper and refrigerate for 1 hour.

❦ Heat the butter with the oil in a large skillet over medium heat. Dust the crab cakes lightly with flour and fry until golden brown, about 4 minutes on each side. Serve immediately with tartar sauce.

SERVES 5

TARTAR SAUCE

1 cup (8 fl oz/250 ml) mayonnaise
½ cup (4 fl oz/125 ml) sour cream
½ teaspoon Dijon mustard
1 small shallot (white onion), finely chopped
1 sour gherkin, finely chopped
1 tablespoon chopped fresh dill
1 teaspoon chopped fresh parsley
½ teaspoon chopped fresh tarragon or pinch of dried tarragon
dash of hot red pepper (Tabasco) sauce
salt and freshly ground pepper to taste

❦ Whisk all the ingredients together in a bowl. Refrigerate, covered, until ready to serve.

MAKES ABOUT 1¾ CUPS (425 ML)

Rhode Island

STEAMED CLAMS

Soft-shell clams are invariably used for steaming, but hard-shell clams work just as well, although they take a few minutes longer to open. Often called "steamers," East Coast soft-shell clams include the Ipswich and Maninose. Out west, the razor clam is the most commonly used, but parts of the large geoduck (pronounced "gooeyduck") are often minced and steamed as well.

18 to 24 soft-shell clams per person
1 tablespoon cornstarch (cornflour)
unsalted butter, melted

❦ Scrub the clams and soak for 30 minutes in a large pot of cold water to which you have added the cornstarch. Rinse well.

❦ Place 2 in (5 cm) cold salted water in a pot and add the clams. Heat to boiling; cook, covered, until the clams open, about 3 minutes. Strain the broth and serve the clams with broth and melted butter.

MARYLAND CRAB CAKES

Maryland

MARYLAND CRAB CAKES

Maryland is renowned for its blue crab dishes, crab cakes being the best known. All crabmeat that is sold as lump crabmeat (merely a term for large pieces of picked crabmeat) has been cooked to some degree and is often sold pasteurized in cans for longer shelf life, although this product does require refrigeration as well. Crabmeat must be gently picked through to remove any bits of shell and cartilage.

1 lb (500 g) cooked crabmeat, picked over
1 cup (2 oz/60 g) fresh breadcrumbs
⅓ cup (3 fl oz/80 ml) milk
¼ cup (2 fl oz/60 ml) mayonnaise
1 egg, lightly beaten
2 tablespoons finely chopped fresh parsley
2 tablespoons finely chopped green (spring) onion with top
½ teaspoon baking powder
½ teaspoon salt
¼ teaspoon freshly ground white pepper
2 tablespoons (1 oz/30 g) unsalted butter
2 tablespoons vegetable oil
all-purpose (plain) flour
tartar sauce (recipe follows)

❦ Place the crabmeat in a large bowl. Cover with the bread-crumbs and pour the milk on top.

❦ Combine the mayonnaise, egg, parsley, green onion, baking powder, salt and pepper in a bowl. Pour over the crab mixture

California

STEAMED MUSSELS

Mussels, greatly unappreciated in the United States, are found on both coasts. They are wonderful steamed in a flavorful broth and are normally served in their shells, which open when cooked. They can be added, scrubbed but unopened, to any seafood stew, to open as they cook. Serve this dish with crusty bread for dipping.

48 mussels in their shells
1 tablespoon cornstarch (cornflour)
½ cup (4 fl oz/125 ml) dry white wine
1½ cups (12 fl oz/375 ml) water
1 onion, chopped
2 garlic cloves, minced
1 sprig fresh cilantro (coriander/Chinese parsley)
1 teaspoon salt

STEAMED MUSSELS (top) AND STEAMED CLAMS (bottom)

½ teaspoon freshly ground pepper
3 tablespoons (1½ oz/50 g) unsalted butter
2 teaspoons lemon juice

❦ Scrub the mussels with a wire brush and pull off the "beards." Soak the mussels for 30 minutes in a large pot of cold water to which you have added the cornstarch. Rinse well.
❦ Place the wine in a large pot and add the water, onion, garlic, cilantro, salt and pepper. Heat to boiling and add the mussels.

Cover and cook over high heat until the mussels open, 4 to 5 minutes. Transfer the mussels to 4 soup bowls, discarding any that have not opened.
❦ Add the butter to the boiling liquid and boil until reduced to about 1 cup (8 fl oz/250 ml). Stir in the lemon juice and strain through several layers of cheesecloth. Add more lemon juice if needed. Pour the liquid evenly over each serving.

SERVES 4 AS AN APPETIZER

OYSTERS ON THE HALF SHELL

Maryland

CLAMS OR OYSTERS ON THE HALF SHELL

Hard-shell clams are reserved for the half shell. The small quahogs of the East include the cherrystone and littleneck. (Large quahogs are used in chowders.) Butter clams are the most common "half-shell" clams out West. The eastern oysters, by far the largest group, are generally named for their location, for example, Blue Points (New York), Cotuits and Wellfleets (Massachusetts), Chincoteagues (Maryland, Virginia), Apalachicolas (Florida) and New Orleans and Grand Isles (Louisiana). The only native West Coast oysters are the tiny Olympias, but Japanese oysters, introduced in the early 1900s, have flourished. You can have your fishmonger open the clams or oysters for you, but they are best eaten as soon as possible after opening.

6 to 8 cherrystone, littleneck or butter (venus) clams or 6 to 8 oysters per person (minimum)
1 tablespoon cornstarch (cornflour)
lemon wedges

❧ Scrub the clams or oysters and soak for 30 minutes in a large pot of cold water to which you have added the cornstarch. Rinse well.

❧ To open a clam, hold it flat side down in the palm of your hand. Insert a blunt-ended clam knife along the groove toward the hinge end of the clam. Curl your fingers over the blade and force into the crack without wiggling. Once the knife is inserted, sever the adductor muscle with a twisting motion and run the knife around the edge of the clam. Cut it free and discard the top half of the shell. Lay the clams flat so you do not lose the juices.

❧ To open an oyster, hold it firmly in one hand and push the blade of an oyster knife between the shells near the hinge. Work the knife around the oyster until you feel it loosen. Force the top shell up.

❧ If you damage the shells of either while opening, strain the juices through cheesecloth and pour back over the clams or oysters. Serve the bivalves with their juices in their shells. Arrange on a bed of crushed ice and garnish with lemon wedges.

Louisiana

OYSTERS ROCKEFELLER

Oysters Rockefeller was invented in 1899 at Antoine's in New Orleans. It came by its name when a respected customer tasted it and exclaimed, "Why, this is as rich as Rockefeller!"

6 tablespoons (3 oz/90 g) unsalted butter, at room temperature
3 green (spring) onions with tops, chopped
½ celery stalk, chopped
½ cup (¾ oz/20 g) chopped parsley
½ cup (¾ oz/20 g) chopped spinach
pinch of dried tarragon
2 to 3 tablespoons Pernod
¼ cup (1 oz/30 g) fine dry breadcrumbs
½ teaspoon salt
dash of hot red pepper (Tabasco) sauce
24 oysters on half shell (previous recipe)

❧ Preheat the oven to 400°F (200°C). Melt 2 tablespoons of the butter in a skillet over medium-low heat. Add the green onions and celery; cook for 4 minutes. Add the parsley, spinach

and tarragon; cook 4 minutes longer. Transfer to a blender or food processor and add 2 tablespoons Pernod. Process until smooth.

❧ Scrape the mixture into a bowl. Stir in the remaining 4 tablespoons butter, the breadcrumbs, salt and hot pepper sauce. Taste and add more Pernod if needed.

❧ Place the oysters on a bed of rock salt on a large, shallow, ovenproof serving platter. Spread each oyster with 1 teaspoon spinach mixture. Bake in the oven for 10 minutes.

SERVES 4 TO 6

Washington

CRAB LOUIS

Some credit the St. Francis Hotel in San Francisco with the recipe for Crab Louis, a first course or salad of cooked Dungeness crab topped with chili-sauced mayonnaise. Northwesterners claim it was invented at the Olympic Club in Seattle and gained fame when Enrico Caruso could not get enough of it when he was in town in 1904.

1 cup (8 fl oz/250 ml) mayonnaise
½ cup (4 fl oz/125 ml) cream, whipped
¼ cup (2 fl oz/60 ml) chili sauce (American-style)
2 tablespoons grated onion
pinch of cayenne pepper
salt and freshly ground pepper
shredded lettuce
1½ lb (750 g) cooked crabmeat, picked over
2 hard-cooked (hard-boiled) eggs, sliced
2 small ripe tomatoes, cut into wedges or slices

❧ Combine the mayonnaise with the whipped cream, chili sauce, onion and cayenne pepper in a bowl. Add salt and ground pepper to taste. Refrigerate until ready to use.

❧ Place shredded lettuce on a platter and mound the crabmeat on top. Pour the mayonnaise dressing over the crabmeat and garnish with eggs and tomatoes.

SERVES 4

CRAB LOUIS

TIFFANY & CO.

California

HANGTOWN FRY

Tall tales abound from the Gold Rush era, when Placerville was called Hangtown for obvious reasons. According to one, this dish was created in return for escaping the noose by a cook caught stealing. The more likely story is that the dish was created when a miner struck it rich and demanded the best meal money (or gold dust) could buy.

4 bacon strips
3 oz (90 g) smoked ham, cut into strips (about ½ cup)
6 eggs
¼ cup (2 fl oz/60 ml) cream
2 tablespoons water
4 tablespoons chopped fresh parsley
3 tablespoons freshly grated Parmesan cheese
1 cup (4 oz/125 g) fine dry breadcrumbs (approximately)
8 to 10 shucked (opened) oysters
1 shallot or small onion, minced
chopped fresh parsley (optional)
salt and freshly ground pepper

❦ Sauté the bacon in a large ovenproof skillet until crisp. Drain on paper towels, crumble and set aside. Sauté the ham strips in the bacon drippings over medium-high heat until lightly browned. Drain on paper towels and set aside.
❦ Beat 4 of the eggs in a bowl until light. Beat in the cream, water, parsley and cheese. Set aside.
❦ Beat the remaining 2 eggs in a shallow bowl and spread the breadcrumbs on a plate. Dip the oysters in the beaten eggs and roll in the breadcrumbs.
❦ Preheat the broiler (griller). Remove all but 2 tablespoons drippings from the skillet. Add the shallot and cook over medium heat for 1 minute. Add the oysters and cook for 1 minute on each side. Stir in the bacon and ham. Pour the egg mixture over the top and let cook, without stirring, until the eggs begin to set, 4 to 5 minutes. Place the skillet under the broiler until lightly browned on top. Sprinkle with parsley and add salt and pepper to taste.

SERVES 6

Maryland

SAUTÉED SOFT–SHELL CRABS

Soft-shell crabs are nothing more than blue crabs that have molted their shells and are harvested before they can grow new ones. The whole crab when young is entirely edible, and most are sold already cleaned.

8 small soft-shell crabs, cleaned
milk
all-purpose (plain) flour
salt and freshly ground pepper
¼ cup (2 oz/60 g) unsalted butter
¼ cup (2 fl oz/60 ml) vegetable oil
lemon wedges
parsley sprigs

❦ Rinse the crabs under cold running water and place in a shallow glass or ceramic dish. Cover with milk and let stand for 30 minutes. Drain.
❦ Dredge the crabs in flour and place them on a plate lined with wax paper. Sprinkle with salt and pepper.
❦ Heat the butter with the oil in a large skillet over medium-high heat. Add the crabs, shell side down, and sauté for 3 minutes on each side. Drain lightly on paper towels. Arrange the crabs on a warm serving platter and garnish with lemon wedges and parsley.

SERVES 4

SAUTÉED SOFT-SHELL CRABS (top)
AND DEVILED CRAB (bottom)

California

DEVILED CRAB

Deviled dishes were common throughout the nineteenth century; deviled crab was one of the most popular. Traditionally it is baked in a casserole, but talented chefs like Mario Rotti of Los Angeles are creating highly original take-offs, such as the following Rotti invention.

1¼ lb (625 g) King crab (or large sandcrab) legs, cooked
3 tablespoons white wine vinegar
1½ tablespoons English dry mustard
½ cup (2 oz/60 g) fine dry breadcrumbs
1 small garlic clove, minced
¼ teaspoon dried oregano
½ teaspoon hot red pepper (Tabasco) sauce
¼ teaspoon salt
¼ teaspoon freshly ground pepper
1 teaspoon chopped fresh parsley
1 cup (8 oz/250 g) unsalted butter, melted

❦ Preheat the oven to 400°F (200°C). With sharp heavy scissors, carefully cut the crab shells lengthwise, trying not to pierce the meat. Remove the crabmeat in one piece. Cut into 2-in (5-cm) segments.
❦ Combine the vinegar and dry mustard in a small bowl. Combine the breadcrumbs, garlic, oregano, hot pepper sauce, salt, pepper and parsley in a bowl and mix thoroughly.
❦ Lightly coat the crabmeat pieces with the vinegar-mustard mixture. Roll in the breadcrumbs and place on a lightly greased ovenproof serving dish. Bake for 10 minutes. Serve with the melted butter.

SERVES 4 AS AN APPETIZER

and hot pepper sauce. Heat to boiling, reduce the heat and simmer, uncovered, for 20 minutes. Let cool.

❧ Place the shrimp in the barbecue sauce and marinate for 30 minutes. Meanwhile, preheat an outdoor grill or broiler.

❧ Cut each whole strip of bacon crosswise into thirds. Remove the shrimp from the sauce and wrap each in a piece of bacon. Secure with water-soaked toothpicks. Place the shrimp on skewers if grilling outdoors. Grill or broil over high heat until the bacon is crisp, about 3 minutes on each side. Reheat the remaining sauce and serve on the side.

SERVES 4 AS AN APPETIZER

Hawaii

GRILLED SHRIMP AND SCALLOPS

Found throughout the world, scallops are a bivalve with a fan-shaped shell. Sea scallops are much larger than the bay variety and better for grilling or broiling. The following fish kabob of scallops and shrimp is marinated in pureed mango and lime juice.

1 large ripe mango
2 tablespoons olive oil
juice of 1 lime
salt and freshly ground pepper
¾ lb (375 g) shucked (opened) sea scallops
½ lb (250 g) large shrimp (green prawns), shelled and deveined
24 snow peas (mangetout)

❧ Peel the mango and cut the flesh from the core. Place the mango flesh in the container of a blender or food processor. Add the olive oil and lime juice. Blend until smooth. Add salt and pepper to taste. (The mixture should be tart; add more lime juice if it is too sweet.)

❧ Combine ¼ cup (2 fl oz/60 ml) of the mango sauce with the scallops in a bowl. In a separate bowl, combine ¼ cup mango sauce with the shrimp. Let both marinate for 1 hour.

❧ Meanwhile, cook the snow peas in boiling salted water for 30 seconds. Rinse under cold water and drain.

❧ Preheat an outdoor grill or broiler. Place the scallops, alternating with shrimp and snow peas, on 4 skewers. Grill or broil for about 4 minutes on each side. Serve with extra mango sauce on the side.

SERVES 4

BACON-WRAPPED BARBECUED SHRIMP (top left), GRILLED SHRIMP AND SCALLOPS (top right) AND GRILLED SAND DABS (bottom)

Texas

BACON-WRAPPED BARBECUED SHRIMP

The following recipe comes from the Settlement Inn, an old stagecoach stop just north of San Antonio. The specialty of the house is barbecue. These shrimp, doused in sauce and wrapped in bacon, are grilled and served as a first course.

1 tablespoon unsalted butter
1 small onion, finely chopped
¾ cup (6 oz/185 g) ketchup (tomato sauce)
3 tablespoons Worcestershire sauce
2 tablespoons A-1 steak sauce (see glossary)
1 tablespoon cider vinegar
3 tablespoons brown sugar
¼ cup (2 fl oz/60 ml) water
dash of hot red pepper (Tabasco) sauce
16 large shrimp (green prawns), shelled and deveined
5⅓ thin bacon strips

❧ Melt the butter in a saucepan over medium-low heat. Add the onion. Cook for 5 minutes but do not brown. Stir in the ketchup, Worcestershire sauce, A-1 sauce, vinegar, sugar, water

California

GRILLED SAND DABS

Sand dabs, the smallest members of the West Coast flounder family, have a delicate, sweet flavor that calls for quick and simple cooking. Grill or broil these fish over high heat to crisp the skin and seal in the juices.

¼ cup (2 oz/60 g) unsalted butter
2 tablespoons olive oil
1 shallot (small white onion), minced
2 teaspoons chopped fresh chervil
8 sand dabs (sole or flounder), 6 to 8 oz (185 to 250 g) each, pan dressed

❧ Preheat an outdoor grill or a broiler. Heat the butter with the oil in a small skillet over low heat. Add the shallot and cook until soft, about 10 minutes. Do not let brown. Remove from the heat, let cool slightly and stir in the chervil.

❧ Dip the fish into the butter mixture and grill or broil over very high heat until crisp, 1 to 2 minutes on each side.

SERVES 4

New York

GARLICKY BAY SCALLOPS

Bay scallops, found in the bays and inlets of the northeastern United States, are considered by locals to be far superior to the larger sea scallops. Sea scallops, stronger in taste than the bay variety, may be used in the following recipe, but cut them into quarters first.

1¼ lb (625 g) shucked (opened) bay scallops
3 tablespoons all-purpose (plain) flour
6 tablespoons (3 oz/90 g) butter
1 tablespoon olive oil
2 garlic cloves, minced
¼ cup (2 fl oz/60 ml) dry white wine
2 tablespoons lemon juice
2 tablespoons chopped fresh parsley
salt and freshly ground pepper
hot cooked rice

❧ Dust the scallops lightly with the flour.

❧ Heat the butter with the oil in a large heavy skillet over low heat. Add the garlic; cook for 2 minutes. Increase the heat to medium and sauté the scallops in batches until golden, 3 to 4 minutes. Transfer to a plate.

❧ Add the wine and lemon juice to the pan, scraping the bottom with a wooden spoon. Heat to boiling and boil until slightly syrupy, about 5 minutes. Reduce the heat and return the scallops to the pan. Sprinkle with parsley and toss gently until warmed through. Add salt and pepper to taste and serve with the rice.

SERVES 4

New York

OYSTER PAN ROAST

The Oyster Bar, situated in New York's Grand Central Station, has been serving this dish since it opened its doors in 1912. The name comes from the fact that large quantities of the dish were made in pans over simmering water. It is almost like a stew and always served with oyster crackers for dunking.

16 shucked (opened) oysters, with liquor
¼ cup (2 fl oz/60 ml) bottled clam juice or fish stock
  (see glossary)
¼ cup (2 oz/60 g) unsalted butter
pinch of celery salt
2 teaspoons Worcestershire sauce
1 cup (8 fl oz/250 ml) milk, room temperature
1 cup (8 fl oz/250 ml) cream, room temperature
paprika

❧ Place the oysters, ½ cup (4 fl oz/125 ml) oyster liquor, the clam juice, half the butter, the celery salt and Worcestershire sauce in the top of a double boiler. Place over boiling water and cook, stirring constantly, until the edges of the oysters begin to curl, 1 to 2 minutes. Add the milk and cream and continue to stir until just below boiling. Do not let boil.

❧ Ladle the mixture into bowls and add 1 tablespoon butter to each bowl. Sprinkle with paprika and serve immediately with oyster crackers.

SERVES 2

GARLICKY BAY SCALLOPS (right) AND OYSTER PAN ROAST (left)

TIFFANY & CO.

CRAWFISH ÉTOUFFÉE (top)
AND SHRIMP CREOLE (bottom)

Louisiana

SHRIMP CREOLE

"Creole" usually indicates a dish made with green peppers and tomatoes and zapped with cayenne or hot pepper sauce. This shrimp dish, popular in New Orleans, is seasoned with filé powder as well. Filé, or sassafras leaves, must never be cooked (add it only off the heat and do not reheat) because it turns stringy and is unappealing, to say the least.

3 tablespoons olive oil
2 onions, chopped
2 garlic cloves, minced
1 green bell pepper (capsicum), seeded and chopped
2 celery stalks, chopped
3 large ripe tomatoes, peeled, seeded and chopped
pinch of sugar
1 bay leaf
½ teaspoon dried thyme
2 lb (1 kg) shrimp (green prawns), shelled and deveined
½ teaspoon cayenne pepper, or to taste
salt and freshly ground pepper
1 teaspoon filé powder (ground dried sassafras leaves)
chopped fresh parsley
hot cooked rice

❦ Heat the oil in a heavy saucepan over medium-low heat. Add the onions; cook for 1 minute. Add the garlic; cook 4 minutes longer. Stir in the bell pepper, celery, tomatoes, sugar, bay leaf and thyme. Cook, covered, for 10 minutes.
❦ Add the shrimp and cayenne pepper. Continue to cook, covered, for 5 minutes. Add salt and pepper to taste. Remove from the heat and stir in the filé powder. Sprinkle with parsley and serve with hot rice.

SERVES 4 TO 6

Louisiana

CRAWFISH ÉTOUFFÉE

Crawfish étouffée, literally "smothered crawfish," is a rich, dark, unctuous stew that is always served over rice. It must be made ahead of time because it needs to be chilled and reheated for the flavors to meld.

2 tablespoons vegetable oil
2 tablespoons all-purpose (plain) flour
¼ cup (2 oz/60 g) unsalted butter
2 onions, finely chopped
1 red bell pepper (capsicum), seeded and finely chopped
2 large garlic cloves, minced
1 teaspoon tomato paste
2 lb (1 kg) peeled fresh or thawed frozen crawfish tails (or marron, scampi or Balmain bugs) with accumulated fat*
2 large hot green (chili) peppers, seeded, deveined and chopped
4 tablespoons chopped chives or green (spring) onion tops
4 tablespoons chopped fresh parsley
salt and freshly ground pepper
hot cooked rice

❦ Whisk the oil with the flour in a small heavy saucepan. Cook over medium-low heat, stirring frequently, until the roux is dark golden brown, about 25 minutes. Set aside.
❦ Meanwhile, melt the butter in a heavy saucepan over low heat and add the onions, bell pepper and garlic. Cover and cook, stirring occasionally, for 25 minutes.
❦ Add the roux and tomato paste to the vegetable mixture. Stir in the remaining ingredients except the rice. Cook, covered, for 30 minutes. Let cool and refrigerate, covered, for 4 hours or overnight.
❦ Reheat the étouffée over low heat for about 30 minutes before serving over rice.

SERVES 6 TO 8

Louisiana

CRAWFISH PIES

Crayfish, always called "crawfish" in Louisiana, resemble tiny lobsters and inhabit the bayous and waterways of Louisiana and elsewhere. Only the tails are eaten, usually just boiled. On special occasions, however, Cajun cooks prepare crawfish dinners in which every dish is made with crawfish. Such a dinner wouldn't be complete without crawfish pies shaped like half moons.

crawfish pie pastry (recipe follows)
½ cup (4 oz/125 g) unsalted butter
all-purpose (plain) flour
2 tablespoons tomato sauce (pureed tomato)
1 onion, finely chopped
½ small green bell pepper (capsicum), seeded and finely chopped
1 celery stalk, finely chopped
4 green (spring) onions, white and green chopped separately
1 garlic clove, minced
2 lb (1 kg) peeled fresh or thawed frozen crawfish tails (or marron, scampi or Balmain bugs) with accumulated fat*
1 teaspoon cayenne pepper
salt
2 egg whites
2 tablespoons cold water
¼ cup (2 fl oz/60 ml) cream

❦ Make the pastry a day in advance.
❦ Melt the butter in a large saucepan over medium heat. Whisk in ¼ cup (1 oz/30 g) flour. Cook, stirring frequently, until the roux turns dark golden brown, about 30 minutes. Stir in the tomato sauce, onion, bell pepper, celery, white part of

Florida

BAKED FISH WITH ORANGES

Oranges and fish go surprisingly well together, as Floridians have known for a long time. Pompano and red snapper are two of Florida's most prized varieties of fish, but other firm-fleshed white fish may be used.

5 tablespoons (2½ oz/80 g) unsalted butter, melted
2 lb (1 kg) fish fillets, cut into 4 pieces
salt and freshly ground pepper
1 small white onion, finely chopped
2 tablespoons cognac
1 teaspoon very fine julienne strips of orange peel
½ cup (4 fl oz/125 ml) cream
2 tablespoons chopped fresh parsley
2 tablespoons orange juice
1 seedless orange, thinly sliced, slices cut in half

❦ Preheat the oven to 350°F (180°C). Brush a shallow baking dish with 1 tablespoon of the butter. Place the fish in the dish and brush with 2 tablespoons of the butter. Sprinkle with salt and pepper. Bake until the fish flakes easily, about 20 minutes.

❦ Meanwhile, heat the remaining 2 tablespoons butter in a skillet over medium-low heat. Add the onion, cognac and orange peel. Cook over low heat for 10 minutes (mixture should barely bubble).

❦ When the fish is done, turn off the oven. Pour any juices from the fish into the skillet and return the fish to the oven. Add the cream to the skillet and heat to boiling; boil until slightly thickened, 3 or 4 minutes. Stir in the parsley and orange juice. Pour over the fish and garnish with orange slices.

SERVES 4

California

PETRALE OR REX SOLE WITH LEMON SAUCE

Petrale is the largest and most succulent of the West Coast flounders. If using the smaller Rex variety in the following recipe, you may wish to add more fillets to the pan.

⅓ cup (1½ oz/45 g) all-purpose (plain) flour
1 egg
½ cup (4 fl oz/125 ml) dry white wine
¾ to 1 cup (3–4 oz/90–125 g) cracker crumbs or fine dry breadcrumbs
4 sole (or flounder) fillets
3 tablespoons (1½ oz/50 g) unsalted butter
2 tablespoons olive oil
2 small lemons, peeled, seeded and thinly sliced
¼ cup (2 fl oz/60 ml) water
salt and freshly ground white pepper
1 tablespoon chopped fresh basil, watercress or chives

❦ Place the flour on a plate. Beat the egg with 1 tablespoon of the wine in a shallow bowl. Place the cracker crumbs on another plate. Dust the fish lightly with flour. Dip in the egg mixture and coat lightly with crumbs.

❦ Heat 2 tablespoons of the butter with the oil in a large heavy skillet over medium heat. Sauté the fillets until golden and the flesh flakes when tested with a fork, about 3 minutes on each side. Transfer to a heatproof serving dish and keep warm in a low oven.

❦ Add the remaining butter to the skillet and add the lemon slices, remaining wine and water. Heat to boiling, reduce the heat and simmer until reduced by half, about 4 minutes. Add salt and pepper to taste. Pour over the fish and sprinkle with herbs.

SERVES 4

BAKED FISH WITH ORANGES

FILAMENTO

BROILED TUNA STEAK (top, recipe page 78), SAUTÉED ABALONE STEAKS (center, recipe page 78) AND SOLE WITH LEMON SAUCE (bottom)

California

SAUTÉED ABALONE STEAKS

Abalone, a univalve, is considered a great delicacy on the West Coast. The meat is tough, however, and must be pounded to tenderize. It is also imperative not to overcook abalone or it will turn rubbery.

¼ cup (1 oz/30 g) all-purpose (plain) flour
½ teaspoon salt
¼ teaspoon freshly ground pepper
1 egg, lightly beaten
1 tablespoon water
4 abalone slices (4–5 oz/125–155 g each), well pounded with
    meat mallet to soften
⅓ cup (1½ oz/45 g) fine dry breadcrumbs
2 tablespoons (1 oz/30 g) unsalted butter
1 tablespoon olive oil
lemon wedges

❧ Combine the flour, salt and pepper on a plate. Combine the egg and water in a shallow bowl. Dust the abalone slices lightly with the flour mixture, dip into the egg, shaking off the excess, and coat lightly with breadcrumbs.
❧ Heat the butter with the oil in a heavy skillet over medium heat. Sauté the abalone for 45 to 50 seconds on each side. Do not overcook. Serve immediately with lemon wedges.

SERVES 4   *Photograph page 77*

California

BROILED TUNA STEAKS

Many California towns developed with tuna fishing as the main industry. Nowadays local fishermen cannot compete with the fishing fleets owned by large companies or even other countries that are virtually floating factories traveling the oceans. Fresh tuna is excellent cut into steaks and grilled. In this recipe fresh swordfish may be substituted.

4 tuna steaks, 1 in (2.5 cm) thick
¼ cup (2 fl oz/60 ml) lemon juice
½ cup (4 fl oz/125 ml) olive oil
1 small garlic clove, minced
pinch of dried oregano, crushed
½ teaspoon finely grated lemon peel
salt and freshly ground pepper

❧ Place the tuna in a glass or ceramic dish. Combine the remaining ingredients in a bowl and pour over the fish. Let marinate for 30 minutes.
❧ Preheat a broiler or griller. Broil or grill the tuna on a lightly greased broiling rack, basting with the marinade, for 5 minutes on each side.

SERVES 4   *Photograph page 77*

Wisconsin

PLANKED LAKE TROUT

Baking fish on wooden planks dates back to the Indians. Originally, fish were tied to the planks and set upright near hot coals until cooked. Wooden planks should be oiled and wet down thoroughly before going into the oven. It is wise to place a baking sheet under the plank to catch juices. The fish may also be baked in a shallow ovenproof platter.

2 lake trout, 2 lb (1 kg) each, pan dressed
salt and freshly ground pepper
juice of 2 large lemons
2 tablespoons (1 oz/30 g) unsalted butter, melted

4 cups hot mashed potatoes (about 5 potatoes)
1 egg yolk, lightly beaten
2 tablespoons freshly grated Parmesan cheese

❧ Preheat the oven to 350°F (180°C). Sprinkle the trout, inside and out, with salt and pepper and lemon juice. Place on a seasoned plank or shallow ovenproof platter. Brush with melted butter and bake until the flesh flakes when tested with a fork, about 35 minutes.

❧ Meanwhile, make the mashed potatoes and beat in the egg yolk.

❧ When the trout is done, place the potatoes in a pastry (icing) bag and pipe around the fish in swirls. Sprinkle the potatoes with cheese and place under a preheated broiler (griller) for a few minutes to brown.

SERVES 4

PICKLED SMELTS

1 boned tail section of salmon, about 4 lb (2 kg),
   or a 5-lb (2.5-kg) salmon, butterfly filleted
   (sliced lengthwise and opened out)
1½ tablespoons light brown sugar
2 tablespoons red wine vinegar
3 tablespoons olive oil
½ teaspoon coarse salt
¼ teaspoon freshly ground pepper
4 tablespoons chopped fresh dill

❧ Open the salmon up and sprinkle the flesh with the brown sugar and vinegar. Close the salmon and refrigerate, covered, overnight.

❧ About 2 hours before cooking, combine the olive oil, salt, pepper and dill in a bowl. Mash together and spread over the outside (skin) of the salmon. Let stand, covered, at room temperature.

❧ Preheat an outdoor grill (or oven to 375°F/190°C). Open the salmon up and place on a greased rack (or large baking sheet in the oven). Cover the fish and cook over medium-hot coals (or in the oven) until the flesh flakes easily, about 10 minutes per inch (2.5 cm) of thickness.

SERVES 6 TO 8   *Photograph pages 58 – 59*

Michigan

PICKLED SMELTS

Smelts are tiny oily fish that thrive in the cold waters of the North, where they were introduced in the early 1900s. The tiniest are sometimes fried to a crisp and eaten bones and all. The larger ones are excellent pickled in the eastern European tradition.

2 qt (2 l) smelts (or small sardines or anchovies), heads
   removed and cleaned
½ cup (4 oz/125 g) coarse or pickling salt
2 onions, sliced
2 teaspoons pickling spices
2 small bay leaves
¾ cup (6 oz/185 g) sugar
2 cups (16 fl oz/500 ml) white vinegar

❧ Sprinkle the smelts with salt. Let stand for 10 hours. Rinse the fish 6 times in cold water and drain. Cut into pieces.

❧ Place the fish in 2 sterilized 1-qt (1-l) jars. Add 1 sliced onion, 1 teaspoon pickling spices and 1 small bay leaf to each jar.

❧ Combine the sugar and vinegar in a small saucepan. Heat to boiling, reduce the heat and simmer, uncovered, for 5 minutes. Pour over the fish. Cover and let cool. Refrigerate at least 3 days before serving. Keep stored in the refrigerator.

MAKES 2 QUARTS/LITERS

Washington

SEATTLE BAKED SALMON

The Indians of the Puget Sound baked salmon tied to vertical boards leaned toward smoldering coals. Alderwood was (and is) used to give the fish a subtle flavor. The following is the modern-day Seattle rendering. If you grill the fish outdoors, try to find alderwood chips, which are sold in bags throughout much of the country. Always soak wood chips in water before adding to hot coals.

Oregon

POACHED SALMON WITH DILL SAUCE

It is said that Abigail Adams, wife of the second president, began the tradition of serving poached salmon on the Fourth of July. Nowhere is this custom more popular than in the Northwest.

1 white onion, sliced
1 lemon slice
½ cup (4 fl oz/125 ml) dry white wine
2 cups (16 fl oz/500 ml) fish stock (see glossary)
4 salmon steaks, about ½ lb (250 g) each
2 tablespoons (1 oz/30 g) unsalted butter
2 tablespoons all-purpose (plain) flour
¼ cup (2 fl oz/60 ml) light (single) cream or half & half
   (half cream and half milk)
1 egg yolk
salt and freshly ground pepper
4 tablespoons chopped fresh dill

❧ Combine the onion, lemon slice, wine and fish stock in a large saucepan. Heat to boiling, boil 1 minute and reduce the heat. Place the salmon in the cooking liquid, cover and poach (do not boil) until the flesh flakes when tested with a fork, about 10 minutes. Remove from the heat.

❧ Meanwhile, melt the butter in a saucepan over medium-low heat. Add the flour and cook, stirring constantly, for 2 minutes. When the salmon is cooked, carefully remove about 1 cup (8 fl oz/250 ml) of the cooking liquid from the pan. Whisk into the butter-flour mixture. Heat to boiling and boil until slightly thickened, about 3 minutes. Reduce the heat to low.

❧ Whisk the cream with the egg yolk in a bowl and slowly stir into the sauce. Cook, stirring constantly, until slightly thickened, about 2 minutes. Do not let boil. Add salt and pepper to taste and stir in the dill. Remove from the heat.

❧ With a slotted spatula, remove the salmon and rest gently on paper towels. Transfer to a platter. Pour the sauce over the top and serve at once.

SERVES 4

POACHED SALMON WITH DILL SAUCE

WILLIAMS-SONOMA INC.

SKILLET TROUT (left) AND CODFISH BALLS (right)

Massachusetts

CODFISH BALLS

Codfish balls are second only to baked beans as a specialty of Boston's culinary past. Dried salt cod is available in packages at most grocers. The cod must be soaked prior to cooking to remove the excess salt.

½ lb (250g) dried salt cod (*bacalhao*)
1½ cups cold mashed potatoes (about 2 potatoes)
1 egg, lightly beaten
1 tablespoon unsalted butter, room temperature
2 tablespoons light (single) cream or half & half (half cream and half milk)
½ teaspoon freshly ground pepper
6 tablespoons (3 oz/90 g) solid vegetable shortening (vegetable lard)
chopped fresh parsley (optional)

❦ Soak the salt cod overnight or for 24 hours in cold water, changing the water several times.
❦ When the cod is soft, drain thoroughly and place in a heavy saucepan. Cover with cold water. Slowly heat to just below boiling. Do not let boil or the fish will toughen. Poach until tender, 15 to 20 minutes. Drain and transfer to a bowl. Break up the pieces with a fork and let cool.
❦ Add the mashed potatoes to the flaked cod and stir in the egg, butter, cream and pepper. Mix well and divide into 12 portions. Form each into a slightly flattened ball or cake.
❦ Heat half the shortening in a large heavy skillet over medium-high heat. Add half the codfish balls and fry until lightly browned, about 1½ minutes on each side. Drain lightly on paper towels, transfer to a platter and keep warm. Fry remaining codfish balls, drain and transfer to the platter. Sprinkle with parsley.

SERVES 4

Wyoming

SKILLET TROUT

As settlers trekked westward, trout and freshwater salmon became an important part of their diet. Trout is, without question, the favorite freshwater fish in America. It is at its best when simply pan-fried in a heavy skillet and even better if cooked outdoors over an open fire.

½ cup (4 fl oz/125 ml) milk
½ cup (2 oz/60 g) all-purpose (plain) flour
½ teaspoon salt
4 brook or rainbow trout or freshwater salmon, 8 to 12 oz (250 to 375 g) each, pan dressed
2 tablespoons (1 oz/ 30 g) unsalted butter
2 tablespoons vegetable oil
lemon wedges

❦ Place the milk in a shallow bowl. Combine the flour and salt on a plate. Dip the fish lightly in the milk, shaking off the excess. Lightly roll in the flour to coat.
❦ Heat the butter with the oil in a large heavy skillet over medium heat. Sauté the fish until crisp and firm, 3 to 4 minutes on each side. Drain lightly on paper towels and serve with lemon wedges.

SERVES 4

Rhode Island

HADDOCK SAUTÉ

Haddock, a member of the cod family, ranges between 2 and 5 pounds (1 to 2.5 kg) in weight. It is often baked, poached and served with egg sauce or simply sautéed in the following manner.

¼ cup (1 oz/30 g) all-purpose (plain) flour
1¼ cups (2½ oz/75 g) fresh breadcrumbs (approximately)
½ cup (4 fl oz/125 ml) milk
1½ to 2 lb (750 g to 1 kg) haddock (or gemfish or cod) fillets
½ cup (4 oz/125 g) unsalted butter
2 tablespoons vegetable oil
1½ tablespoons malt or red wine vinegar
lemon wedges
chopped fresh parsley

❦ Preheat the oven to 350°F (180°C). Place the flour on a plate, the breadcrumbs on another plate and the milk in a shallow bowl. Dust the fish lightly with flour, dip into the milk and coat lightly with breadcrumbs.

❦ Heat half of the butter with 1 tablespoon of the oil in a large heavy skillet over medium heat. Sauté the fish until golden, about 2 minutes on each side, adding more butter and oil as needed. Transfer to a heatproof serving platter.

❦ Sprinkle the vinegar over the fish and place in the oven until the fish flakes when tested with a fork, about 8 minutes. Garnish with lemon wedges and sprinkle with parsley.

SERVES 4

Massachusetts

BAKED HADDOCK OR CODFISH

This recipe from Massachusetts is a fairly standard one for baking fish. Any firm-fleshed fish, even bluefish, can be prepared this way.

2 tablespoons (1 oz/30 g) unsalted butter
1 small yellow (brown) onion, chopped
1½ lb (750 g) haddock (or gemfish) or cod (or ling) fillets
1 tablespoon chopped fresh herbs (parsley, tarragon, chervil)
½ teaspoon salt
¼ teaspoon freshly ground pepper
½ cup (4 fl oz/125 ml) cream
paprika

❦ Preheat the oven to 350°F (180°C). Melt the butter in a small skillet over medium-low heat. Add the onion and cook until soft, about 8 minutes. Spread over the bottom of a shallow baking dish large enough to hold the fish in one layer.

❦ Place the fish over the onions and sprinkle with the herbs, salt and pepper. Drizzle the cream over the top and sprinkle lightly with paprika. Bake, covered, for 15 minutes. Remove the cover and continue to bake until the fish flakes when tested with a fork, 10 to 15 minutes longer, depending on the thickness of the fillets.

SERVES 4

HADDOCK SAUTÉ (top)
AND BAKED CODFISH (bottom)

THE SOUTH

THE SOUTH

T he Muskogean Indians reigned in the South, although the Cherokees of the Iroquoian family controlled the mountainous regions. Some of the more familiar tribes of the Muskogean family were the Choctaws, Chickasaws, Creeks, Natchez and Seminoles. The one food that these southern tribes will always be remembered for is hominy, which is made from corn. Thanks to the warmer climate, the Indians could plant corn at various times of the year, giving them, in effect, three annual harvests to celebrate. Making hominy requires lye, which the Indians obtained from wood ashes. The corn kernels were soaked in lye until they swelled, then washed many times in spring water to remove the poisonous substance. Much of the hominy was dried whole for future use or dried and ground into "grits." The Indians used cornmeal to make crisp pones, ash cakes, hoecakes (all thin breads) and an oblong-shaped cornbread containing huckleberries.

They grew sunflowers, pumpkins and other squash and beans. Some historians say that they also grew sweet potatoes and melons. Sweet potatoes probably, but not melons, which were introduced by the Spanish from the West Indies. The woods were full of blackberries, strawberries, persimmons, pecans and hickory nuts. The Indians boiled hickory nuts in water to produce a sweet, rich liquid they used for enriching soups and cornbread. They also flavored their foods with spicebrush, wild mint and sassafras. For meat, the Indians hunted opossums, squirrels, rabbits, deer, snakes, frogs and wild fowl. The rivers and bayous provided catfish and crawfish; the coastal waters, all manner of fish, shellfish and sea turtles. Fish were grilled over fires, smoked or turned into stews.

Virginia was the first British colony in North America, although at the time the land belonged to the London Company. Tobacco grew well there, and after a

STREET MUSICIANS ARE PART OF THE CONSTANT FESTIVAL OF THE FRENCH QUARTER IN NEW ORLEANS, AN AREA JUSTLY FAMOUS FOR FRENCH ARCHITECTURE AND ORNATE BALCONIES AS WELL AS TRADITIONAL JAZZ, BLUES AND BRASS SOUNDS.

PREVIOUS PAGES: A SHRIMP FLEET AT SUNSET IN DELCAMBRE, LOUISIANA. SHRIMP ARE THE MOST POPULAR SHELLFISH IN AMERICA, AND THE MAJORITY COME FROM ATLANTIC OR GULF WATERS.
PHOTO: TOM ALGIRE/TOM STACK & ASSOCIATES

KENTUCKY FARMERS HAVE A SOUTHERN PRIDE THAT CHARACTERIZES THE
REGION'S GENTEEL BUT DOWN-HOME RURAL STYLE.

new method for curing tobacco was discovered in 1617, the colony changed from backwater poor to plantation rich in a very short period. When the colony prospered, the British government stepped in and simply revoked the London Company's charter. Virginia came under direct control of the crown in 1624, causing many early settlers to flee to neighboring frontiers. "Royalist" rule gave rise to an elitist class in Virginia and elsewhere, and thus the rich plantation life was enjoyed by the few rather than the many. It should be remembered that much of the lavish entertaining that went on in the South before the Civil War was made possible by slavery.

Carolina (originally there was just one) was part of a grant given by Charles II to his supporters. Charlestown (now Charleston) was the first settlement, and since it possessed one of the finest harbors on the Atlantic coast, the town flourished. After 1685, when Louis XIV revoked the Edict of Nantes, which protected Protestants' rights, the French Huguenots, as they were called, fled. Most sought refuge in Acadia (Nova Scotia), along the St. Lawrence River and in Quebec and Maine, but a great many found their way to Charleston, which at one point was more than twenty percent French. Vast political differences developed between the northern part of the colony and the southern, and so the colony was split in two. South Carolina, like Virginia, boomed. Large plantations and aristocratic ways prevailed. North Carolina, on the other hand, remained a collection of small farms inhabited by independent frontiersmen. North Carolina was often referred to as "the Valley of Humility between two Peaks of Arrogance."

Georgia was the last colony to be set up by the English. When James Oglethorpe, a philanthropist, deigned to establish a colony for Protestants persecuted in Catholic countries, as well as for men languishing in English jails, the crown agreed—not, however, out of any goodness of heart. England viewed the new colony and its "disposable" occupants as protection for South Carolina from Indian attacks encouraged by the Spanish, a buffer between the other colonies and Spanish Florida.

As of 1783, after the Treaty of Paris was signed, the United States reached west to the Mississippi River. Spain, however, controlled Florida and the Gulf Coast all the way to New Orleans. Since the area south of the

Ohio River was so well settled by 1792, Kentucky was admitted to the Union, followed by Tennessee in 1796, but Spain was still in control of the lower Mississippi, blocking the most important river route to the Midwest. Shortly after an agreement with Spain was signed in 1795 for free use of the port of New Orleans, Spain ceded the area to France. Thomas Jefferson, then president, urged Congress to offer France two million dollars for the city. The French, under Napoleon Bonaparte, having just suffered defeat in Haiti due to uprisings and disease, surprised the Americans by offering the whole Louisiana Territory for fifteen million dollars. That territory covered much of what is now the middle United States, sweeping northwest from Louisiana to Montana and extending eastward to the Mississippi River. Florida was purchased from Spain in 1819.

The Indians grew and cooked corn of all colors, but white corn became the favorite of Southerners. Since wheat flour had to be imported from England or the Middle Atlantic region, cornmeal became the basis of many southern breads. Those who could not afford flour, even when it was available, adapted Indian methods for hoecake, ash cake and corn pone. Because cornmeal does not contain the gluten needed for traditional yeast-rising breads, a soufflé-like mixture called spoon bread became a good substitute. Early southern desserts were based on English recipes. Pound cakes, chess pies, fruit and custard desserts were all English. Sweet potato pie, however, is a true American original.

Rice was a very important crop in the Carolinas in the early eighteenth century, but today most of the southern rice is grown in Louisiana and Arkansas (the other two major rice-growing states being Texas and California). Many a rice dish such as dirty rice, jambalaya and hopping John came out of the South. Hopping John, a complete protein-providing mix of rice and black-eyed peas eaten for good luck at New Year's, was an African invention. The African slaves, by the mere fact of being in plantation kitchens, added a great deal to southern cuisine. Okra, sesame seeds, melons and hot spices can be attributed to the slaves.

Pork was eaten in the South on a regular basis, and southern barbecued pork is legendary. In Smithfield, Virginia, hogs were raised on a diet of peanuts, and hams cured and smoked over hickory wood fires—a specialty of the region even today. Fried chicken with creamed gravy is another of the South's famous dishes. Others include ham with redeye gravy accompanied by grits and biscuits in Tennessee. Kentucky has contributed bourbon and the meat and vegetable stew called burgoo. Georgia is famous for peaches, pecans and Country Captain, a chicken dish seasoned with curry. Alabama and Mississippi have catfish and fried pies. Florida, with its Spanish heritage, combines citrus fruits and fresh seafood. Which brings us to Louisiana.

Although much of Louisiana's cuisine is similar to that in the rest of the South, New Orleans and the area west of the city are unique. New Orleans was originally settled by the French, then came under Spanish rule. The city was always (and remains) a major port and therefore cosmopolitan in nature. New Orleans Creole cooking, as it is called, is based on classic French cookery but has been heavily influenced by Spanish taste through the years. Moreover, the spices and vegetables incorporated into many dishes can be traced to Choctaw Indian and black heritages. New Orleans remains one of the best "eating" cities in America.

CATHERINE KARNOW

A YELLOW SCHOOL BUS WINDS ITS WAY ALONG THE MISTY
COUNTRY ROADS NEAR PARIS, IN NORTHERN VIRGINIA.

A NEW ORLEANS FRUIT VENDOR TENDS TO HIS COLORFUL DISPLAY OF
SIGNS AND FRESH PRODUCE THAT ARE SURE TO TEMPT THE PASSERBY.

ANNE RIPPY/THE IMAGE BANK

Cajun country stretches in a rough triangle across the southern portion of the state, from the Sabine River on the west to the Mississippi on the east, with its apex near Alexandria. *Cajun* is a derivation of *Acadian*. The Cajuns are, in fact, descendants of the French Huguenots who fled to Acadia in 1685. When England took over Canada, the Acadians refused to pledge allegiance to the English flag or to give up their French language. The story of their deportation in 1755 is well known. Families were separated, men from women, women from children, and sent off in every direction—often never to see one another again. Many came to Louisiana, which at the time was under French rule. So Cajun cookery also has its roots firmly established in French cuisine, but it is more of a country style of cooking, spicy and gutsy. Both Creole and Cajun food depends on local agricultural and Gulf Coast bounty: shrimp, crawfish, oysters, crabs, hot peppers, rice and filé powder, to name just a few. Louisiana has contributed gumbos, jambalayas, Creole shrimp and fish dishes, pain perdu (French toast) and myriad other specialties to American cuisine.

One trait that all Southerners seem to have in common is the appreciation of good food, especially good food shared with good friends. One of the reasons for this is that the South, for the most part, is still rural and agrarian. When people get together, they do so over food.

POULTRY AND GAME BIRDS

WILD DUCKS AND GEESE WERE VERY POPULAR WITH THE EARLY SETTLERS WHO LEARNED FROM THE INDIANS HOW TO ROAST THE BIRDS OVER OPEN FIRES OR COOK THEM IN HOT EMBERS.

POULTRY AND GAME BIRDS

The English had plenty of game to choose from when they arrived in America. Although most of them knew little about hunting wild game birds and could not hit the broad side of a barn with their clumsy muskets, they learned quickly—to survive. From the Indians they learned not only how to trap wild turkeys, ducks, geese, quail, larks, pigeons, partridges and even sea gulls, but also how to roast the birds over open fires and how to bake them buried in hot embers, the fowl often stuffed with herbs, vegetables, nuts or fruits.

The turkey originally ranged throughout Mexico, the Southwest, the Midwest and the East. Whereas the midwestern and eastern Indian tribes caught the birds in the wild, the Indians of the Southwest, like the Aztecs, domesticated the fowl long before the Spaniards arrived. From the moment the settlers first chomped on a drumstick, turkey became the favorite wild bird in the American diet. In the seventeenth and eighteenth centuries it was served as often as two or three times a week. In fact, the bird was so associated with the American way of life that Benjamin Franklin once remarked, "I wish the Bald Eagle had not been chosen as the representation of our country. The turkey is a much more respectable bird, and withal a true original native of America." In his opinion the bald eagle was "a Bird of poor moral character, like those among men who live by sharpening and robbing." His goal was to make the turkey the national bird. Needless to say, he failed. As progress took hold, wild turkeys became scarce. Domesticated birds, however, took up the slack. Today most Americans eat turkey only once a year at Thanksgiving, although that is beginning to change.

New settlers did eventually bring chickens with them on their long ocean crossings. During the seventeenth and eighteenth centuries, however, chickens were hard to come by, expensive, and considered a luxury. By the mid-1800s the breeding of chickens had become well established, and breeders developed several superior crossbreeds, including the White Plymouth Rock, the Rhode Island White, the Rhode Island Red and the Wyandotte. The Cornish game hen is actually a cross between the Cornish game cock and the Plymouth Rock chicken. As chicken became more available, special dishes evolved in different parts of the country. New Englanders made pot pies, Southerners enjoyed fried chicken, Southwesterners made Mexican dishes with chicken, Midwesterners barbecued theirs, and Californians, by and by, presented the world with tetrazzini.

Most of today's "supermarket" chickens are mass-produced and lack the flavor of farm-raised birds. Fortunately, this state of affairs is changing, primarily because of the elevation of chefs to "star" status in this country. Good chefs constantly seek out the best ingredients. As a result, the demand for old-fashioned farm-raised chickens is on the rise, and small chicken farmers have found a new market. Ducks and geese, although in little demand in this day and age, were very popular with our European forefathers. Wild ducks once were plentiful, and canvasbacks in particular were relished for their distinctive flavor. In 1873 domesticated Peking ducks were introduced, and raising ducks became a major industry on Long Island, which is why domesticated ducks are known as Long Island ducklings. Geese, too, were important in early America, and not just for their meat. Goose fat was used as a medicinal ointment for chest colds, and goose feathers supplied down for bedding and quills for pens. The noisy birds were even used as "watchdogs," as they honked loudly at any intruders, whether four-legged or two-legged. Traditionally served at Christmas, geese are almost always roasted. Wild geese and ducks still migrate across a large portion of the United States and are a favorite target of hunters. Wild birds have a stronger taste than domesticated and not nearly as much fat.

Besides ducks and geese, wild game birds that are in favor today include pheasant, grouse, quail and squab. The ring-necked pheasant was introduced from Europe and Asia in the eighteenth century. In fact, George Washington may have been first when he imported pheasants to stock his Mount Vernon estate. In any case, pheasants proliferated and are now found in more than thirty states. Grouse is another favorite with hunters, not only because of its taste, but because it is extremely wily and difficult to bag. The ruffed grouse, sometimes called partridge in the Northeast and ruffy in the upper Midwest, is the tastiest of the lot. Grouse are also abundant in the plains states, where they are commonly referred to as prairie chickens.

Quail, tiny birds averaging about half a pound, are found throughout the United States. The bobwhite, the most common quail, gets its name from the sound the bird makes. Southerners often call quail partridge, which is somewhat confusing because America has no true partridge. Squab is another story. Although young chickens are often referred to as squab, wild squabs are actually young pigeons. The types of pigeons in the United States include the mourning dove of the East, the white-winged dove of the South, and the band-tailed pigeon of the West. It should be noted that mourning doves are protected as song birds in some northeastern states.

GEORGE OLSON

NEW SETTLERS BROUGHT CHICKENS WITH THEM ON THEIR LONG OCEAN CROSSINGS, AND BY THE MID-NINETEENTH CENTURY CHICKEN BREEDING HAD BECOME WELL ESTABLISHED IN AMERICA.

BECAUSE THE DEMAND FOR FLAVORFUL, OLD-FASHIONED, FARM-RAISED CHICKENS IS ON THE RISE, SMALL CHICKEN FARMERS HAVE FOUND A NEW MARKET.

JIM BRANDENBURG

FRIED CHICKEN

Maryland

FRIED CHICKEN

There are so many recipes for fried chicken, it is impossible to choose "the one" that will please everybody. This recipe has a light egg dip, but that amenity can be omitted if you are so inclined.

1 egg
2/3 cup (5 fl oz/160 ml) milk
1 chicken, about 4 lb (2 kg), cut into serving pieces
salt and freshly ground pepper
2 cups (8 oz/250 g) plus 1½ tablespoons all-purpose
   (plain) flour
1 cup (8 oz/250 g) lard
1 cup (8 oz/250 g) solid vegetable shortening (vegetable lard)
2 cups light (single) cream

❦ Whisk the egg with the milk in a shallow bowl until light. Dip the chicken pieces into the mixture and allow the excess to drain off. Place the chicken on a large plate. Sprinkle both sides generously with salt and pepper.

❦ Place the 2 cups (250 g) flour on a large plate. Roll the chicken pieces in the flour, pressing the flour onto the chicken.

❦ Preheat the oven to 250°F (120°C). Melt the lard with the vegetable shortening in a large cast-iron skillet over medium-high heat. Gently place the chicken in the skillet; do not crowd. Fry until golden brown, about 7 minutes on each side. Reduce the heat to medium-low, cover the skillet partially and cook, turning the chicken several times, for 20 minutes. (The chicken will be deep copper in color; reduce the heat if browning too fast.) Drain the chicken pieces on paper towels. Keep warm in the oven.

❦ Drain all but 2 tablespoons drippings from the skillet. Stir in 1½ tablespoons flour. Cook, stirring constantly, over low heat for 2 minutes. Whisk in the cream. Heat to boiling, stirring and scraping the bottom and sides of the skillet, and boil until thickened. Add salt and pepper to taste. Serve with the chicken.

SERVES 3 TO 4

New Mexico

CHICKEN POT PIE

Pot pies were once made in heavy pots and cooked slowly over burning coals—hence, the name. Although originally made with top and bottom crusts, today's pies generally are bottomless and made in shallow pans rather than deep pots.

1 whole chicken, about 3½ lb (1.75 kg)
1 large yellow (brown) onion (unpeeled), halved
2 carrots, 1 sliced, 1 diced
1 celery stalk, chopped
1 white turnip, chopped
1 parsnip, chopped
4 parsley sprigs
4 cups (1 qt/1 l) chicken stock (see glossary)
1 teaspoon red wine vinegar
2 tablespoons vegetable oil
20 small mushroom caps
1 large leek, washed and chopped (about 1 cup)
1 small potato, peeled and diced (about ½ cup)
2 tablespoons (1 oz/30 g) unsalted butter
1½ tablespoons all-purpose (plain) flour
1 cup (8 fl oz/250 ml) cream
pinch of ground mace
pinch of freshly grated nutmeg
salt and freshly ground pepper
1 cup (4 oz/125 g) shelled green peas
1 tablespoon milk

PIE PASTRY

1½ cups (6 oz/185 g) all-purpose (plain) flour
¼ teaspoon salt
¼ cup (2 oz/60 g) cold unsalted butter
¼ cup (2 oz/60 g) cold solid vegetable shortening or lard
2 tablespoons water

❦ Place the chicken in a large pot or Dutch oven and add the onion, sliced carrot, celery, turnip, parsnip, parsley, chicken stock and water to cover. Heat to boiling, reduce the heat and simmer, partially covered, until the chicken is tender, about 50 minutes. Remove from the heat, stir in the vinegar and let the chicken cool in the stock for about 30 minutes.

❦ Meanwhile, make the pastry: Combine the flour with the salt in a large bowl. Cut in the butter and shortening until the texture of coarse crumbs. Using a fork, mix in the water to form a soft dough. Cover and chill for 1 hour before using.

❦ When the chicken is cool enough to handle, remove the skin and bones and cut the meat into bite-size pieces. Strain the stock and set aside.

❦ Heat the oil in a skillet. Sauté the mushroom caps, turning once, until nicely browned. Transfer to a bowl.

❦ Combine the leek with 1½ cups (12 fl oz/375 ml) of the stock in a saucepan and heat to boiling. Stir in the diced carrot and reduce the heat. Cook, uncovered, over medium-low heat for 5 minutes. Add the potato and cook 5 minutes longer. Strain the vegetables and set aside. Add more stock, if necessary, to the cooking liquid to make 1 cup (8 fl oz/250 ml).

❦ Melt the butter in a saucepan over medium-low heat. Whisk in the flour. Cook, stirring constantly, for 2 minutes. Add the reserved cooking liquid, heat to boiling and boil for 3 minutes. Whisk in the cream, mace, nutmeg and salt and pepper to taste. Remove from the heat and let cool, stirring occasionally, for 10 minutes. Stir in the chicken, vegetables, mushrooms and peas. Transfer to a lightly greased 10-in (25-cm) round baking dish 1½ to 2 in (4 to 5 cm) deep.

❦ Preheat the oven to 400°F (200°C). Roll out the pastry on a lightly floured board and cover the dish. Trim and flute the edges. Brush the top with the milk and cut a slash in the center. Bake until golden brown, about 25 minutes.

SERVES 4 TO 6

BARBECUED CHICKEN

Ohio

BARBECUED CHICKEN

Barbecue sauces vary from one end of the country to the other, but most are ketchup-based and should be applied near the end of the cooking time to prevent burning. The following recipe originated in northern Ohio, where it is not unusual to find maple syrup sweetening the sauce at maple festival time. The sauce that accompanies the bacon-wrapped barbecued shrimp on page 68 may be substituted.

2 tablespoons (1 oz/30 g) unsalted butter
1 tablespoon dry mustard
½ cup (4 fl oz/125 ml) maple syrup
1 cup (8 oz/250 g) chili sauce (American-style)
½ cup (4 oz/125 g) ketchup (tomato sauce)
½ cup (4 fl oz/125 ml) cider vinegar
1 teaspoon celery seed
1 teaspoon cayenne pepper
½ teaspoon salt
2 chickens, about 3 lb (1.5 kg) each, cut into serving pieces
vegetable oil

❦ Melt the butter in a saucepan over medium heat. Stir in the mustard, syrup, chili sauce, ketchup, vinegar, celery seed, cayenne pepper and salt. Heat to boiling, reduce the heat and simmer, uncovered, for 20 minutes. Let cool.
❦ Place the chicken in a large glass or ceramic bowl. Toss the pieces with just enough sauce to lightly coat, ½ to ¾ cup (125 to 180 ml). Refrigerate, covered, overnight.
❦ About 1 hour before grilling, remove the chicken from the refrigerator and pat dry. Brush lightly with oil.
❦ Preheat an outdoor grill and brush the rack lightly with oil. Place the chicken pieces over medium-hot coals and cover. Cook with the vents open for 15 minutes on each side. Remove the cover and continue to grill, basting with the sauce, until the chicken is crisp, about 5 minutes on each side. Or the chicken may be broiled (grilled) indoors for 20 minutes on each side. Reheat the remaining sauce and serve on the side.

SERVES 6 TO 8

Texas

TEXAS CHICKEN

This dish is fairly typical of grilled or broiled chicken Texas-style. It requires an overnight stint in the refrigerator for the seasonings to blend.

3 garlic cloves, finely minced
2 teaspoons cayenne pepper
1 teaspoon chili powder
juice of 1 lemon
2 tablespoons sweet paprika
¼ cup (2 fl oz/60 ml) olive oil
1 chicken, 3½ to 4 lb (1.75 to 2 kg), cut into serving pieces

❦ With the back of a wooden spoon, mash the garlic with the cayenne pepper and chili powder in a small bowl. When pasty, stir in the lemon juice. Whisk in the paprika and olive oil.
❦ Spread the garlic mixture over the chicken pieces and place in a glass or ceramic dish. Refrigerate, covered, overnight. Remove from the refrigerator 1 hour before cooking.
❦ Preheat the broiler (griller). Broil the chicken pieces about 6 in (15 cm) from the heat until crisp and the juices run clear when the chicken is pricked, about 20 minutes on each side.

SERVES 3 TO 4

Texas

FLAUTAS

One of the easiest Mexican-style dishes to prepare, flautas are rolled-up chicken-filled tortillas. Corn tortillas are difficult to make without practiced hands but can be found in almost every supermarket.

peanut oil for frying
3 cups (1 lb/500 g) roughly chopped cooked chicken
12 corn tortillas
1 head iceberg lettuce, shredded
guacamole (recipe follows)
2 cups (16 fl oz/500 ml) sour cream
4 oz (125 g) Monterey Jack (mild melting) cheese, shredded

❦ Heat ½ in (1 cm) oil in a large heavy skillet until hot but not smoking.
❦ Place about ¼ cup (1½ oz/50 g) chicken in a strip on one side of each tortilla. Roll up the tortillas as tightly as possible, using toothpicks to secure them if needed. Fry them, a few at a time, in the hot oil until crisp, 1 to 2 minutes. Drain well on paper towels and keep warm in a low oven until all have been fried.
❦ To serve, arrange the flautas on lettuce on a serving platter. Spoon guacamole over the top. Or sprinkle with lettuce and top with sour cream and cheese. Serve immediately.

SERVES 4 TO 6

GUACAMOLE

2 ripe avocados
1 tablespoon plus 1 teaspoon lime juice
1 large ripe tomato, seeded and chopped
2 tablespoons finely chopped onion
½ red onion, finely chopped (about ¼ cup)
1 small hot green (chili) pepper, seeded, deveined and finely chopped
2 tablespoons chopped fresh cilantro (coriander)

❦ Peel and pit the avocados, saving the pits. Place the avocados in a bowl and mash to a "chunky" texture. Add the remaining ingredients and mix thoroughly. Press the pits into the guacamole (this helps prevent it from turning brown) and refrigerate, covered, for 1 hour. Remove the pits and mix once more before serving.

MAKES ABOUT 2 CUPS (1 PT/500 ML)

CHICKEN WITH DUMPLINGS

Ohio

CHICKEN WITH DUMPLINGS

A nineteenth-century recipe, this old-fashioned supper was served all over America, generally using hens whose laying days were over.

6 tablespoons (3 oz/90 g) cold unsalted butter
1 tablespoon vegetable oil
2 small chickens, 2½ lb (1.25 kg) each, cut into serving pieces
1 onion, finely chopped
1 cup (8 fl oz/250 ml) dry white wine
chicken stock (see glossary)
2 celery stalks with leaves, chopped
¾ teaspoon salt
½ teaspoon freshly ground pepper
¼ teaspoon ground allspice
2 cups (8 oz/250 g) plus 1 tablespoon all-purpose (plain) flour
2½ teaspoons baking powder
1 teaspoon sugar
⅔ cup (5 fl oz/160 ml) milk
¼ cup (2 fl oz/60 ml) cream
chopped fresh parsley (optional)

Heat ¼ cup (2 oz/60 g) of the butter with the oil in a large heavy pot or Dutch oven. Sauté the chicken, a few pieces at a time, until well browned on all sides, about 15 minutes. Do not let the butter burn. Transfer them to a plate as they are done.

Add the onion to the pot; cook for 1 minute. Stir in the wine, scraping the bottom and sides of the pot. Return the chicken and add stock to cover. Add the celery, ½ teaspoon of the salt, the pepper and the allspice. Heat to boiling, reduce the heat, cover and cook until the chicken is tender, about 30 minutes.

Meanwhile, combine the 2 cups (8 oz/250 g) flour with the baking powder, sugar and ¼ teaspoon salt in a bowl. Mix well and add the remaining 2 tablespoons (1 oz/30 g) butter. Blend with a pastry blender to incorporate the butter and stir in the milk to form a soft dough. Roll the dough out ½ in (1 cm) thick on a floured board and cut into 2-in (5-cm) circles.

Preheat the oven to 250°F (120°C). Transfer the chicken pieces to a large shallow baking dish and cover loosely with foil. Keep warm in the oven.

Strain the cooking juices and return to the pot. Combine the 1 tablespoon flour with 2 tablespoons of the cream until smooth. Add to the cooking juices along with the remaining 2

98

tablespoons cream. Heat to simmering and place the dumplings on top. Cook, covered, over medium-low heat until firm, about 18 minutes.

🐦 To serve, remove the dumplings with a slotted spoon and place over the chicken. Spoon the sauce on top. Sprinkle with parsley.

SERVES 6 TO 8

California

GARLICKY GRILLED CHICKEN

Based on a Thai recipe, the following dish comes from Los Angeles. Note that the roots of the cilantro (coriander) are called for, which impart more flavor than just the leaves.

1 chicken, 3½ to 4 lb (1.75 to 2 kg), cut into serving pieces
1 teaspoon salt
2 tablespoons whole black peppercorns
6 garlic cloves
1 small hot green pepper, seeded, deveined and chopped
4 whole sprigs fresh cilantro (coriander/Chinese parsley) with roots, washed, dried and chopped
2 tablespoons lemon juice
2 tablespoons vegetable oil

🐦 Place the chicken pieces in a bowl. Place the remaining ingredients in a food processor or blender and process until very smooth. Pour over the chicken, toss well to coat and let stand for 1 hour.

🐦 Preheat the broiler or an outdoor grill. Broil or grill the chicken about 6 in (15 cm) from the heat until crisp and the juices run clear when the chicken is pricked, about 20 minutes on each side.

SERVES 3 TO 4

California

CHICKEN WITH ANCHOVIES

Chicken breasts are quick and easy to prepare. The version below may be topped with Parmesan cheese, as is sometimes done in San Francisco, and run under a hot broiler (griller) at the last minute to brown. The dish may also be served cold with mayonnaise.

⅓ cup (1½ oz/45 g) all-purpose (plain) flour
½ teaspoon salt
¼ teaspoon freshly ground pepper
3 large chicken breasts, skinned, boned and halved
1 garlic clove, bruised
1½ to 2 teaspoons anchovy paste (essence)
¼ cup (2 oz/60 g) unsalted butter
2 tablespoons vegetable oil
juice of 1 large lemon
chopped fresh parsley (optional)

🐦 Combine the flour with the salt and pepper on a plate.

🐦 Rub the chicken breasts well with the bruised garlic. Then rub the top of each with about ¼ teaspoon anchovy paste. Lightly coat each piece with the seasoned flour.

🐦 Heat the butter with the oil in a large heavy skillet over medium-high heat. Sauté the chicken breasts until lightly browned, about 3 minutes on each side. Drain lightly on paper towels and transfer to a serving platter. Keep warm.

🐦 Pour off all but 2 tablespoons drippings from the skillet and stir in the lemon juice, scraping the bottom and sides of the pan. When hot but not boiling, pour over the chicken. Sprinkle with parsley.

SERVES 4 TO 6

CHICKEN TETRAZZINI (left), GARLICKY GRILLED CHICKEN (top) AND CHICKEN WITH ANCHOVIES (bottom)

California

CHICKEN TETRAZZINI

This dish was named after the Italian opera singer Luisa Tetrazzini, who was quite popular in America after 1908. Reportedly, a San Francisco chef created it in her honor. Leftover Thanksgiving turkey is often substituted.

5 tablespoons (2½ oz/80 g) unsalted butter
½ lb (250 g) mushrooms, sliced
½ lb (250 g) thin spaghetti
2 tablespoons all-purpose (plain) flour
2 cups (16 fl oz/500 ml) hot chicken stock (see glossary)
1 cup (8 fl oz/250 ml) cream
3 tablespoons dry sherry
good pinch of freshly grated nutmeg
salt and freshly ground pepper
2 cups (10 oz/315 g) roughly chopped cooked chicken or turkey
½ cup (2 oz/60 g) freshly grated Parmesan cheese

🐦 Melt 3 tablespoons of the butter in a large skillet over medium-high heat. Add the mushrooms and cook, stirring constantly, until golden. Set aside.

🐦 Cook the spaghetti in boiling salted water until tender. Rinse under cold running water; drain thoroughly.

🐦 Preheat the oven to 350°F (180°C). Melt the remaining 2 tablespoons butter in a saucepan over medium-low heat. Whisk in the flour. Cook, stirring constantly, for 2 minutes. Whisk in the stock. Raise the heat slightly; cook for 2 minutes. Add the cream and sherry and continue to cook until thick, about 8 minutes. Add nutmeg and salt and pepper to taste.

🐦 Spread the spaghetti over the bottom of a greased shallow baking dish. Pour half the sauce on top. Spread the chicken and mushrooms over the spaghetti and pour the remaining sauce on top. Sprinkle with the cheese. Bake until golden, about 20 minutes.

SERVES 4 TO 6

SHAKER CHICKEN WITH APPLE RINGS

Massachusetts

SHAKER CHICKEN WITH APPLE RINGS

The Shakers were members of a religious sect that originated in England and was brought to America in the mid-eighteenth century. Known today for their handcrafts, the Shakers believed in communal living and celibacy. Eventually their communities died out, although a handful of Shakers still exist. This recipe is from Hancock Village, which endured until 1960.

1 chicken, 3½ to 4 lb (1.75 to 2 kg), cut into serving pieces
salt and freshly ground pepper
½ cup (4 oz/125 g) unsalted butter
1 tablespoon vegetable oil
½ cup (4 fl oz/125 ml) plus 3 tablespoons apple cider
2 large red sweet apples
juice of 1 lemon
1 cup (8 oz/250 g) sugar
1 cup (8 fl oz/250 ml) cream
2 teaspoons grated lemon peel
chopped fresh parsley (optional)
hot cooked rice

❧ Preheat the oven to 350°F (180°C). Pat the chicken pieces dry with paper towels and sprinkle with salt and pepper. Heat half of the butter with the oil in a large heavy skillet over medium heat. Sauté the chicken pieces, half at a time, until golden brown, 10 minutes on each side. Transfer to a plate.
❧ Discard all but 2 tablespoons fat from skillet. Stir in 3 tablespoons of the cider, scraping the bottom and sides of the pan. Return the chicken to the skillet, cover and cook over low heat, turning once, until tender, about 30 minutes.
❧ Meanwhile, core the apples and cut into rings ½ in (1 cm) thick. Sprinkle with lemon juice. Place the sugar on a plate and press the apple rings into the sugar, coating well on both sides.
❧ Melt the remaining butter in a large skillet over medium

heat. Quickly sauté the apple rings, a few at a time, until golden, about 2 minutes on each side. Place on an ovenproof platter and bake for 15 minutes. Remove from the oven and reduce the temperature to 250°F (120°C).
❧ When the chicken is tender, transfer the pieces to a large ovenproof serving dish. Surround with the apple rings and keep warm in the oven.
❧ Add the remaining ½ cup (4 fl oz/125 ml) cider to the juices in the skillet and stir in the cream and lemon peel. Heat to boiling; boil until slightly thickened, about 5 minutes. Add salt and pepper to taste and pour over the chicken. Sprinkle with parsley and serve with rice.

SERVES 4

Delaware

ROAST CHICKEN WITH VEGETABLES

Delaware is an important poultry-producing state. Although most supermarket chickens lack the taste and texture of farm-raised (often called free-range) chickens, a strong cottage industry of small chicken farmers is making more flavorful birds available. The following recipe is fairly standard throughout the United States.

½ cup (4 oz/125 g) unsalted butter
1 onion, chopped
2 potatoes, peeled and diced
2 carrots, peeled and diced
1 zucchini (courgette), diced
¼ cup chopped fresh parsley
1 tablespoon soy sauce
salt and freshly ground pepper
2 whole chickens, about 3 lb (1.5 kg) each
1 garlic clove, bruised
4 bacon strips
1 cup (8 fl oz/250 ml) water
1 cup (8 fl oz/250 ml) chicken stock (see glossary)
1 tablespoon all-purpose (plain) flour
1 cup (8 fl oz/250 ml) cream
1 tablespoon bourbon
parsley

❧ Preheat the oven to 400°F (200°C). Melt ¼ cup (60 g) of the butter in a large skillet over medium-low heat. Add the onion; cook for 5 minutes. Add the potatoes, carrots and zucchini; cook 5 minutes longer. Stir in the parsley, soy sauce and salt and pepper to taste. Remove from the heat.
❧ Rinse the chickens and pat dry with paper towels. Rub the chickens, inside and out, with the bruised garlic. Spoon half the vegetable mixture into the cavity of each chicken. Truss.
❧ Place the chickens on a rack in a roasting pan. Rub each with 1 tablespoon butter and lay 2 bacon strips on top. Roast in the oven for 15 minutes. Pour the water into the pan and reduce the temperature to 375°F (190°C). Baste the chickens with stock and roast 15 minutes longer. Pour the remaining stock into the pan and continue to roast, basting the chickens with pan juices every 20 minutes, until the juices run clear when the chickens are pricked, about 1 hour. Remove the trussing from the chickens and keep warm. Skim fat from the pan juices.
❧ Melt the remaining 2 tablespoons butter in a saucepan over medium-low heat. Stir in the flour and cook, stirring constantly, for 2 minutes. Whisk in the pan juices and cream. Heat to boiling, reduce the heat and simmer until slightly thickened, about 5 minutes. Add the bourbon and salt and pepper to taste. Spoon some of the gravy over the chickens. Sprinkle with parsley. Serve the remaining gravy on the side with the remaining vegetables.

SERVES 6

Virginia

RICHMOND FRIED CHICKEN

This is an old recipe that has not changed much through the years. It is unusual because the chicken is "peeled" before it hits the pan. Some might argue that this is actually a chicken sauté rather than fried chicken, but no one would argue that it doesn't taste wonderful.

1 chicken, about 4 lb (2 kg), cut into serving pieces
½ cup (2 oz/60 g) all-purpose (plain) flour
salt and freshly ground pepper
pinch of ground allspice
⅛ teaspoon freshly grated nutmeg
½ cup (4 oz/125 g) unsalted butter
2 tablespoons vegetable oil
1 cup (8 fl oz/250 ml) chicken stock (see glossary)
1 cup (8 fl oz/250 ml) cream
1 teaspoon bourbon (optional)
chopped fresh parsley

❦ Remove the skin from the chicken pieces. Combine the flour, ½ teaspoon salt, ¼ teaspoon pepper, the allspice and nutmeg in a large paper bag. Place the chicken, a few pieces at a time, in the bag and shake to coat evenly with the flour mixture. Set aside 2 tablespoons of the flour mixture.

❦ Preheat the oven to 275°F (135°C). Melt the butter with 1 tablespoon oil in a large cast-iron skillet over medium-low heat. Gently place the chicken in the skillet; do not crowd. Sauté until golden brown, 12 to 15 minutes on each side. Reduce the heat if browning too fast; add more oil if needed.

❦ When the chicken is crisp, drain on paper towels. Transfer to a shallow heatproof serving platter and place, uncovered, in the oven for at least 30 minutes but no longer than 1 hour.

❦ Meanwhile, drain all but 2 tablespoons drippings from the skillet. Stir in the reserved flour and cook, stirring constantly,

for 2 minutes. Whisk in the stock, scraping the bottom and sides of the skillet. Whisk in the cream and cook, stirring occasionally, for 20 minutes. Add salt and pepper to taste. Stir in the bourbon. Spoon some of the gravy over the chicken and sprinkle with parsley. Serve the remaining gravy on the side.

SERVES 3 TO 4

Nebraska

OVEN-FRIED CHICKEN

The secret to oven-fried chicken, a midwestern and Plains states specialty, is to place the chicken on a large rack (or two) over a roasting pan so that the chicken sits over the pan and is heated from all sides. Broiler (griller) trays have a tendency to turn the chicken soggy.

1 chicken, about 4 lb (2 kg), cut into serving pieces
1½ cups (12 fl oz/375 ml) milk
2 teaspoons hot red pepper (Tabasco) sauce
2 teaspoons soy sauce
½ cup (2 oz/60 g) crushed bran flakes (cereal flakes)
¼ cup (1 oz/30 g) all-purpose (plain) flour
½ teaspoon salt
¼ teaspoon freshly ground pepper
⅛ teaspoon ground allspice
½ cup (4 oz/125 g) unsalted butter
½ cup (4 fl oz/125 ml) water

❦ Place the chicken in a shallow glass or ceramic dish. Combine the milk, hot pepper sauce and soy sauce in a bowl. Pour over the chicken pieces. Refrigerate, covered, for 3 hours, turning once. Remove from the refrigerator 30 minutes before baking.

Preheat the oven to 375°F (190°C). Drain the chicken pieces and pat dry. Combine the crushed bran flakes with the flour, salt, pepper and allspice in a paper bag. Place the chicken pieces, a few at a time, in the bag and shake to coat evenly. Place the coated chicken, skin side down, on a greased rack over a roasting pan. Bake for 5 minutes.

 Meanwhile, melt the butter with the water in a small saucepan. Baste the chicken with the butter mixture. Continue to bake the chicken, basting every 5 minutes, for 25 minutes. Turn the chicken over and continue to bake, basting every 5 minutes with the butter mixture and pan juices, until crisp and the juices run clear when the chicken is pricked—about 30 minutes longer.

SERVES 3 TO 4

Florida

ROAST CHICKEN WITH ORANGES

Floridians cook just about anything with oranges and there is nothing like a fresh orange picked off the tree in one's own backyard. Roast chicken takes naturally to orange and is particularly satisfying when filled with an old-fashioned bread stuffing and served with a sweet-and-sour sauce.

1 whole chicken, 3½ to 4 lb (1.75 to 2 kg)
1 garlic clove, bruised
salt and freshly ground pepper
2 small oranges
1 cup toasted bread cubes (2 slices)
1 large celery stalk, thinly sliced
¼ cup (2 oz/60 g) unsalted butter, melted
¼ teaspoon dried tarragon
¼ teaspoon dried thyme or rosemary
2 cups (16 fl oz/500 ml) chicken stock (see glossary)
¼ cup (2 fl oz/60 ml) white wine vinegar
3 tablespoons sugar
1 tablespoon cornstarch (cornflour)
parsley or rosemary sprigs (optional)

 Preheat the oven to 375°F (190°C). Rinse the chicken and pat dry with paper towels. Rub inside and out with the bruised garlic. Sprinkle inside and out with salt and pepper.

 Using a vegetable peeler, remove the outer peel of 1 orange and cut into slivers; set aside. Squeeze the juice from the orange; set aside. Peel the other orange and cut into segments, removing seeds if necessary.

 Combine the bread cubes, celery, butter, ½ teaspoon salt, ¼ teaspoon pepper and half the herbs in a bowl. Stir in the orange segments and dampen with 2 or 3 tablespoons stock. Spoon into the cavity of the chicken. Truss. Roast the chicken, basting occasionally with a few tablespoons stock and pan juices, until the juices run clear when the chicken is pricked, about 1½ hours.

 Meanwhile, combine the vinegar, sugar and 1½ cups (12 fl oz/375 ml) stock in a heavy saucepan. Heat to boiling; boil until reduced to half. Stir in the orange juice and remaining herbs. Simmer for 10 minutes.

 Transfer the chicken to a serving platter and keep warm. Mix the pan juices with the cornstarch in a bowl and whisk into the sauce. Cook over medium heat, stirring constantly, until thickened. Strain the sauce and add the orange peel. Add salt and pepper to taste. Pour some of the sauce over the chicken and surround the chicken with parsley sprigs. Serve the remaining sauce on the side.

SERVES 3 TO 4

COUNTRY CAPTAIN (top) AND
ROAST CHICKEN WITH ORANGES (bottom)

Georgia

COUNTRY CAPTAIN

Georgians claim that Country Captain was invented in Savannah, an important port in the days of the spice trade. Others insist the dish was brought to the South by a British captain who spent time in India. The spices in the dish are indeed more Indian than southern.

½ cup (2 oz/60 g) all-purpose (plain) flour
salt and freshly ground pepper
1 chicken, 3½ to 4 lb (1.75 to 2 kg), cut into serving pieces
2 tablespoons (1 oz/30 g) unsalted butter
2 tablespoons vegetable oil
1 large onion, chopped
1 large garlic clove, minced
1 green bell pepper (capsicum), seeded and chopped
3 ripe tomatoes, seeded and chopped
½ teaspoon sugar
1½ teaspoons curry powder
¼ teaspoon dried thyme
⅓ cup (2 oz/60 g) dried currants
½ cup (2 oz/60 g) toasted slivered almonds
chopped fresh parsley
hot cooked rice

 Season the flour with 1 teaspoon salt and ½ teaspoon pepper and lightly coat the chicken pieces with it.

 Heat the butter with the oil in a large heavy skillet over medium heat. Sauté the chicken pieces, half at a time, until golden brown, about 10 minutes on each side. Transfer to a plate.

 Discard all but 2 tablespoons drippings from the skillet and add the onion, garlic and bell pepper. Cook, stirring frequently, over medium-low heat for 5 minutes. Add the tomatoes, sugar, curry powder and thyme. Mix well and return the chicken pieces to the skillet. Heat to boiling, reduce the heat, cover and cook until the chicken is tender, about 30 minutes. Raise the heat if needed to evaporate any liquid.

 Stir in the currants and sprinkle with almonds and parsley. Serve with rice.

SERVES 3 TO 4

BUFFALO CHICKEN WINGS WITH CREAMY BLUE CHEESE DRESSING

CREAMY BLUE CHEESE DRESSING

2 tablespoons minced onion
1 garlic clove, crushed
4 tablespoons chopped fresh parsley
1 cup (8 fl oz/250 ml) mayonnaise
½ cup (4 fl oz/125 ml) sour cream
1 tablespoon lemon juice
1 tablespoon red wine vinegar
6 oz (185 g) creamy blue cheese, cut into pieces
salt and freshly ground pepper to taste

❦ Whisk all the ingredients together in a bowl until smooth. Chill well before serving.

MAKES ABOUT 2½ CUPS (625 ML)

New Mexico

CHICKEN MOLE

The traditional mole, *flavored with chocolate, was said to have been made with wild turkey and was popularized in the Southwest by Spanish nuns who had traveled north from Mexico. It is now most often made with chicken.*

2 small chickens, 2½ lb (1.25 kg) each, cut into serving pieces
1 garlic clove, bruised
salt and freshly ground pepper
2 tablespoons (1 oz/30 g) unsalted butter
1 tablespoon olive oil
1 onion, chopped
1 tablespoon red wine vinegar
1 fresh jalapeño (hot green chili) pepper, seeded, deveined and roughly chopped
1 can (28 oz/875 g) plum (egg) tomatoes with juice
3 large canned mild green chilies
1 oz (30 g) unsweetened (cooking) chocolate, grated
chopped fresh parsley (optional)

❦ Rub the chicken pieces well with the bruised garlic. Sprinkle with salt and pepper.
❦ Heat the butter with the oil in a large heavy skillet over medium heat. Sauté the chicken pieces until golden brown on both sides, about 10 minutes on each side. Transfer to a large pot or Dutch oven.
❦ Discard all but 2 tablespoons drippings from the skillet. Add the onion and cook over medium-low heat until golden, about 5 minutes. Sprinkle with the vinegar, scraping the bottom and sides of the skillet, and transfer to the pot.
❦ Place the jalapeño pepper, tomatoes and green chilies in a food processor or blender and process until smooth. Pour over the chicken. Heat to boiling, reduce the heat and stir in the grated chocolate. Cook, covered, over medium-low heat until the chicken is tender, about 30 minutes. Transfer the chicken to a serving dish. Add salt and pepper to taste to the sauce and pour over the chicken. Sprinkle with parsley.

SERVES 6 TO 8

Arizona

CHICKEN WITH SAUSAGE AND RICE

Arroz con pollo, *or chicken with rice, is popular throughout the Southwest. Its Mexican heritage is evident. This particular recipe from Arizona uses Spanish sausages as well as chicken. The sausages are available at any Mexican or Spanish grocer, as well as many gourmet shops.*

New York

BUFFALO CHICKEN WINGS

Although Buffalo chicken wings did not make their debut until the 1960s, this specialty of the Anchor Bar & Grill in Buffalo, New York, has become a popular treat from coast to coast. The chicken wings are spicy, so don't forget the celery and blue cheese dressing; they help cool the palate between bites. If Frank's Louisiana Red Hot Sauce is unavailable, any spicy barbecue-type sauce may be substituted.

20 to 24 small chicken wings
oil for frying
¼ cup (20 oz/60 g) unsalted butter
¾ cup (6 fl oz/180 ml) Frank's Louisiana Red Hot Sauce (hot barbecue sauce)
4 celery stalks, cut into strips 3 in (7.5 cm) long and ¼ in (6 mm) thick
creamy blue cheese dressing (recipe follows)

❦ Cut the tips off the chicken wings and save for use in stocks. Cut the wings in half at the joint. Pat dry.
❦ Heat enough oil in a heavy saucepan to deep-fry the wings. When hot but not smoking, add the wings. Fry until crisp and cooked through, about 12 minutes.
❦ Meanwhile, heat the butter and hot sauce in another saucepan large enough to hold the wings. When the wings are crisp, drain on paper towels and stir into the sauce, tossing well to coat. Serve immediately with the celery sticks and individual bowls of blue cheese dressing.

SERVES 4

CHICKEN MOLE (top) AND CHICKEN WITH SAUSAGE AND RICE (bottom)

1 lb (500 g) *chorizos* (Spanish sausages), cut into ½-in
  (1-cm) slices
2 tablespoons vegetable oil
1 chicken, about 4 lb (2 kg), cut into pieces
1 large onion, chopped
2 garlic cloves, minced
1 large green bell pepper (capsicum), seeded and cut into strips
1 hot green (chili) pepper, seeded, deveined and minced
2 large ripe tomatoes, seeded and chopped
½ teaspoon sugar
1 tablespoon chopped fresh cilantro (coriander/Chinese
  parsley)
½ teaspoon chopped fresh thyme or pinch of dried thyme
2 cups (16 fl oz/500 ml) chicken stock (approximately)
  (see glossary)
1 cup (5 oz/155 g) long-grain rice
1 cup (4 oz/125 g) corn kernels
¼ cup (2½ oz/80 g) chopped pimientos
salt and freshly ground pepper
2 tablespoons chopped fresh parsley (optional)

❦ Sauté the sausage in a greased large pot or Dutch oven over medium-low heat until rendered of fat and golden, about 15 minutes. Transfer to a plate.

❦ Pour off all but 1 tablespoon fat and add the oil to the pot. Sauté the chicken pieces over medium heat until golden brown, about 8 minutes on each side. Transfer to the plate with the sausages.

❦ Add the onion to the pot. Cook over medium-low heat for 2 minutes, scraping the bottom and sides of the pot. Add the garlic; cook 4 minutes longer. Add the peppers, tomatoes, sugar, cilantro and thyme. Cook for 4 minutes. Stir in the stock, rice, corn and pimientos, heat to boiling and remove from the heat.

❦ Preheat the oven to 375°F (190°C). Return the chicken and sausage to the pot, pressing gently into the mixture. Cover and bake for 35 minutes. Remove the cover and bake 5 minutes longer. Add salt and pepper to taste and serve sprinkled with parsley.

SERVES 4 TO 6

Connecticut

ROAST THANKSGIVING TURKEY WITH CORNBREAD STUFFING

The first Thanksgiving was celebrated by the Plymouth colonists in 1621 after surviving their first hard year in the New World. It became an annual event in New England, although each colony celebrated it on different days. George Washington, as president, proclaimed November 26 to be the nationally observed holiday. President Lincoln changed the date to the last Thursday in November. No one is quite sure if turkey was actually served at the first Thanksgiving, but the bird definitely appeared at the second celebration and has been served ever since. In early America, the stuffing was made with cornbread and oysters. The cornbread should be made a day or two in advance.

1 fresh turkey, 18 to 20 lb (9 to 10 kg)
2 large garlic cloves, bruised
salt and freshly ground pepper
cornbread stuffing (recipe follows)
3 bacon strips
½ cup (4 fl oz/125 ml) dry white wine
4 cups (1 qt/1 l) water
1 onion
1 celery stalk, broken
3 parsley sprigs, plus extra for garnish
¼ teaspoon salt
4 whole black peppercorns
1½ tablespoons (1 oz/30 g) unsalted butter
1½ tablespoons all-purpose (plain) flour
¼ cup (2 fl oz/60 ml) cream

❦ Preheat the oven to 325°F (165°C). Remove the giblets from the turkey; set aside (but discard the liver) for the gravy if desired. Wipe the turkey inside and out with a damp cloth. Rub well inside and out with 1 bruised garlic clove, salt and pepper. Stuff the cavity with the cornbread stuffing. Truss.
❦ Place the turkey on a rack in a roasting pan and lay the bacon strips across the breast. Cut a piece of cheesecloth large enough to fit over the turkey, soak it in the wine and place over the turkey. Pour any extra wine over the top. Roast in the oven for 30 minutes.
❦ Meanwhile, combine the giblets (except the liver), water, onion, celery, remaining garlic clove, parsley, salt and peppercorns in a large saucepan. Heat to boiling, reduce the heat and simmer, uncovered, until the liquid is reduced to 2 cups (16 fl oz/500 ml). Strain.
❦ Baste the turkey with the stock and continue to roast, basting every 30 minutes, until the legs move freely and the juices run clear when the inner thigh is pierced, 5½ to 6 hours total. During the last half hour of roasting, remove the cheesecloth by first wetting it with basting juices. It should lift off easily. Raise the oven temperature to 375°F (190°C) to crisp the skin. Transfer the turkey to a carving board; let stand for 15 minutes.
❦ Meanwhile, strain the turkey drippings, skimming off the fat if necessary. Melt the butter in a saucepan over medium-low heat. Whisk in the flour. Cook, stirring constantly, for 2 minutes. Whisk in the drippings and cream; simmer for 5 minutes. Adjust the seasonings if necessary. Garnish the turkey with the remaining sprigs of parsley. Serve with gravy and stuffing.

SERVES 8 TO 10   *Photograph pages 90 – 91*

CORNBREAD STUFFING

½ lb (250 g) pork sausage meat
½ cup (4 oz/125 g) unsalted butter, melted
1 large onion, chopped
2 celery stalks, chopped
1 small green or red bell pepper (capsicum), seeded and finely chopped
½ cup (¾ oz/20 g) chopped fresh parsley
1 pint (500 ml) shucked (opened) oysters with liquor
1 8-in (20-cm) square cornbread (page 155)
1 teaspoon minced fresh sage or ¼ teaspoon dried sage
salt and freshly ground pepper

❦ Sauté the sausage in a large skillet over medium heat, stirring to break up the lumps, until lightly browned, about 10 minutes. Transfer to a large bowl.
❦ Discard all but 2 tablespoons drippings from the skillet. Add ¼ cup (2 oz/60 g) of the melted butter, the onion, celery and bell pepper. Cook, stirring frequently, for 10 minutes. Remove from the heat and stir in the parsley. Drain the oysters, reserving their liquor, and stir into the vegetable mixture.
❦ Crumble the cornbread into the bowl with the sausage meat. Add the vegetable mixture, sage and salt and pepper to taste. Toss to combine. Slowly add the oyster liquor and remaining butter to the stuffing, tossing until the mixture is moist but not wet. Cool before stuffing the turkey.

MAKES ENOUGH FOR A 20-LB (10-KG) TURKEY

Alabama

GAME HEN CUSTARD

Game bird baked in custard is a dish that was popular throughout the South in the seventeenth and eighteenth centuries. The following is an updated version that includes vodka to give the marinade punch. Any game bird can be successfully substituted for the Cornish hens.

2 Cornish game hens, about 2 lb (1 kg) each, cut into serving pieces
salt and freshly ground pepper
3 tablespoons chopped fresh mint
¼ cup (2 fl oz/60 ml) vodka
1 small eggplant (aubergine), about ¼ lb (125 g)
4 oz (125 g) salt pork or bacon, diced
3 tablespoons vegetable oil
1 tablespoon butter
1 onion, finely chopped
2 garlic cloves, minced
2 small hot green (chili) peppers, seeded and finely chopped
¾ cup (6 fl oz/180 ml) chicken stock (see glossary)
¾ cup (6 fl oz/180 ml) cream
¾ cup (3 oz/90 g) all-purpose (plain) flour
pinch of ground allspice
6 eggs, lightly beaten

❦ Place the game hens in a large bowl. Sprinkle with salt and pepper; add the mint and vodka and toss well. Leave for 1 hour.
❦ Cut the eggplant into ½-in (1-cm) cubes and sprinkle with salt. Drain in a colander for 30 minutes; pat dry.
❦ Cook the salt pork in boiling water for 2 minutes. Drain and pat dry.
❦ Sauté the salt pork in a large heavy skillet over medium-low heat until crisp and rendered of fat. Transfer with a slotted spoon to a plate. Pour off all the fat and set aside.
❦ Add 2 tablespoons of the oil to the skillet and sauté the hens in batches until well browned on all sides. Transfer to the plate with the salt pork. Add the drippings from the pan to the salt pork drippings (about 4 tablespoons altogether); do not scrape the pan.
❦ Melt the butter in the same skillet over medium-high heat. Add the onion; cook for 1 minute. Add the garlic; cook 4 minutes longer. Stir in the peppers. Return the hen pieces and salt pork to the skillet and add the stock. Heat to boiling, reduce the heat and simmer, covered, until the hens are tender, about 25 minutes.

GAME HEN CUSTARD (left, baked in individual bowls) AND CAPITOLADE OF ROAST FOWL (top right)

❦ Sauté the eggplant cubes in the remaining 1 tablespoon oil over medium heat until golden. Drain on paper towels.

❦ Preheat the oven to 375°F (190°C). With a slotted spoon, transfer the hen pieces, along with the salt pork, peppers and onions, to a lightly greased 12-in (30-cm) round baking dish. Sprinkle with the eggplant cubes.

❦ Pour the reserved drippings into a blender. Add the cooking juices from the skillet, the cream, flour, allspice and eggs. Blend until smooth. Pour over the hens in the dish and bake until puffed and golden, about 35 minutes.

SERVES 4

Virginia

CAPITOLADE OF ROAST FOWL

Capitolade, the precursor of chicken hash, was a favorite of Thomas Jefferson's. He ate it for breakfast, spooned over biscuits.

3 tablespoons (1½ oz/50 g) unsalted butter
1 green (spring) onion, finely chopped

pinch of dried thyme
1½ tablespoons all-purpose (plain) flour
1½ cups (12 fl oz/375 ml) chicken stock (see glossary)
⅓ cup (3 fl oz/80 ml) dry white wine
2½ to 3 cups (1 lb/500 g) leftover roast fowl, roughly chopped
pinch of freshly grated nutmeg
salt and freshly ground pepper
½ cup (4 fl oz/125 ml) cream
1 egg yolk
2 tablespoons lemon juice
2 teaspoons chopped fresh dill
2 teaspoons chopped fresh parsley

❦ Melt the butter in a large saucepan over medium-low heat. Add the onion and thyme; cook for 3 minutes. Stir in the flour; cook, stirring constantly, for 2 minutes. Whisk in the stock and wine. Heat to boiling; reduce the heat and simmer for 10 minutes.

❦ Add the fowl to the sauce, tossing to coat the pieces. Add the nutmeg and salt and pepper to taste.

❦ Combine the cream with the egg yolk and lemon juice. Stir into the meat mixture. Cook over low heat until slightly thickened, but do not let boil. Sprinkle with dill and parsley.

SERVES 4

107

New York

ROAST GOOSE WITH FRUIT AND NUT DRESSING

The Dutch first brought domestic geese to America, and the birds flourished on Long Island. But because of their fattiness and the fact that they must be raised on small farms and are difficult to "mass-produce," geese have never achieved the popularity they deserve. A stuffing made with fruits and nuts helps absorb some of the fatty richness.

1 lb (500 g) dried prunes
1 cup (8 fl oz/250 ml) dry white wine
1 cup (5 oz/155 g) dried apricot halves
½ cup (4 fl oz/125 ml) orange juice
2 tablespoons sugar
2 tart apples, peeled, cored and coarsely chopped
1 lemon
1 tablespoon very fine julienne strips of lemon peel
1 cup (5 oz/155 g) chopped dates
3 tablespoons (1½ oz/50 g) unsalted butter
1½ cups (6 oz/185 g) finely chopped walnuts
¼ teaspoon ground cinnamon
⅓ cup (3 fl oz/80 ml) port wine (approximately)
1 goose, 9 to 10 lb (4.5 to 5 kg)
boiling water
2 tablespoons cognac
salt and freshly ground pepper

☙ Soak the prunes in hot water for 5 minutes; drain. Pit and slice in half. Place in a small saucepan and add the wine. Heat to boiling, reduce the heat and cook, covered, for 10 minutes. Drain, saving both prunes and liquid.

☙ Place the apricots, orange juice and sugar in a saucepan. Heat to boiling, reduce the heat, and simmer, uncovered, for 15 minutes. Drain, saving both apricots and liquid.

☙ Place the apples in a large bowl. Sprinkle with the juice of half the lemon and add the prunes and apricots, lemon peel and dates. Cut 1 tablespoon of the butter into small pieces and add

to the fruit mixture along with the walnuts, cinnamon and enough port to moisten the mixture.

☙ Preheat the oven to 425°F (220°C). Remove the giblets and all loose fat from the goose. Rub the skin with the other lemon half. Wipe out the cavity and stuff with the fruit and nut dressing. Truss. Prick the skin of the thighs, back and lower breast with a fork. Place breast side up in a roasting pan and roast for 15 minutes.

☙ Reduce the oven temperature to 350°F (180°C). Turn the goose on its side; roast for 1 hour, basting every 15 minutes with 2 tablespoons boiling water. Remove accumulating fat from the pan with a bulb baster. Turn the goose over and continue to roast for 1 hour, basting every 15 minutes with boiling water.

☙ Raise the oven temperature to 425°F (220°C) and place the goose breast side up. Roast until the skin is crisp, about 15 minutes. Turn off the oven.

☙ Remove the stuffing from the goose and place in an ovenproof bowl. Transfer the goose to an ovenproof serving platter and place both in the oven with the door ajar.

☙ Skim any remaining fat from the roasting pan and add the reserved fruit liquids. Heat to boiling and cook until slightly reduced. Add the cognac; cook for 1 minute. Add salt and pepper to taste. Remove from the heat and stir in the remaining 2 tablespoons butter. Serve with the goose and dressing.

SERVES 4 TO 6

Michigan

ROAST WILD DUCK

Wild ducks are much smaller than their domesticated cousins. They also lack their fat, making it a good idea to place a layer of bacon over the birds as they roast. A hunter will tell you that the only way to cook wild duck is rare, but medium is fine with most people. Do not, however, cook wild duck until well-done or you will be serving leather on a plate.

ROAST GOOSE WITH FRUIT AND NUT DRESSING

ROAST PHEASANT WITH WILD RICE STUFFING (right)
AND ROAST WILD DUCK (left)

4 wild ducks, 1¼ to 1½ lb (625 to 750 g) each
salt and freshly ground pepper
4 small onions
4 parsley sprigs
4 bacon strips, halved

❧ Preheat the oven to 500°F (240°C). Pat the ducks dry with paper towels and sprinkle inside and out with salt and pepper. Place 1 onion and 1 parsley sprig in each cavity. Place 2 bacon halves over the breast of each duck.

❧ Place the ducks on a rack in a roasting pan and roast about 20 minutes for rare. If medium is preferred, reduce the heat after 15 minutes to 350°F (180°C) and roast about 15 minutes longer.

SERVES 4

Minnesota

ROAST PHEASANT OR GROUSE WITH WILD RICE STUFFING

Although not a native bird, pheasant is so abundant that it has become one of America's favorite game birds. Grouse, a true native, has many enthusiasts too. Depending on the variety, grouse weigh slightly less than pheasants, so if you can get them, add an extra one or two for the table.

½ cup (3 oz/90 g) wild rice
salt
1½ cups (12 fl oz/375 ml) water
10 tablespoons (5 oz/155 g) unsalted butter, melted
2 shallots (small onions), chopped
3 oz (90 g) mushrooms, cleaned, stems removed, caps thinly sliced
¼ teaspoon chopped fresh rosemary or pinch of dried rosemary

freshly ground pepper
2 pheasants or grouse, 2½ to 3 lb (1.25 to 1.5 kg) each
2 bacon strips, halved
1 tablespoon all-purpose (plain) flour
½ cup (4 fl oz/125 ml) chicken stock (approximately) (see glossary)
1 tablespoon cream
pinch of freshly grated nutmeg

❧ Rinse the wild rice under cold water and drain. Place in a saucepan with the salt and water. Heat to boiling, reduce the heat and cook, covered, over medium-low heat until tender, 35 to 60 minutes, depending on the rice. Drain.

❧ Meanwhile, heat 2½ tablespoons butter in a saucepan over medium-low heat. Add the shallots; cook for 5 minutes. Stir in the mushrooms and cook, tossing constantly, until softened, about 2 minutes. Remove from the heat.

❧ Preheat the oven to 375°F (190°C). Add the rice to the mushroom mixture. Stir in the rosemary and salt and pepper to taste.

❧ Wipe the pheasants or grouse with a damp cloth and sprinkle inside and out with salt and pepper. Spoon the rice stuffing into each cavity. Truss. Place the birds on a rack in a roasting pan and lay the bacon over the breasts.

❧ Roast the birds, loosely covered with foil, for 40 minutes, basting often with the remaining melted butter. Remove the foil and continue to roast, basting with pan juices, for 30 minutes. Remove the pheasants or grouse and keep warm.

❧ Discard all but 2 tablespoons drippings from the pan. Place the pan over medium-low heat and whisk in the flour. Cook, stirring and scraping up the brown bits, for 2 minutes. Whisk in the stock. Heat to boiling, reduce the heat and simmer until slightly thickened. Whisk in the cream, nutmeg and salt and pepper to taste. Serve the sauce on the side.

SERVES 6

North Dakota

BRAISED QUAIL OR SQUAB

The average quail weighs about 4 ounces (125 g) dressed, so serve two per person. Although small birds may be roasted, they are delicious braised, which assures tender, juicy results. Quail are found throughout North America. Squabs are young pigeons, less than one month old.

8 quail or squabs
1 lemon, halved
all-purpose (plain) flour
3 tablespoons (1½ oz/50 g) unsalted butter
1 tablespoon vegetable oil
2 green (spring) onions, chopped
2 tablespoons finely chopped green and/or red and yellow
    bell pepper (capsicum)
2 garlic cloves, minced
2 cups (16 fl oz/500 ml) chicken stock (see glossary)
¼ cup (2 fl oz/60 ml) dry red wine
8 slices trimmed toast
salt and freshly ground pepper
½ teaspoon chopped fresh rosemary
chopped fresh parsley (optional)

❦ Rub the quail or squabs inside and out with lemon juice. Lightly dust with flour.

❦ Heat the butter with the oil in a heavy pot or Dutch oven large enough to hold the birds in one layer. Brown the quail, 4 at a time, over medium heat until browned on all sides, about 10 minutes. Transfer to a large plate as they are done.

❦ Preheat the oven to 325°F (165°C). Add the green onions, bell pepper and garlic to the pot, scraping the bottom and sides. Reduce the heat to medium-low and stir in 2 tablespoons flour. Cook, stirring constantly, for 2 minutes. Whisk in the stock and wine, heat to boiling and reduce the heat. Return the quail to the pot. Cover and bake until tender, about 30 minutes.

❦ Transfer the pot to the top of the stove. Arrange the toast over the bottom of a warmed platter. Using a slotted spoon, place a quail on each piece of toast. Add salt and pepper to taste to the

sauce. Stir in the rosemary, heat to boiling and remove from the heat. Spoon about 1 tablespoon sauce over each bird and sprinkle with parsley. Serve the remaining sauce on the side.

SERVES 4

Oklahoma

ROAST DUCKLING WITH HOT PEPPER JELLY

A plains state to be sure and western at heart, Oklahoma is also influenced by the South and by the spicier offerings of Texas, where pepper jelly is on the hot side compared to the sweeter concoctions of Georgia and Alabama.

2 fresh domestic ducks, about 5 lb (2.5 kg) each
salt
½ teaspoon lemon juice
2 garlic cloves, bruised
freshly ground pepper
1 onion, sliced
½ cup (4 fl oz/125 ml) hot pepper jelly (jam) (recipe follows)
watercress stems

❦ Remove all fat and excess skin from the neck and cavity of the ducks. Make sure the fat glands at the base of the tail have been removed. Remove any residue and rub the area with salt and lemon juice. Pierce the skin at ½-in (1-cm) intervals along the thighs, back and lower part of the breast. Place on a rack; let stand, uncovered, in a *very cool* place (or refrigerate) overnight.

❦ Rub the ducks inside and out with bruised garlic. Rub the cavities with salt and pepper. Place 1 bruised garlic clove and half the onion in each cavity. Truss. Coat each duck with half of the hot pepper jelly. Let stand for 1 hour.

❦ Preheat the oven to 375°F (190°C). Place the ducks breast side up in a roasting pan and roast for 20 minutes. Turn on their sides and roast 30 minutes longer. Remove accumulating

BRAISED QUAIL

TIFFANY & CO.

ROAST DUCKLING WITH HOT PEPPER JELLY

fat from the pan with a bulb baster. Turn the ducks over and roast another 30 minutes. Turn breast side up and continue to roast until the juices run clear when a thigh is pricked, about 25 minutes longer. Cut the ducks into pieces and arrange on a platter. Garnish with watercress.

SERVES 6 TO 8

HOT PEPPER JELLY

1½ lb (750 g) juicy red apples
1½ cups (12 fl oz/375 ml) water
2-in (5-cm) strip lemon peel
7 cups (3½ lb/1.75 kg) sugar, or to taste
¼ lb (125 g) hot red (chili) peppers, seeded, deveined
    and finely chopped
¼ lb (125 g) hot green (chili) peppers, seeded, deveined
    and finely chopped
1 large onion, finely chopped
1 cup (8 fl oz/250 ml) cider vinegar

❦ Remove the stems from the apples and cut into quarters. Place in a large saucepan and add the water and lemon peel. Heat to boiling, reduce the heat and simmer, covered, for 30 minutes. Pour apples and liquid into a jelly bag or towel-lined colander over a pot. Let stand until the dripping stops. Do not squeeze or mash the apples. There should be about 2½ cups (20 fl oz/625 ml) liquid.

❦ Heat the liquid to boiling and add 2 cups (16 fl oz/500 g) of the sugar. Reduce the heat and simmer until the liquid sets when tested on a small cold plate, about 20 minutes. Remove from the heat.

❦ Place the peppers and onion in another saucepan. Add the vinegar. Heat to boiling and add the remaining sugar. Boil for 4 minutes, stirring to dissolve the sugar. Add the apple liquid and reduce the heat. Simmer, uncovered, until the mixture sets when tested on a small cold plate, 10 to 15 minutes. Pour into sterilized jars and seal. Shake the jars gently as the jelly cools to distribute the peppers evenly. Store unused jelly in a cool, dark place.

MAKES ABOUT 3 PINTS (1.5 L)

THE MIDWEST
AND THE GREAT PLAINS

THE MIDWEST AND THE GREAT PLAINS

As settlers pushed west, they encountered the three Indian families of what is now the Midwest and Great Plains: the Algonquians, Siouans and Caddoans. They also discovered odd-shaped, manmade mounds of earth. Modern science has identified these large mounds— built in square, octagonal, circular and even animal shapes —as the burial grounds, fortifications and places of worship of the Indians' prehistoric ancestors. Studies have shown that these peoples, whom history has recorded as the Mound Builders, ate much the same food as their descendants.

In the Great Lakes region, the Ojibwas, Winnebagos and Chippewas discovered the joys of the grass we know as wild rice. These tribes were highly skilled in working with birch bark and built waterproof canoes to fish the lakes and harvest the rice. The rice was collected by the women, two to a canoe, much the same way it is harvested today. One sits in the front of the canoe, paddling slowly, while the other uses two long pointed sticks to bend the delicate stems over the boat, shaking the loose grains into the bottom. The rice is then cured over smoky fires and literally danced upon to loosen the chaff. Although the tribes were hunters as well, they never strayed far from their wild rice sources. Along the great rivers that ran throughout the area, the land was fertile, and tribes such as the Osage, Caddos, Omahas, Wichitas and Shawnees farmed for their livelihood.

Little or no agriculture was pursued by the Indians who lived on the Great Plains. Dubbed the Buffalo Hunters, they included the Blackfoot, Cheyenne and Arapaho tribes of the Algonquian family; the Sioux, Dakotas and Crows of the Siouan family; and the Pawnees of the Caddoan family. Although game birds, mostly grouse, supplied some meat and eggs, it was the buffalo that was the source of life for these tribes. They used every part of

IN THE NATIVE AMERICAN LANGUAGE OF THIS REGION, IOWA MEANS THE BEAUTIFUL COUNTRY, AND FROM THE OLD ROADS THAT WIND THROUGH GREEN MEADOWS AND HILLS, THIS BEAUTY IS EVIDENT.

PREVIOUS PAGES: THE LANDSCAPE OF NORTHERN IOWA WAS REMINISCENT OF THE OLD COUNTRY FOR MANY IMMIGRANT FARMERS FROM GERMANY AND SCANDINAVIA WHO SETTLED HERE IN THE NINETEENTH CENTURY AND WHOSE DESCENDANTS POPULATE MUCH OF THE RURAL AREA TODAY.
PHOTO: TALIS BERGMANIS

115

JOE ROSSI

THESE RIVERBOATS ON THE ICY MISSISSIPPI RIVER IN ST. PAUL, CAPITAL OF MINNESOTA, SERVE TOURISTS WITH A REMINDER OF THEIR GLORIOUS PAST.

the animal for food, clothing or shelter. To preserve the meat, the Buffalo Hunters cut it into thin strips and set it in the sun to dry, just as other tribes did with venison. They later taught the pioneers how to make this "jerky," though beef eventually replaced buffalo and venison. The Indians also made pemmican, a mixture of dried buffalo or venison ground with berries and fat and pressed into small cakes. One of the major seasonings on the plains was the buffalo berry, similar in size to the cranberry, which was harvested only after the first frost, when it was somewhat sweeter. Most of the cooking on the plains was done outdoors, either over open fires or in rock-lined pits.

After the Revolution several states, including Massachusetts and Virginia, laid claim to the vast region surrounding the Great Lakes. Fearing that it would be underrepresented in the new government, Maryland, along with some other older hemmed-in states, insisted that the lands be ceded to the central government. In 1785 Congress provided funding for surveying the lands northwest of the Ohio River, and the Northwest Territory was born. The five states that grew out of the Northwest Territory are Ohio, Indiana, Illinois, Michigan and Wisconsin, but what we now call the Midwest (technically, the region from Ohio westward through Iowa and from the Ohio and Missouri rivers northward through the Great Lakes) not only includes these five but also encompasses Minnesota, Iowa and Missouri. These rolling prairies of rich farmland today are often called the "corn belt."

Beyond the prairies lie the Great Plains. The climate is much drier here, and although the area appears flat, it actually increases in elevation as the plains approach the Rocky Mountains to the west. Because the Great Plains were deemed unsuitable for habitation by pioneers heading west, the plains states of the Dakotas, Nebraska, Kansas and Oklahoma were among the last to be settled. Incredible as it may seem, it has been less than one hundred years since the famous homesteading "run" into the Cherokee Strip Territory in Oklahoma took place. In the early 1900s more people arrived, prompted by a campaign waged by the governors of the empty states, the railroads and even politicians in overcrowded eastern states. The Great Plains were advertised here and abroad as

a garden spot. Early arrivals found instead a harsh land subject to long, cold winters and dry, hot summers with occasional droughts. Worse, during severe dry spells violent wind storms whipped through the area, removing the topsoil and covering everything with a layer of dirt. Yet, even though times can still be hard on the plains, the good years bring such enormous wheat harvests that the area is known as the "wheat belt."

For the early pioneers life was almost as rough as it was for the early colonists. The land had to be cleared and planted in the Midwest, the tough soil cultivated on the plains. There was a scarcity of metals, pottery and tools; supplies from the East were difficult to get, and many plains settlers first lived in earthen houses with nothing but roofs of sod over their heads. As time went by, however, great cities were built on the major rivers that became the lifeline of the area. The Midwest began to thrive as pioneers were trickling onto the plains. It was a time of house and barn raisings, quilting bees, taffy pulls and husking bees.

Aside from the overall problems of settling a new territory, those who came to the Midwest and Great Plains had to face a more serious problem: the Indians. They were becoming more and more fierce as white settlers pushed farther and farther into their lands. The Shawnees in Indiana were particularly resistant and formed an alliance with the British in what was to be the losing cause known as the War of 1812. On the plains white hunters slaughtered millions of buffalo for their hides, robbing the Plains Indians of their way of life. Trouble continued until well after the Civil War. Most Indians were banished to reservations by the end of the 1880s, and although uprisings occurred after that time, the cavalry quickly squelched the Indians' efforts.

The cooking of the Midwest and Great Plains is a combination of many cultures. The first influence came from pioneers from the East and South who headed to the Northwest Territory to start a new life on the fertile land. The area in Ohio near the Great Lakes was settled mostly by New Englanders who brought Yankee cooking with them. Settlers also moved into the territory from the southern states, many coming from Kentucky, Tennessee, West Virginia and Arkansas and bringing their preference for southern cooking with them. Other settlers of English background included the Shakers, a religious sect founded in England that practiced communal living and celibacy. They located in Ohio and Indiana. All their food was raised or grown in the community and cooked in a spacious central kitchen. The Shakers ate balanced meals and were ahead of their time in nutritional concerns. They learned about herbs and plants from the Indians and sold 350 kinds of medicinal plants, herbs and flowers to the public, as well as extracts, elixirs and ointments. Shaker tools and furniture are greatly admired for their craftsmanship. It was a Shaker, incidentally, who invented the apple parer.

German immigrants flocked to the Midwest and Great Plains in the nineteenth century. The descendants of the German Amish and Moravians of Pennsylvania had already spilled over into Ohio and Indiana, but it was the new immigrants who had a profound effect on the Midwest. Germans, along with the Swiss, were responsible for the dairy and cheese production that is still a major part of the midwestern economy. Germans also became the brewmasters of America, but more importantly, they had great butchering skills, which enabled them to turn fragile fresh meat into smoked products like sausage and ham that could be shipped east.

To this day most livestock is sent to the Midwest and Great Plains states for butchering and shipping.

Immigrants from the Scandinavian countries settled throughout the Midwest. The Swedes also pushed out onto the plains and were joined by the Norwegians in the Dakotas. Hungarians, Romanians, Poles and other eastern Europeans came to work in the steel mills and eventually settled in urban Michigan, Illinois and Ohio. Czechs can also be found in Nebraska. A fair number of Russians, taken in by the plains advertising blitz, ended up in Kansas. Detroit's auto industry attracted a variety of twentieth-century immigrants, including Arabs. Significant communities of Irish, Greeks and Italians populated Chicago.

The Midwest and Great Plains gave America a potpourri of dishes—sorrel soups and pickled smelts from Michigan, chicken and dumplings from Ohio, whole wheat batter breads from Kansas, chicken-fried steak from Oklahoma and Missouri, braised quail from North Dakota and much more. The Midwest also has the distinction of being the regional home of the hamburger and hot dog, both introduced at the 1904 World's Fair in St. Louis. This region can truly be called the melting pot of American cuisine.

GEORGE OLSON/THE PHOTOFILE

LIFE CAN MOVE AT AN EASY, FRIENDLY PACE IN KANSAS, HEART OF THE GREAT PLAINS REGION, WHERE MOST OF AMERICA'S GRAIN AND LIVESTOCK IS RAISED.

HIGHWAY 160 LINKS COLORADO WITH SOUTHWEST KANSAS. KANSAS PRODUCES MORE WHEAT THAN MOST SMALL NATIONS AND MORE THAN ANY OTHER STATE IN THE U.S.

MEAT AND GAME

CATHERINE KARNOW

COWBOYS TAKE TIME TO LUNCH ON A HEARTY MEAL OF
BEEF AND BEANS DURING A CATTLE DRIVE IN NEW MEXICO.

MEAT AND GAME

WEST VIRGINIA'S MAIN ECONOMIES ARE MANUFACTURING AND
TOURISM, BUT IN THE MOUNTAINS, FARMING COMMUNITIES LOOK
MUCH THE SAME AS THEY DID AT THE TURN OF THE CENTURY.

NICK NICHOLSON/THE IMAGE BANK

Bear, deer, elk, the occasional moose, squirrels, rabbits, raccoons, otters, possums and a snake here and there provided the Indians in the East with plenty of meat. Farther west, buffalo, armadillos, bighorn sheep and even beavers were hunted for food. It took a while, but once the settlers became skilled hunters, the colonies began to flourish. Wild game provided meat for Americans well into the 1800s in the East and a great deal longer in the West. By the late nineteenth century, pork was fairly abundant, and beef was certainly starting to hold its own, but game was still hunted on a regular basis. In fact, it was so much a staple in markets and restaurants that the first hunting quotas had to be introduced to protect animals from extinction. Thanks to strict preservation laws, game animals are once again flourishing in more rural areas, and hunting remains a major sport in this country. Many states have laws prohibiting the sale of wild game to the general public, however, and therefore much of our game, including deer and rabbits, is raised on preserves. The animals are not domesticated but raised under controlled circumstances. The vast majority of Americans, however, rely on domesticated animals for their meat supply and consider game a delicacy.

The first domesticated animals introduced to America were hogs. They were brought to Florida from Spain in 1539 (some say 1542) by Hernando de Soto. Southerners like to believe that all swine in this country came from the stock of those original three, but the English brought them in as well, a few at a time, to New England and Virginia. North and south, hogs flourished. Requiring little care, they were allowed to roam the woods foraging

PREVIOUS PAGES: HONOLULU SPARE RIBS (left, recipe page 128) AND
BARBECUE PORK (right, recipe page 132)
TIFFANY & CO.

120

for nuts, which gave their meat a distinctive flavor. Many of the hogs actually went wild, and their descendants, often mistakenly called wild boars, still roam certain areas of the American countryside. It did not take long for Southerners to realize that the peanut was particularly well suited to feeding hogs, and many areas in the South to this day specialize in peanut-raised pork products. When German immigrants came to the Midwest in the 1800s, their butchering skills were in high demand. Hogs were raised throughout the Midwest, and Cincinnati, Ohio, became the first meat-packing center. So much pork was turned into German delicatessen specialties that the city was nicknamed "Porkopolis." Pork became the most important domestic meat and remained so until after the Civil War, when the West was opened up and beef began reaching eastern markets in great quantities via refrigerated railway cars.

Spanish settlers brought the first cattle into Florida in 1550, long before they took them to the Southwest. The English introduced cattle into the colonies; Jamestown had them by 1611, and the first slaughterhouse opened in Boston in 1662. Cattle required more care than hogs, however, and much more land for grazing. For this reason, beef, while certainly available, was quite a luxury. Most beef was salted or pickled in the early days, and virtually no meat was shipped until after the Civil War, when the railroads were completed. The first beef cattle were shipped live by rail from Kansas to the East in 1867. Although it was not an easy (or inexpensive) feat, this important event sparked the age of the great cattle drives. Soon after, in 1871, G. H. Hammond invented the refrigerator rail car and changed history. It was now possible to ship beef carcasses; live cattle no longer had to make the trip all the way east. Chicago, being closer to the West than Cincinnati, seemed like a natural jumping-

off point, and so the meat industry moved to that city. (Today Omaha is the country's major meat-packing center.) The animals were butchered in Chicago and then shipped east in one of Hammond's spanking-new railway cars.

Americans, particularly those of English descent, had such a yearning for beef that by the early 1900s beef overtook pork in popularity at the dining table and still leads in annual consumption. It should be noted that Jewish immigrants, who could not eat pork for religious reasons, played a major role in popularizing beef charcuterie. Veal, however, has never entered the mainstream of American cookery, perhaps because of its expense. It is found only in ethnic dishes from Italy and France.

Lamb, likewise, has not made much of an inroad into American home cooking. It has had more acceptance in recent years, but remains far behind beef and pork in consumption. The reason may be historical: the range wars that occurred between ranchers and sheepherders in the West when sheep were first introduced left a lingering ill will toward this meat. It is more likely, however, that because lamb used to be slaughtered close to maturity and the meat cooked until well-done, it had an objectionable "muttony" taste. This is no longer the case. America raises excellent lamb, far superior, in many a cook's mind, to the frozen lamb shipped in from New Zealand. Sheep and goats were introduced to this country by the Spanish. Both sheep and goats supplied the southwestern Indians with dairy products, and goat meat became the centerpiece of the Spanish Southwest's barbecues. As sheep raising spread over the mountain regions (to the fury of cattle ranchers), Basque sheepherders were imported to tend them, and today, in Nevada and Idaho, Basque family-style restaurants do a booming business.

THE SPANISH INTRODUCED LIVESTOCK TO THE SOUTHWEST, AND THE MEXICANS WHO WERE EMPLOYED TO TEND THE HERDS WERE THE FIRST "COWBOYS."

HAM WITH REDEYE GRAVY (top) AND
CHICKEN-FRIED STEAK

Tennessee

HAM WITH REDEYE GRAVY

Ham with redeye gravy is served all over the South, and the recipe varies from state to state, even from county to county. Coffee and water are the usual gravy components, but many cooks add a splash of cream to enrich the sauce. "Redeye" refers to the bubbling center of the gravy as it is reduced.

2 ham steaks, ¼ in (5 mm) thick
¼ cup (2 fl oz/60 ml) water
¼ cup (2 fl oz/60 ml) brewed coffee
1 tablespoon cream (optional)

❦ Trim the excess fat from the ham steaks and sauté in a large heavy skillet until rendered of fat. Pan off the fat and sauté the ham steaks over medium-high heat until the edges turn slightly golden, 2 to 3 minutes on each side. Transfer to a shallow serving platter and keep warm.
❦ Add the water, coffee and, if using, the cream to the skillet. Heat quickly and boil, scraping the bottom of the pan, until slightly thickened. Pour over the ham and serve immediately.

SERVES 2

Wyoming

ROAST LAMB WITH BUTTERMILK AND ROSEMARY

Although lamb has never gained the appreciation it deserves, some of the world's best is raised in this country. The next recipe comes from Cheyenne.

1 leg of lamb, about 6 lb (3 kg)
1 garlic clove, cut into fine slivers
2 garlic cloves, crushed
1 tablespoon Dijon mustard
½ teaspoon freshly ground pepper
3 tablespoons olive oil
¼ cup (2 fl oz/60 ml) buttermilk
½ cup (4 fl oz/125 ml) dry white wine
1½ cups (12 fl oz/375 ml) beef stock (approximately)
   (see glossary)
2 rosemary sprigs
1 tablespoon unsalted butter
salt and freshly ground pepper

❦ Pierce the top of the lamb at 1½-in (4-cm) intervals with an ice pick or sharp, pointed knife. Insert a sliver of garlic into each hole. Combine the crushed garlic with the mustard, pepper, oil and buttermilk and spread over the lamb. Let stand at least 6 hours, basting the lamb frequently with the marinade that runs off.
❦ Preheat the oven to 400°F (200°C). Place the lamb on a rack in a roasting pan. Set aside the marinade. Roast the lamb for 15 minutes. Combine the marinade with the wine and ½ cup (4 fl oz/125 ml) of the stock. Pour into the roasting pan and add the rosemary. Reduce the oven heat to 300°F (150°C) and continue to roast the lamb, 15 minutes per pound for medium-rare. Add the remaining stock as the pan juices dry up. Let stand for 10 minutes.
❦ Meanwhile, skim off the fat from the pan juices and stir in the butter. Add salt and pepper to taste. Serve with the lamb.

SERVES 6 TO 8

Missouri

CHICKEN-FRIED STEAK

Pounded beefsteak was relished by the English even before they settled here. Chicken-fried steak, standard fare in the Midwest, Great Plains and some southern regions, is simply pounded beefsteak coated and cooked like fried chicken; hence, the name.

2 lb (1 kg) ½-in (1-cm) thick beef round (topside) steaks,
   pounded thin
2 eggs, lightly beaten
3 tablespoons milk
dash of hot red pepper (Tabasco) sauce (optional)
1 cup (4 oz/125 g) all-purpose (plain) flour, fine dry breadcrumbs or cracker crumbs
1 teaspoon salt
½ teaspoon freshly ground pepper
3 tablespoons (1½ oz/30 g) bacon drippings
1 cup (8 fl oz/250 ml) cream

❦ Cut the meat into 4 to 6 pieces. Combine the eggs, milk and hot sauce in a shallow bowl. Combine the flour or crumbs with the salt and pepper on a plate.
❦ Dip the meat into the egg mixture, shaking off the excess. Press into the flour or crumbs, coating the meat well. Transfer to a plate lined with wax paper.
❦ Heat the drippings in a large heavy skillet over medium-high heat. Quickly brown the steaks for 1 to 2 minutes on each side. Drain lightly on paper towels and transfer to a heatproof serving platter. Keep warm in a low oven.
❦ Stir the cream into the drippings, scraping the bottom and sides of the skillet. Heat to boiling and cook until slightly thickened, 3 or 4 minutes. Pour over the steaks.

SERVES 4 TO 6

ROAST LAMB WITH BUTTERMILK AND ROSEMARY

Vermont

LOIN OF PORK WITH APPLES

Pork was the most widely eaten meat in America until the turn of the century. After the Civil War, as people moved west, beef became increasingly available and surpassed pork in popularity. In the East pork is still greatly appreciated, and generations of cooks have passed down their favorite recipes, many using the apples that grow so abundantly in New England.

1 loin of pork, about 4 lb (2 kg)
salt and freshly ground pepper
all-purpose (plain) flour
1 cup (8 oz/250 g) sugar
⅓ cup (3 fl oz/80 ml) cider vinegar
4 tart apples, peeled, cored and quartered
2 teaspoons sugar
1 cup (8 fl oz/250 ml) cream, room temperature

❧ Preheat the oven to 450°F (230°C). Lightly score the top of the pork. Rub with salt, pepper and flour. Place bone side down on a rack in a roasting pan. Roast for 15 minutes.

❧ Meanwhile, combine the sugar and vinegar in a saucepan. Heat, stirring, until boiling. Reduce the heat and simmer for 5 minutes.

❧ Baste the pork with the vinegar-sugar mixture and reduce the oven temperature to 350°F (180°C). Pour enough water in the pan to film the bottom. Continue to roast, basting every 20 minutes with the vinegar-sugar mixture, about 1 hour 45 minutes longer (30 minutes per pound). Add more water to the bottom of the pan as needed.

❧ About 30 minutes before the pork is done, add the apples to the pan, turning to coat with the juices. Sprinkle with sugar and, turning occasionally, cook with the pork until it is tender.

❧ Transfer the meat to a serving platter and surround with the apples. Skim the fat from the pan juices and add the cream. Heat to boiling and serve with the roast.

SERVES 4

Arizona

GREEN CHILIED PORK

Pork and smoked green peppers are often combined in the cuisine of the Southwest. Dishes like the one that follows may be served with rice or with burritos stuffed with refried beans. If you can find the pungent yet mild poblano chilies, use them in place of the bell peppers.

3 large green bell peppers (capsicums)
¼ cup (2 oz/60 g) bacon drippings
2½ lb (1.25 kg) boneless pork shoulder, cut into ½-in (1-cm) cubes
2 large onions, chopped
2 large garlic cloves, minced
2 tablespoons all-purpose (plain) flour
4 cans (4 oz/125 g each) mild green chilies, drained and chopped
4 cups (1 qt/1 l) chicken stock (see glossary)
salt and freshly ground pepper
hot cooked rice

❧ Roast the peppers over a gas flame or under a broiler (griller) until charred all over. Carefully wrap in paper towels and place in a plastic bag. Let stand until cool. Rub off the skins with paper towels. Seed, chop and set aside.

❧ Heat the bacon drippings in a large heavy pot or Dutch oven over medium heat. Sauté the pork in batches until lightly browned. Transfer to a plate.

❧ Add the onions to the bacon drippings; cook for 1 minute. Add the garlic; cook 2 minutes longer. Return the meat to the pot and reduce the heat to medium-low.

❧ Sprinkle the pork with the flour. Cook, stirring constantly, for 2 minutes. Stir in the roasted peppers, canned chilies and chicken stock. Heat to boiling, reduce the heat and simmer, partially covered, until the pork is tender, about 1 hour 15 minutes. Raise the heat slightly if the chili is too thin. Add salt and pepper to taste and serve with hot cooked rice.

SERVES 6

LOIN OF PORK WITH APPLES (left) AND GREEN CHILIED PORK (right)

VILLEROY & BOCH

VILLEROY & BOCH

NEW ENGLAND BOILED DINNER

New Hampshire

NEW ENGLAND BOILED DINNER

Salt or pickled beef (corned beef), the mainstay of a traditional boiled dinner, was put on to boil right after breakfast and eaten at the noonday meal. Not only did this dish provide a hearty dinner, but it freed the housewife to do the many other chores that fell to her. Leftovers were always turned into red flannel hash (see page 238) for the following day's breakfast.

1 corned beef brisket (salt beef), 4 to 4½ lb (2 to 2.5 kg)
12 small carrots, peeled
6 small turnips, peeled
6 potatoes, peeled
8 small beets (beetroot), trimmed but not peeled
1 small head cabbage, chopped
1½ tablespoons (¾ oz/20 g) unsalted butter
1½ tablespoons all-purpose (plain) flour
1½ tablespoons dry mustard
1 teaspoon Dijon mustard
1 tablespoon red wine vinegar
½ cup (4 fl oz/125 ml) sour cream, room temperature
salt and freshly ground pepper

❦ Rinse the brisket with cold water and place in a large heavy pot or Dutch oven. Cover with cold water and heat to boiling, skimming the surface if needed. Reduce the heat and simmer, covered, for 2½ hours.

❦ Add the carrots, turnips and potatoes to the pot and continue to simmer, covered, until the vegetables and meat are tender, about 40 minutes longer.

❦ Meanwhile, place the beets in a saucepan and cover with cold water. Heat to boiling, reduce the heat and simmer, uncovered, until tender, about 30 minutes. Rinse quickly under cold running water. Peel and transfer to a heatproof bowl. Keep warm in a low oven.

❦ After the beets have cooked for about 15 minutes, place the cabbage in a saucepan. Remove ½ cup (4 fl oz/125 ml) cooking liquid from the corned beef and add to the cabbage. Heat to boiling, reduce the heat and cook, partially covered, until the cabbage is tender and all the liquid has evaporated, about 15 minutes. (Remove cover if mixture is too wet.) Reduce the heat to low and keep warm.

❦ When tender, transfer the corned beef to a heatproof platter and carrots, turnips and potatoes to a heatproof bowl. Cover and keep warm in a low oven. Save the cooking liquid.

❦ Melt the butter in a saucepan over low heat. Stir in the flour and both mustards. Cook, stirring constantly, for 3 minutes. Whisk in 1½ cups (12 fl oz/375 ml) of the corned beef cooking liquid and the vinegar. Heat to boiling and boil until slightly thickened, about 4 minutes. Remove from the heat and whisk in the sour cream. Add salt and pepper to taste.

❦ To serve, slice the meat and arrange on the platter. Surround with the carrots, potatoes and turnips. Serve the cabbage and beets in separate bowls. Pass the gravy on the side.

SERVES 6

Wyoming

SMOTHERED VENISON

Venison, the mainstay of many an early settler's diet, is rarely served at home these days, unless it's the home of an avid hunter. Much of the venison sold at butcher shops comes from preserves, as most states have laws regulating the killing and handling of game to be sold on the market.

½ cup (2 oz/60 g) all-purpose (plain) flour
1 teaspoon salt
½ teaspoon pepper
4 venison steaks, about ½ lb (250 g) each, cut 1 in (2.5 cm) thick
2 tablespoons (1 oz/30 g) unsalted butter
2 tablespoons vegetable oil
1 large onion, chopped
1 garlic clove, minced
⅓ cup (3 fl oz/80 ml) dry red wine
1 can (17 oz/530 g) plum (egg) tomatoes with juices
3 large fresh tomatoes, seeded and chopped
1 small carrot, finely chopped
1 small celery stalk, finely chopped
1 tablespoon Worcestershire sauce
chopped fresh parsley (optional)

❦ Preheat the oven to 325°F (165°C). Combine the flour with the salt and pepper. Coat the venison steaks with the flour, pounding it into both sides of the steak with a wooden mallet. Save the excess flour.

❦ Heat the butter with the oil in a large heavy pot or Dutch oven and brown the meat well on both sides. Transfer the meat to a plate.

❦ Discard all but 2 tablespoons fat from the pot and add the onion. Cook for 2 minutes, scraping the bottom and sides of the pot. Add the garlic and cook 3 minutes longer. Stir in 2 tablespoons of the reserved flour. Cook, stirring constantly, for

2 minutes. Whisk in the wine, canned and fresh tomatoes, carrot, celery and Worcestershire sauce. Heat to boiling, reduce the heat and simmer for 10 minutes.

❦ Return the venison to the pot, pressing into the mixture, and transfer to the oven. Cover and bake until the meat is tender, about 1½ hours, depending on the meat. Remove the cover and bake 30 minutes longer. Sprinkle with parsley.

SERVES 4

California

GRILLED BUTTERFLIED LAMB

Outdoor cooking is more popular in America than ever before, as backyard cooks have discovered the pleasure of cooking many foods outside. Lamb is particularly delicious grilled. Butterflied, the meat cooks quickly, like a thick steak, and should be served as such—rare to medium-rare.

1 leg of lamb, 5 to 6 lb (2.5 to 3 kg), boned and butterflied (cut open lengthwise and flattened)
16 fl oz (500 ml) plain yogurt
4 garlic cloves, crushed
½ cup (1 oz/30 g) chopped fresh mint
¼ teaspoon freshly ground pepper

❦ Place the lamb in a shallow glass or ceramic dish. Combine the yogurt, garlic, mint and pepper. Spread over both sides of the lamb. Refrigerate, covered, overnight. Let stand at room temperature for 1 hour before cooking.

❦ Preheat an outdoor grill. Place the lamb on a greased rack and close the cover with the vents open. Cook over medium heat for 15 minutes on each side for medium-rare. Let stand for 10 minutes before serving.

SERVES 6 TO 8

Hawaii

HONOLULU SPARERIBS

Polynesians began arriving in Hawaii about 2,000 years before the English set off for Massachusetts. They came prepared, bringing their favorite foods with them. They introduced taro, the banana, plantain, breadfruit, the yam, coconut and even sugar cane, which they chewed raw. They also brought a good supply of the animals they liked most to eat: dogs, chickens and pigs. The following spicy recipe for pork ribs depends on a mixture of Chinese origin called five-spice powder, which can be purchased or made at home.

4 to 5 lb (2 to 2.5 kg) meaty pork ribs
1 lemon, sliced
4 parsley sprigs
1 oregano sprig or pinch of dried oregano
1 garlic clove, minced
¼ teaspoon freshly ground pepper
1 teaspoon minced fresh ginger
2 tablespoons soy sauce
2 tablespoons dry sherry
1½ tablespoons honey
1½ teaspoons five-spice powder*
¼ cup (2 oz/60 g) chili sauce (American–style)
¼ cup (2 fl oz/60 ml) peanut oil

❦ Place the ribs in a large pot or Dutch oven. Add water to cover, then the lemon slices, parsley and oregano. Heat to boiling, reduce the heat and simmer, partially covered, for 45 minutes. Drain and transfer to a shallow glass or ceramic dish.

❦ Combine the garlic, pepper, ginger, soy sauce, sherry, honey, five-spice, chili sauce and oil in a bowl. Mix well and pour over the ribs. Let stand, covered, for 1 hour.

❦ Preheat an outdoor grill or broiler. Grill or broil the ribs over medium heat, basting often with the marinade, until crisp, 6 to 8 minutes on each side.

*To make your own five-spice, combine 1 teaspoon ground cinnamon, 1 teaspoon crushed aniseed, ¼ teaspoon crushed fennel seed, ¼ teaspoon freshly ground pepper and ⅛ teaspoon ground cloves. Store in an airtight container. Makes about 2½ teaspoons.

SERVES 6   *Photograph pages 118 – 119*

Texas

TEXAS SHORT RIBS

Short ribs, sometimes called flanken, are cut ends of the rib roast and contain a great deal of fat. The meat is very tender when cooked in the style of East Texas: stewed in peppers, tomato and beer. If you make the dish a day ahead and refrigerate it overnight, you can easily remove the fat from the top.

½ cup (2 oz/60 g) all-purpose (plain) flour
salt and freshly ground pepper
¼ teaspoon ground allspice
3 to 3½ lb (1.5 to 1.75 kg) beef short ribs (or brisket, top skirt or thin flank)
¼ cup (2 oz/60 g) unsalted butter
1 tablespoon vegetable oil
2 large onions, chopped
2 garlic cloves, minced
1 small hot green (chili) pepper, seeded, deveined and minced
1 small green bell pepper (capsicum), seeded and chopped
1 celery stalk, chopped
2 tablespoons brown sugar
½ teaspoon sweet paprika
2 tablespoons chili powder
½ teaspoon dry mustard
¼ cup (2 fl oz/60 ml) lemon juice
½ cup (4 oz/125 g) chili sauce

½ cup (4 fl oz/125 ml) dark beer (ale)
1 can (17 oz/530 g) plum (egg) tomatoes, chopped
chopped fresh parsley (optional)

❦ Preheat the oven to 350°F (180°C). Combine the flour with ½ teaspoon salt, ½ teaspoon pepper and the allspice on a large plate. Roll the ribs in the mixture, patting the flour into the meat. Set aside 1 tablespoon flour mixture.

❦ Heat 3 tablespoons (1½ oz/45 g) butter with the oil in a large heavy pot or Dutch oven over medium-high heat. Brown the ribs well, a few at a time, on all sides. Transfer to a plate.

❦ Reduce the heat and add the remaining tablespoon butter to the pot. Stir in the onions, garlic and peppers, scraping the bottom and sides of the pot. Cook, stirring occasionally, for 5 minutes. Sprinkle in the reserved 1 tablespoon flour mixture; cook 2 minutes longer.

❦ Add the celery, brown sugar, paprika, chili powder, mustard, lemon juice, chili sauce and beer to the pan, stir well and add the tomatoes. Return the ribs to the pot and heat to boiling. Cover and transfer to the oven. Bake for 1½ hours, turning the meat once. Uncover and bake 15 minutes longer. Skim off the fat and sprinkle with parsley.

SERVES 4 TO 6

Texas

CHILI CON CARNE

Although Texas is associated with chili, the dish dates back to Inca, Aztec and Mayan cuisines. These Indians had discovered that hot peppers preserved the meat they hunted, so quite naturally the chilies went right into their stews along with the meat and beans. The dish was popularized in San Antonio during the era of the Texas Republic, when "ladies" (called Chili Queens) stirred up pots of the stuff by lantern light for the militia.

1 lb (500 g) dried pinto (*borlotto* or red kidney) beans
6 tablespoons (3 oz/90 g) unsalted butter
1 tablespoon vegetable oil
1½ lb (750 g) beef chuck steak, cut into 2 x ½-in (5 x 1-cm) strips
1½ lb (750 g) lean ground (minced) beef
2 large onions, chopped
2 garlic cloves, minced
¼ cup (2 oz/60 g) chili powder (see glossary)
2 large tomatoes, seeded and chopped
1 can (10 oz/315 g) mixed tomatoes and green chilies (or 9-oz/280-g can crushed tomatoes and 2–3 cans green chilies)
1 teaspoon brown sugar
1 bay leaf
pinch of dried thyme
1 teaspoon cayenne pepper, or to taste
1 tablespoon Worcestershire sauce
1¼ cups (10 fl oz/315 ml) beef stock (approximately) (see glossary)
1 teaspoon salt
½ teaspoon freshly ground pepper

❦ Soak the beans overnight in cold water.

❦ Preheat the oven to 300°F (150°C). Heat half of the butter with the oil in a large heavy skillet over medium heat. Pat the beef strips dry with paper towels and sauté in batches until well browned. Transfer to a large heavy pot or Dutch oven.

❦ Add the ground beef to the skillet. Cook over medium-high heat, breaking up the lumps, until lightly browned. Transfer to the pot with the beef strips.

❦ Discard all fat from the skillet. Add the remaining butter and stir in the onions, scraping the bottom and sides of the skillet. Cook over medium heat for 3 minutes. Add the garlic and cook 2 minutes longer. Transfer to the pot with the meat.

CHILI CON CARNE (top) AND TEXAS SHORT RIBS

❧ Stir the chili powder into the meat mixture. Add all the remaining ingredients except the beans and mix well. Heat to boiling, cover and transfer to the oven. Bake until the meat strips are tender, 1½ to 2 hours.

❧ Meanwhile, drain the beans and place in a heavy saucepan. Cover with cold water. Heat to boiling, reduce the heat and simmer, stirring occasionally, until tender, about 1 hour. Drain.

❧ When the meat is tender, stir in the beans and return to the oven. Bake, uncovered, for 30 minutes. (Add more beef broth if the chili gets too dry.)

SERVES 6 TO 8

129

YANKEE POT ROAST

Connecticut

YANKEE POT ROAST

The English, Dutch and French brought this style of cooking to our shores, although in the early days the pot more than likely contained venison or bear. At first cooked over coals, pot roasts eventually were baked in brick ovens in earthenware vessels. The edges of the vessels were sealed with pastry to compensate for the lack of tight-fitting lids. Some cooks brown the meat first, but this step is not necessary. The best cuts of meat for this style of cooking are chuck and brisket.

1 large or 2 medium onions, chopped
1 boneless chuck (neck) roast, about 4 lb (2 kg) (rolled roast is
   suitable)
1 cup (8 fl oz/250 ml) beef stock (approximately) (see glossary)
4 potatoes, peeled
4 carrots, cut into sticks
4 small parsnips
chopped fresh parsley (optional)

❧ Preheat the oven to 350°F (180°C). Spread the onions over the bottom of a large heavy pot or roaster. Place the meat on top of the onions. Cover and bake for 1 hour. Add half of the stock and bake, covered, 1 hour longer.

❧ Arrange the vegetables around the meat, turning to coat with the juices. Continue to bake, covered, adding more stock if needed, until the meat and vegetables are tender, about 1 hour longer.

❧ Slice the meat and arrange on a platter. Surround with the vegetables and sprinkle with parsley. Strain the juices (add more stock to the pan if there is not enough and heat to boiling) and serve on the side.

SERVES 4

Colorado

BARBECUED POT ROAST

Out west, pot roast is often cooked in an old beat-up, smoke-scarred pot on an outdoor grill, which gives it the smoky taste of real barbecue. If you are so inclined, cover the pot with aluminum foil rather than a lid, because smoke can permeate foil.

1 small onion, chopped
1 boneless chuck (neck) roast, 3½ to 4 lb (1.75 to 2 kg)
   (rolled roast is suitable)
1 small garlic clove, bruised
½ cup (4 fl oz/125 ml) beef stock (approximately) (see
   glossary)
1 can (8 oz/250 g) tomato sauce (pureed tomatoes)
2 tablespoons brown sugar
¼ teaspoon sweet paprika
½ teaspoon dry mustard
¼ cup (2 fl oz/60 ml) lemon juice
¼ cup (2 oz/60 g) ketchup (tomato sauce)
¼ cup (2 fl oz/60 ml) cider vinegar
1 tablespoon Worcestershire sauce
chopped fresh parsley (optional)

❧ Preheat the oven to 350°F (180°C). Sprinkle the onion over the bottom of a large heavy pot or Dutch oven. Rub the meat well with garlic and place on top of the onions. Cover and bake for 1½ hours. Add some stock if the juices in bottom of pan begin to dry up.

❧ Combine the tomato sauce, brown sugar, paprika, mustard, lemon juice, ketchup, vinegar and Worcestershire sauce in a bowl. Pour over the meat. Continue to bake, covered, basting every 20 minutes, until the meat is tender, about 2 hours longer.

❧ Slice the meat and arrange on a serving platter. Spoon some of the sauce on top and sprinkle with parsley. Serve the remaining sauce on the side.

SERVES 4 TO 6

BARBECUED POT ROAST

New York

GRILLED PORTERHOUSE STEAK

Porterhouse is the most popular cut of beef for steaks in this country. The name derives from the taverns (called "porter houses") where porters once congregated to drink dark ale. The cut is from the thick end of the short loin and contains the T-bone and part of the tenderloin. Other cuts of prime steak are the T-bone, club, tenderloin and strip or shell.

2½ to 3 lb (1.25 to 1.5 kg) porterhouse steak (or boneless short loin/strip loin), about 2 in (5 cm) thick
1 garlic clove, bruised
2 teaspoons olive oil
¼ teaspoon freshly ground pepper

❦ Trim all but ¼ in (6 mm) fat from the sides of the steak.

Slash the remaining fat with a knife at 1-in (2.5-cm) intervals. Pat the steak dry with paper towels and rub with the garlic. Mix the oil with the pepper and spread over both sides of the steak. Let stand for 1 hour.

❦ Preheat an outdoor grill. Brush the rack lightly with vegetable oil. Secure the tail section of the steak with water-soaked toothpicks so that the steak cooks evenly. Sear the steak over hot coals for 1 minute on each side, then place over medium-hot coals (raise the rack or use the outer edges of the coals to reduce the heat). Grill for 7 to 8 minutes on each side for rare, 8 to 10 minutes on each side for medium-rare. (If the coals flare up, remove the steak and spray the fire with water.) To serve, let the steak stand a few minutes before cutting the meat from the bones. Cut the meat across the grain into slices about ¼ in (6 mm) thick.

SERVES 4

North Carolina

BARBECUE PORK

Barbecue socials have played an important role in this country, dating back to Tidewater Jamestown. Wild boar was the staple in the seventeenth century. As the pig flourished, so did the barbecue cookouts that seemed to go hand-in-hand with the burgeoning political scene. Barbecue in the South means pork. No arguing the point, except whether to serve it sliced, chopped or "pulled." The recipe below is for the genuine stuff, made in a smoker. You can roast the pork in the oven (at 350°F/180°C), but if you do, don't call it barbecue.

2 teaspoons salt
2 tablespoons sugar
1 tablespoon sweet paprika
½ teaspoon cayenne pepper
½ teaspoon dry mustard
1 teaspoon freshly ground pepper
⅔ cup (5 fl oz/160 ml) water
¼ cup (2 fl oz/60 ml) Worcestershire sauce
⅔ cup (5 fl oz/160 ml) red wine vinegar
½ cup (4 oz/125 g) unsalted butter, cut into bits
1 fresh pork shoulder (blade) or butt (leg), about 6 lb (3 kg)
2 cans (12 fl oz/375 ml each) beer (lager)

❦ Combine the salt, sugar and spices in a medium saucepan. Stir in the water, heat to boiling and remove from the heat. Add the Worcestershire sauce, vinegar and butter, stirring to melt the butter. Place the pork in a bowl and pour on 1 cup (8 fl oz/250 ml) of the mixture. Cover and let stand, turning occasionally, for 3 hours.

❦ Preheat a water smoker and add presoaked wood chips to the heat source. Put the water pan in place and add the beer. Add water to fill the pan. Place the pork on the highest rack. Cover and cook, keeping the temperature between 200° and 225°F (95° and 110°C) and basting every hour with the sauce, until fork tender, about 6½ hours. (Add water to the pan and more wood chips or charcoal to the smoker as needed.) Serve the meat sliced or "pulled" (shredded) with the remaining sauce, reheated.

SERVES 6 TO 8   *Photograph pages 118 – 119*

Pennsylvania

SCHNITZ UND KNEPP

One way the early settlers stored apples for the winter was to slice and dry them. While most of the country used dried apples in pies, the Pennsylvania Dutch also used them in one of their most famous ham dishes, Schnitz und Knepp. Schnitz refers to the sliced apples; a knepp is a dumpling.

2 cups (4 oz/125 g) dried apple slices (or 1 cup dried diced apples)
2 cups (16 fl oz/500 ml) water
2 lb (1 kg) porkette (boneless rolled ham)
2 tablespoons brown sugar
2 cups (8 oz/250 g) all-purpose (plain) flour
4 teaspoons baking powder
½ teaspoon salt
1 egg, lightly beaten
2 tablespoons unsalted butter, melted
½ to ¾ cup (4–6 fl oz/125–180 ml) milk
freshly ground pepper
chopped fresh parsley (optional)

❦ Place the apples in a bowl and cover with the water. Refrigerate, covered, overnight.

❦ Place the ham in a large pot and cover with water. Heat to boiling, reduce the heat and simmer, partially covered, for 1 hour. Transfer the ham to a board and save the cooking water. Remove any net casing and slice the ham about ½ in (1 cm) thick.

❦ Place the apples with their liquid in a large, preferably shallow, pot. Stir in 3 cups (24 fl oz/750 ml) of the ham cooking liquid and the brown sugar. Tuck the ham slices into the apples. Heat to boiling, reduce the heat and simmer, covered, for 30 minutes.

❦ Meanwhile, combine the flour, baking powder and salt in a large bowl. Beat in the egg, butter and enough milk to form a soft, sticky dough.

❦ After the apples and ham cook for 30 minutes, drop the batter in by the spoonful. Cook, covered, until the dumplings are just firm, about 12 minutes. Sprinkle with pepper and parsley and serve in shallow bowls, spooning some of the liquid into each bowl.

SERVES 6

Missouri

PORK WITH SAUERKRAUT

Sauerkraut is generally associated with German communities, yet people of all ethnic backgrounds can be seen lining up for hot dogs and sauerkraut on city streets and at baseball games everywhere. Pork (including the hot dog) seems to have an affinity for the pickled stuff.

2½ lb (1.25 kg) boneless pork, cut into 1½-in (4-cm) cubes
salt and freshly ground pepper
3 tablespoons vegetable oil
1 large onion, chopped
1 large garlic clove, minced
1 teaspoon caraway seed
3 large fresh tomatoes, seeded and chopped
pinch of sugar
6 juniper berries, crushed
1 cup (8 fl oz/250 ml) chicken stock (approximately) (see glossary)
2 lb (1 kg) sauerkraut, rinsed and drained

❦ Preheat the oven to 375°F (190°C). Sprinkle pork with salt and pepper. Heat the oil in a large heavy pot or Dutch oven over medium heat. Sauté the pork in batches until well browned. Transfer to a plate.

❦ Discard all but 2 tablespoons fat from the pot. Add the onion and cook for 2 minutes, scraping the sides and bottom of the pot. Add the garlic and cook 3 minutes longer. Return the meat and stir in the caraway seed, tomatoes, sugar, juniper berries and ½ cup (4 fl oz/125 ml) of the stock. Heat to boiling, cover and transfer to the oven. Bake for 1 hour, adding more stock if needed.

❦ Stir the sauerkraut into the pork mixture and bake for another 30 minutes. Remove the cover if the mixture is too wet.

SERVES 4 TO 6

Connecticut

BEEF BOUILLI

Beef bouilli (literally, boiled beef) was a favorite dish of the British colonists, and Thomas Jefferson doted on it. Root vegetables were often added to the pot in New England, but they are entirely optional. To vary the sauce, omit the mushrooms and add a crushed anchovy, one minced gherkin and a tablespoon of capers to the egg enrichment.

SCHNITZ UND KNEPP (top) AND PORK WITH SAUERKRAUT (bottom)

¼ cup (2 oz/60 g) unsalted butter
1 beef rump roast, about 4 lb (2 kg) (rolled roast is suitable)
8 cups (2 qt/2 l) cold water
1 large onion, chopped
2 turnips, peeled and chopped
4 celery stalks with leaves, chopped
2 large carrots, chopped
1½ teaspoons salt
10 peppercorns
4 whole cloves
½ lb (250 g) mushrooms, sliced
2 tablespoons all-purpose (plain) flour
1 egg yolk
juice of ½ lemon
salt and freshly ground pepper
chopped fresh parsley
croutons

❦ Melt 2 tablespoons butter in a large pot or Dutch oven over medium heat. Add the meat and brown well on all sides. Stir in all but ½ cup (4 fl oz/125 ml) of the water, scraping the bottom and sides of the pan. Heat to boiling, skimming foam from the surface. Add the remaining cold water and skim the surface once more. Add the onion, turnips, celery, carrots, salt, peppercorns and cloves. Return to boiling, reduce the heat and simmer, covered, until the meat is tender, about 3½ hours.

❦ Transfer the meat to a carving board. Let stand for 5 minutes. Strain the stock, pressing the vegetables to release their juices. Slice the meat and arrange on a platter. Cover loosely with foil and keep warm in a low oven.

❦ Melt the remaining 2 tablespoons butter in a large skillet over medium heat. Quickly brown the mushrooms. Reduce the heat and sprinkle the mushrooms with the flour. Cook, stirring constantly, for 2 minutes. Add 1 cup (8 fl oz/250 ml) of the strained beef stock. Cook over medium heat until slightly thickened, about 8 minutes.

❦ Combine ¼ cup (2 fl oz/60 ml) stock with the egg yolk and lemon juice. Stir into the sauce. Cook over low heat, stirring frequently, until slightly thickened, about 5 minutes. Do not let boil. Add salt and pepper to taste and pour over the meat. Sprinkle with parsley and surround with croutons.

SERVES 6 TO 8   *Photograph page 134*

SOURED BEEF (left) AND BEEF BOUILLI (right, recipe page 133)

Pennsylvania

SOURED BEEF

The Germans brought their own version of pot roast with them, which they called Sauerbraten. *This dish, with its mingling of sweet and sour, has always been popular with Americans of every background. For the authentic flavor it is imperative to marinate the meat for three days prior to cooking.*

1 beef brisket (or beef topside, boned and rolled), 3½ to 4 lb
   (1.75 to 2 kg)
1 cup (8 fl oz/250 ml) red wine vinegar
1 cup (8 fl oz/250 ml) water
1 onion, sliced
2 garlic cloves, minced
2 celery stalks, chopped
1 medium carrot, chopped
6 parsley sprigs
2 bay leaves
6 whole cloves
¼ cup (about 2 oz/60 g) diced salt pork or bacon
1 cup (8 fl oz/250 ml) beef stock (see glossary)
2 cans (8 oz/250 g each) tomato sauce (pureed tomatoes)
1 tablespoon dark brown sugar
1 tablespoon lemon juice
8 gingersnaps, crushed

1 tablespoon Worcestershire sauce
chopped fresh parsley
salt and freshly ground pepper

❧ Place the brisket in a large shallow glass or ceramic dish. Add the vinegar, water, onion, garlic, celery, carrot, parsley, bay leaves and cloves. Cover and refrigerate, turning the meat occasionally, at least 3 days.
❧ Preheat the oven to 325°F (165°C). Remove the meat from the marinade and pat dry. Set the marinade aside.
❧ Sauté the salt pork in a large heavy pot or Dutch oven over medium-low heat until golden, about 5 minutes. Remove with a slotted spoon and discard. Raise the heat under the pot to medium-high, add the meat and brown well. Transfer to a plate.
❧ Discard all but 1 tablespoon drippings from the pot. Place over medium heat and stir in the stock, scraping the bottom and sides of the pan. Return the meat to the pot and pour the marinade on top. Add the tomato sauce, brown sugar, lemon juice, gingersnaps and Worcestershire sauce. Heat to boiling and transfer to the oven. Bake, covered, until the meat is tender, 2½ to 3 hours.
❧ Slice the meat and arrange on a serving platter. Sprinkle with parsley. Add salt and pepper to taste to the cooking juices. Strain and serve with the meat.

SERVES 6

Indiana

Midwestern Meat Loaf

Early meat loaves were generally made entirely of veal, although that is a luxury of a bygone era. In the late 1800s, "All-U-Kan-Eat-For-A-Nickel" lunch counters sprang up in every major city in the country, and meat loaf was always on the menu. Many cooks use only ground beef to make meat loaf these days, but it is best to use a combination of beef, veal and pork because beef alone can result in a dry loaf.

1 tablespoon unsalted butter
¼ cup (2 oz/60 g) finely chopped shallots or green (spring)
    onions
1½ lb (750 g) ground (minced) beef
½ lb (250 g) ground (minced) veal
¼ lb (125 g) lean ground (minced) pork
1 teaspoon salt
1 teaspoon freshly ground pepper
2 tablespoons chopped fresh parsley
½ teaspoon chopped fresh basil or ¼ teaspoon dried basil
⅓ cup (1½ oz/45 g) fine dry breadcrumbs
¼ cup (2 oz/60 g) chili sauce (American-style)
½ teaspoon soy sauce
1 egg, lightly beaten
¼ cup (2 fl oz/60 ml) milk
3 bacon strips

❦ Preheat the oven to 400°F (200°C). Melt the butter in a small skillet over medium-low heat. Add the shallots and cook for 5 minutes.

❦ Combine the meats in a large bowl. Add the shallots, salt, pepper, parsley, basil, breadcrumbs, chili sauce, soy sauce, egg and milk. Mix thoroughly. Form into a loaf on a shallow baking dish and lay the bacon strips over the top. Bake for 15 minutes. Reduce the oven temperature to 350°F (180°C) and bake 1 hour longer.

SERVES 6 TO 8

Connecticut

Connecticut Ham Loaf

"Country-style" hams, cured and smoked in the old-fashioned manner, are an American specialty. Everyone seems to have a favorite, be it a Smithfield or Surry ham from Virginia or a cob-smoked one from Vermont. Many states are dotted with smokehouses, each with its own way of doing things. Country hams (uncooked) must be soaked overnight and boiled until tender. Then they are usually roasted briefly, topped with a glaze of brown sugar and mustard. The following is an old "receipt" from Connecticut that uses up leftover ham.

1 cup (2 oz/60 g) fresh breadcrumbs
½ cup (3 oz/90 g) light brown sugar
2 teaspoons Dijon mustard
1½ lb (750 g) uncooked smoked ham (or bacon pieces), ground
    (minced)
1½ lb (750 g) ground (minced) pork
1 cup (8 fl oz/250 ml) milk
2 eggs, lightly beaten
¼ teaspoon salt
¼ teaspoon freshly ground pepper

❦ Preheat the oven to 350°F (180°C). Combine the breadcrumbs with the sugar in a medium bowl. Toss with a fork until well mixed. Add the mustard and mix with your hands until crumbly. Set aside one-third of the mixture.

❦ Combine the remaining crumb mixture with the ham, pork, milk, eggs, salt and pepper. Mix thoroughly.

❦ Shape the meat mixture into a loaf and place in a shallow baking dish. Sprinkle the reserved crumb mixture over the top and sides, lightly pressing into the meat. Bake for 1 hour 10 minutes. Serve warm, at room temperature or well chilled.

SERVES 8

POMPEY'S HEAD (left, recipe page 136),
CONNECTICUT HAM LOAF (right) AND
MIDWESTERN MEAT LOAF (bottom)

Virginia

POMPEY'S HEAD

Pompey's Head, a round meat loaf with a hole in the center, was reportedly an easy dish to prepare in brick ovens. Because the outside of the loaf would get very crusty, the meat could cook for hours without drying out. The name refers to the broad head of Pompey the Great (106-48 B.C.), but nobody is quite sure why.

1 lb (500 g) ground (minced) beef
1 lb (500 g) ground (minced) veal
½ lb (250 g) pork sausage meat
2 onions, finely chopped
1 tablespoon Dijon mustard
1 teaspoon salt
½ teaspoon freshly ground pepper
⅛ teaspoon dried sage, crumbled
pinch of dried thyme
dash of hot red pepper (Tabasco) sauce
2 eggs, lightly beaten
1¼ cups (10 fl oz/315 ml) beef stock (see glossary)
all-purpose (plain) flour
7 tablespoons (3½ oz/110 g) unsalted butter, melted

❧ Preheat the oven to 500°F (260°C). Combine the meats in a large bowl. Add the onions, mustard, salt, pepper, sage, thyme, pepper sauce, eggs and ½ cup (4 fl oz/125 ml) of the stock. Mix thoroughly.

❧ Shape the meat mixture into a ball and roll in flour to coat. Place on a lightly greased, shallow baking dish, pressing gently

to form a large mound. Make a hole 1 in (2.5 cm) wide halfway through the center. Bake for 10 minutes.

❧ Reduce the oven temperature to 350°F (180°C). Drizzle the loaf with melted butter (set aside 1 tablespoon for the sauce). Bake for another 10 minutes. Remove from the oven and sprinkle lightly with flour. Bake, basting every 15 minutes with butter and pan juices, 1 hour longer. Use a bulb baster to baste with juices from the center of the loaf. Carefully transfer the loaf to a platter and keep warm. Remove all the scum from the baking dish and skim the fat from the pan juices.

❧ Heat 1 tablespoon butter in a saucepan over medium-low heat. Add 1 tablespoon flour. Cook, stirring constantly, for 2 minutes. Add the meat juices and the remaining ¾ cup (6 fl oz/180 ml) stock. Simmer until slightly thickened and serve with the loaf.

SERVES 6 TO 8   *Photograph page 135*

Connecticut

BEEF POT PIE

The English brought their love of meat pies to this country. As far back as the fourteenth century, London was chockablock with cookshops selling deep-dish meat pies laden with heavy crusts called "coffins." Beef pies have been particularly popular in America in the present century. The following recipe is for a top-crust-only pie. For a more substantial, old-fashioned version, line the dish first with pastry before filling with the meat mixture.

FOR THE PASTRY

1½ cups (6 oz/185 g) all-purpose (plain) flour
¼ teaspoon salt
6 tablespoons (3 oz/90 g) cold unsalted butter
6 tablespoons (3 oz/90 g) cold lard
2 to 3 tablespoons cold water

FOR THE FILLING

¼ cup (2 oz/60 g) diced salt pork or bacon
1 onion, chopped
¼ cup (1 oz/30 g) all-purpose (plain) flour
1½ cups (12 fl oz/375 ml) hot beef stock (see glossary)
2 cups (10 oz/315 g) cubed roasted beef
4 small carrots, cooked and sliced
3 potatoes, peeled, cooked and cubed
⅛ teaspoon ground mace
salt and freshly ground pepper
1 egg white, lightly beaten

❧ To make the pastry, combine the flour with the salt in a large bowl. Cut in the butter and lard until the texture of coarse crumbs. Using a fork, mix in enough water to form a soft dough. Chill for 1 hour.

❧ Preheat the oven to 400°F (200°C). Sauté the salt pork in a large heavy skillet over medium heat until crisp. Pour off all but 3 tablespoons drippings and add the onion. Cook, stirring occasionally, over medium-low heat until golden and soft, about 8 minutes. Sprinkle in the flour and continue to cook, stirring constantly, for 3 minutes. The mixture will be quite thick. Stir in the stock. Heat to boiling, stirring constantly. Reduce the heat and simmer until thick, about 4 minutes. Remove from the heat and let cool to lukewarm.

❧ Stir the meat, carrots and potatoes into the onion mixture. Add the mace and salt and pepper to taste. Transfer to a greased 1½- to 2-qt (1.5- to 2-l) baking dish about 2 in (5 cm) deep.

❧ Roll out the pastry on a lightly floured board and cover the dish. Trim and flute the edges. Brush with the egg white. Cut a hole in the center of the pie. Bake for 30 minutes.

SERVES 4 TO 6

BEEF POT PIE

North Dakota

STEWED RABBIT

After venison, rabbit is the most accepted game meat. Again, however, the supermarket freezer or butcher shop generally carries only preserve-raised rabbits. Rabbit can be fried just like chicken and served with cream gravy, as it is in the South, or it can be stewed, as it is in North Dakota.

1 rabbit, cut into serving pieces
1 garlic clove, bruised
hot paprika
salt and freshly ground pepper
1 tablespoon unsalted butter
1 tablespoon vegetable oil
2 onions, halved and thinly sliced
1 celery stalk, finely chopped
2 carrots, peeled and chopped
1/2 teaspoon chopped fresh thyme or pinch of dried thyme
1/2 cup (4 fl oz/125 ml) chicken stock (see glossary)
1/4 cup (2 fl oz/60 ml) dry white wine
1 small green bell pepper (capsicum), seeded and chopped
1 small red bell pepper (capsicum), seeded and chopped
2 teaspoons all-purpose (plain) flour
1 egg yolk
chopped fresh parsley (optional)

❦ Rub the rabbit well with the bruised garlic. Mince the garlic and set aside. Sprinkle the rabbit pieces with paprika, salt and pepper.

❦ Heat the butter with the oil in a large heavy skillet over medium heat. Sauté half the rabbit pieces at a time until well browned. Transfer to a plate.

❦ Set aside 2 teaspoons drippings in a small saucepan. Discard all but 1 tablespoon of the remaining drippings from the skillet. Add the onions to the skillet and cook over medium heat for 2 minutes. Add the reserved minced garlic, celery, carrots and thyme and stir in the stock and wine, scraping the bottom and sides of the skillet. Return the rabbit pieces to the skillet. Heat to boiling, reduce the heat and cook, covered, over medium-low heat for 25 minutes. Add the peppers and continue to cook, covered, 25 minutes longer. Remove 1/4 cup (2 fl oz/60 ml) juices from the skillet.

❦ Heat the reserved drippings over medium-low heat. Stir in the flour. Cook, stirring constantly, for 2 minutes. Whisk in the juices. Heat to boiling and remove from the heat. When the juices stop bubbling, whisk in the egg yolk.

❦ Remove the rabbit from the heat and stir in the egg mixture. Place over low heat and cook, stirring gently, until the sauce thickens, about 2 minutes. Do not let boil. Sprinkle with parsley.

SERVES 4

THE SOUTHWEST

THE SOUTHWEST

T he Spanish called the Indians of the arid Southwest "Pueblos," naming them for the cliff dwellings and villages of stone and adobe buildings in which they lived. Many of the tribes belonged to the Uto-Aztecan family (as did the Aztecs), including the Pima and Hopi, although the Tano and Zuni tribes were linguistically separate groups. Drought and raids by the nomadic Apaches eventually scattered the Pueblos. The Apaches, along with the Comanches and Utes, who were also Uto-Aztecans, were hunters and raiders—and, after the horse was introduced, a danger to everyone, including the Spanish who brought the horse with them.

In good times the Pueblo Indians harvested pumpkins, gourds, melons, corn, squash and beans. Beans, in fact, were so important that the Hopis developed at least twelve varieties ranging from black to white. The most prized were the yellow, blue, red, white, multicolored and black, which represented the six cardinal directions: east, west, north, south, up and down. They also made use of the prickly pear (cactus fruit), pine nuts and the mesquite bean (the pod), which they ground into flour. Chili peppers, so prevalent in the cuisine of the Southwest today, may have been introduced into the diet from farther south by the Spanish. Every Pueblo village had several *hornos,* beehive-shaped outdoor ovens, for baking bread. Corn was ground on flat stones called *metates,* crushed with stone rolling pins called *manos.*

The Spanish had established Santa Fe as a royal city by 1609 and from there set up missions throughout the region, eventually stretching from mid-Texas into California. The name Santa Fe, according to author Huntley Dent, actually stands for "The Royal City of the Holy Faith of St. Francis of Assisi." Although the attempt to foist Christianity on the native Indians did not meet with overwhelming success, the Spanish fit in well with

DOWNTOWN DALLAS, TEXAS, IS A GIANT CLUSTER OF SLEEK OFFICE BUILDINGS AND FREEWAYS THAT CONTRASTS WITH THE RUGGED DESERT LANDSCAPE AT ITS DOORSTEP.

PREVIOUS PAGES: THE SPECTACULAR 1,000-FOOT RED ROCK FORMATIONS OF MONUMENT VALLEY IN ARIZONA, A STATE BLESSED WITH SOME OF THE WORLD'S MOST AWE-INSPIRING NATURAL SCENERY.
PHOTO: GRANT JOHNSON

the natives, and intermarriage was common. The Spanish also provided employment. They brought in livestock and hired the locals to tend the herds. The Texas longhorn, descendant of the Andalusian cattle the Spanish brought with them, did not make the best eating to be sure and was raised mainly for its hide. Nevertheless, herds of them needed tending, and the Mexicans who took care of the wild-natured beasts were, in fact, the first "cowboys." Eventually there were groves of citrus, avocados, apricots, pears and olives to look after as well. As Anglos pushed into the territory, Mexicans were recruited to do all kinds of labor, from building railroads to working in copper mines to tending the vast ranches. Much of the land was simply taken from the natives, most often by underhanded means. The people were treated like immigrants in their own land, and prejudice ran high against them, as it still does in much of the Southwest.

Americans began pushing into Texas in earnest in the 1820s after Mexico won its independence from Spain. Conflicts soon broke out over government, land and slavery. In 1836 the American colonists revolted against the Mexican government and bloody battles ensued, including the legendary loss of the Alamo and Sam Houston's victory at San Jacinto. After Texas became an independent republic, its residents asked for permission to join the Union. The state was admitted in 1845 over strong objections in the North concerning slavery in Texas. Once admitted, it was not long before more fighting broke out with Mexico over disputed lands claimed by both sides. It was only after General Winfield Scott captured Mexico City that a treaty was signed giving the United States what is now the Southwest for an indemnity of fifteen million dollars. The Gadsden Purchase of 1853 added a portion of Arizona and New Mexico. However, the territory of New Mexico (which included Arizona) remained the last region of the continental United States to be granted statehood. New Mexico and Arizona were not admitted until 1912.

In the 1860s the great cattle drives began. By this time shorthorns and Herefords were being bred with success in the West, but most of the five million or so head of cattle ranging wild on the wide-open Texas ranges were offshoots of the original Spanish herds mixed with various other cattle that had been free to roam the land during the Civil War. With the completion of the railroads, the beef market was thriving. Most of the trails began at San Antonio, the most famous being the Chisholm Trail to Abilene, Kansas. Over one and a half million head of cattle were moved over this one trail in four years alone. When the Santa Fe Railroad slashed across lower Kansas en route to New Mexico, the railheads at Wichita, Ellsworth and Dodge City added another two and a half million animals to the list. It was a rowdy lot of cowboys that herded these drives, and the ensuing lawlessness of the western plains has become part of American folklore.

The one person who could order cowboys around like little children was the chuckwagon "cookie," providing, of course, he was any good. Most trail dishes were stewlike affairs, the most famous being "son-of-a-bitch stew" (called "son-of-a-gun stew" in the company of preachers and women). Where the name came from, nobody knows, but it was the customary meal that began the drives. The stew was made with the innards of a freshly slaughtered steer. Salt pork, beans, jerky and flour were the main provisions a cook packed into the chuckwagon. A limited supply of fresh beef was taken to start the drive, but it would not last long in the hot, arid climate of Texas. Baked beans and sourdough biscuits were the mainstay of the cowboy diet. Chili was also a big hit with the men, and cooks took to planting herbs, onions and peppers along the trails so they would always have a supply on hand. When the meat ran out, hares, rattlesnakes, even armadillos found their way into the pot. Ranch food is still very much a part of southwestern cuisine. Barbecue, now available at smoke pits in almost every Texas city, began with ranchers. Germans and other settlers made their presence felt, but it is the Mexicans, with dishes like tacos, enchiladas, frijoles and tamale pie, who had the most influence on southwestern cuisine.

The cuisine of the Southwest is actually a combination of Spanish, Mexican and Indian cooking styles, although

THE ADOBE WALLS AND PAINTED DETAILS OF THIS BUILDING IN TAOS REPRESENT THE MOSAIC OF CULTURES (HISPANIC, ANGLO-AMERICAN AND NATIVE AMERICAN) THAT MAKE UP NEW MEXICO.

BRUCE HANDS

THE COLORADO RIVER WINDS ITS WAY THROUGH MARBLE CANYON, ARIZONA,
SOME OF THE DRIEST, MOST BARREN LANDSCAPE IN AMERICA'S SOUTHWEST.

the food varies from state to state and has, in some cases, been anglicized by other hands stirring the pot as well. Most Americans are hard put to note the subtleties between Tex-Mex, Cal-Mex, New Mexico style or Arizona style, but Southwesterners can clearly taste the difference. Often it is a matter of ingredients: Monterey Jack cheese as opposed to longhorn Cheddar, cumin versus oregano, which types of chili peppers are used in which dishes and so on. Everyone, it seems, has a favorite method of preparing tacos, enchiladas, tamales, guacamole, salsa and the like. One of the more widely acknowledged controversies centers on chili con carne (peppers with meat)—whether to make it with or without beans.

Tortillas, the bread of the Southwest, form the base of many southwestern dishes, and both corn and flour types may be purchased in supermarkets everywhere. While it is not easy to make corn tortillas without the right equipment and practice, flour tortillas are not at all difficult to prepare, and homemade are far superior to the commercial variety (except in the Southwest, where decent locally made tortillas can be purchased). It is the pepper, however, that truly lies at the heart of southwestern cuisine.

The most commonly used fresh cooking pepper is the bright green California Anaheim, which grows six to eight inches long. It is seldom hot, although a bit zippier if grown in New Mexico. One of the most flavorful of all fresh peppers is the poblano, a large, dark green chili that ranges from mild to medium hot. Outside the Southwest, these peppers are generally found only in specialty food stores. Green bell peppers (capsicums), the mildest of all, are the most readily available peppers in the United States and may be used in conjunction with canned mild or hot green chilies. Hot jalapeño peppers, small green or red peppers about two inches long, are available everywhere. The serrano chili, smaller and lighter than the jalapeño, is also much hotter. The guero is a yellow pepper about the size of the jalapeño and is very hot. With interest in the cuisine of the Southwest growing, dried peppers are becoming easier to find. The Anaheim comes in a dried state and is sometimes called pasilla or cascabel. The ancho is the dried poblano. The japone is the dried hot serrano, which gets hotter in the drying process. Then there are the very small and very hot, dried red pequins and tepins. Chipotles are smoked, dried jalapeños, found canned throughout the country. Canned "green chilies" are most often the mild California or hotter New Mexico Anaheims.

The cooking of the Southwest has long been romanticized, and with good reason. It is a colorful, spicy cuisine that natives say is addictive. Addictive or not, it is a style of cooking that has influenced many young American chefs, and their dishes have become more assertive as these chefs have discovered the pleasing effect of peppers on the palate.

WHEAT FIELDS AND STORM CLOUDS IN THE TEXAS PANHANDLE, EAST OF AMARILLO.

TALIS BERGMANIS

BEANS AND GRAINS

CORN HARVESTING IN ILLINOIS, A GREAT LAKES STATE THAT HAS MUCH IN COMMON WITH THE RURAL MIDWEST, WHERE CORN AND WHEAT ARE THE MAJOR CROPS.

BEANS AND GRAINS

Grains and beans were among the first cultivated plants in history, and no wonder. They were easy to grow, were filling and, most importantly, were energy giving (or totally nutritious). Europeans were familiar with many grains before they landed here but had never run across corn (known as *maize* in the European lexicon; most of the world uses the term *corn* to refer to many grains). Corn was, along with the bean, the mainstay of the Indians' diet, and both became staples of the settlers as well. The Indians of the Northeast grew mainly white beans, including the small pea bean and the large plump bean called the Great Northern. The Indians of the Southwest developed the darker beans that are an integral part of southwestern cuisine.

Europeans accepted beans into their daily regimen without difficulty. After all, they were familiar with the broad bean of the Old World and did not realize that the beans of the New World actually were of a different genus. Indian specialties such as succotash and baked beans immediately became a part of the settlers' kitchen repertoires. Corn, however, was alien. Although the colonists may not have taken to it so readily, they had little choice but to use it. Even after rye, barley, oats and wheat were planted in the seventeenth century, the poor crops failed to replace corn in the everyday diet. Cornmeal, stone-ground by hand until the water wheel was introduced, was used as a thickening agent in soups and baked into breads, cakes—even puddings. Although all the Indians seemed to be familiar with hominy (corn treated with wood ash), it was particularly important to

the tribes of the South and Southwest. They used hominy fresh, dried or ground into grits like cornmeal. Even today hominy is very much a part of these two regional styles of cooking.

Wheat was introduced into the Southwest by Spanish missionaries who brought it from Mexico, where Cortez had introduced it in 1519. The grain finally took hold in the Middle Atlantic states, and by the Civil War the North was growing enough to easily supply the Union army. After the Civil War came the move westward. Eventually wheat flourished in the plains states, now often referred to as the "wheat belt."

Rice was being grown in South Carolina as early as 1647, but, according to one story, when the British captured Charleston during the Revolution, they shipped the entire rice crop back to England, leaving nary a seed behind. It was Thomas Jefferson, our first ambassador to France, who smuggled rice out of Italy and put American rice growers back in business, or so the story goes.

America has also been blessed with another grain—wild rice. Technically, not a grain but a grass, wild rice is considered a delicacy in most of the world. Though it is now being cultivated in the West, most of our wild rice comes from the Great Lakes region, mainly Minnesota, where it is still harvested by Indians in much the same way they have always done it—by canoe. The natural wild rice areas in the upper Midwest are mainly on Indian land, and the harvest remains an Indian domain as protected by law.

The earliest breads in America were made with cornmeal, most of them unleavened. When wheat flour first

TALIS BERGMANIS

SUNFLOWERS, THEIR SEEDS USED IN THE PRODUCTION OF
OIL, CREATE A CARPET OF COLOR IN A KANSAS FIELD.

CHARACTERISTIC OF ALL THE FARMLANDS IN THE GREAT PLAINS
ARE THESE SHINY, STAINLESS STEEL WHEAT SILOS IN IOWA.

GEORGE OLSON

became available, it was expensive, so cooks mixed it
with cornmeal to lighten the batter. As wheat spread, its
flour surpassed cornmeal in household usage. Every early
American housewife knew how to make homemade
yeast, but the move west gave rise to a serious problem.
Making a fresh batch of yeast on demand was impossible
on the trail, and thus sourdough was born. A trail cook
(whether pioneer housewife or chuckwagon "cookie")
depended on a "starter dough," which was used and then
replenished every time bread or biscuits were made. This
yeasty mixture was indeed very sour and it was
imperative that a batch be maintained for day-to-day
usage, come rain, shine, heatwave, or blizzard. On
particularly cold nights, it was not uncommon for the
responsible party to actually sleep with the starter to
keep it warm.

At the end of the eighteenth century, pearl ash, a
derivative of the potassium carbonate in wood ashes, was
found to produce carbon dioxide in heated dough, which
made it rise. Pearl ash, unfortunately, had a very bitter
taste, and the first commercial baking soda marketed in
1840 was not much better. Chemists soon discovered,
however, that by adding acidic salts to baking soda, the
bitterness abated. The resulting formula, marketed as
baking powder, hit the market in 1856 and was an
immediate success. Quick breads, particularly biscuits,
became part of daily life. Even the heavy cornbreads of
the day benefited from the new product.

The following recipes represent some of the traditional
beans and grains dishes that Americans enjoy, along with
a good selection of homemade breadstuffs.

Illinois

STICKY BUNS

Although sweet caramelized yeast rolls were popular in Philadelphia in the nineteenth century, the following recipe for the ultimate "sticky bun," made with a mashed-potato dough, comes from farther west, in Illinois. It is a recipe that has been passed down for generations and certainly qualifies for what the donor, Karen Haram, editor of the San Antonio Express-News, *calls the "rich farm food of America's Heartland."*

1 cup (8 fl oz/250 ml) milk
½ cup (4 oz/125 g) sugar
2 teaspoons salt
1 package (¼ oz/7 g) dry yeast
2 eggs, lightly beaten
1 cup mashed potatoes (about 2 small potatoes)
5½ cups (22 oz/700 g) all-purpose (plain) flour
    (approximately)
1¾ cups (14 oz/440 g) unsalted butter
2½ cups (13 oz/410 g) packed dark brown sugar
2 teaspoons ground cinnamon
1½ cups (6 oz/185 g) chopped pecans

❦ Scald the milk; cool to lukewarm and pour into a large bowl. Stir in the sugar, salt and yeast. Let stand for 2 minutes. Beat in the eggs, mashed potatoes and 1½ cups (6 oz/185 g) flour until just mixed. Do not overbeat. Let stand for 10 minutes.
❦ Meanwhile, melt ½ cup (4 oz/125 g) of the butter and cool to lukewarm.
❦ Add the melted butter to the yeast mixture. Stir in the remaining flour, 1 cup (4 oz/125 g) at a time, until smooth and not sticky. Transfer the dough to a floured board and knead for 2 minutes, adding more flour if needed. Transfer to a greased bowl, turning to coat. Cover and let rise in a warm place until tripled in volume, about 2 hours.
❦ Melt another ½ cup (4 oz/125 g) of butter in a small saucepan. Divide the dough in half and roll each half into a rectangle ¼ in (5 mm) thick. Brush with the melted butter. Combine ½ cup (3 oz/90 g) of the brown sugar with the cinnamon and sprinkle over the dough. Roll up like a jelly roll and slice into 1-in (2.5-cm) pieces. You should get 9 pieces per roll.
❦ Melt the remaining ¾ cup (6 oz/180 g) butter with the remaining 2 cups (10 oz/350 g) brown sugar in a saucepan over medium heat. Divide the mixture between 2 greased 8-in (20-cm) square pans. Sprinkle the nuts evenly over the sugar mixture. Place the rolls, flat side down, on top of the nuts, 9 rolls per pan. Cover with a flour-rubbed dish towel and let rise in a warm place until doubled in volume, about 1 hour.
❦ Preheat the oven to 350°F (180°C). Bake the rolls until golden brown, 25 to 30 minutes. When done, cover with a serving platter and invert. Carefully remove the pan, allowing the caramel to run down over the rolls.

MAKES 18 ROLLS

New Jersey

BLUEBERRY MUFFINS

Muffins originally were made with cornmeal and were nothing more than small corn cakes served most often with the breakfast meal. Today wheat flour has taken the place of cornmeal, and fruit is frequently added, blueberries being the most popular choice by far. The United States grows three-fourths of the world's blueberry crop, with Michigan, New Jersey and Maine the top three producers.

1 cup (4 oz/125 g) blueberries, picked over
2 cups (8 oz/250 g) all-purpose (plain) flour
½ cup (4 oz/125 g) sugar
3 teaspoons baking powder
½ teaspoon salt
1 egg, lightly beaten
1 teaspoon finely grated orange peel
¼ cup (2 oz/60 g) unsalted butter, melted
1 cup (8 fl oz/250 ml) milk (or half milk and half buttermilk)

❦ Preheat the oven to 375°F (190°C). Toss the blueberries with ¼ cup (30 g) flour in a bowl. Set aside.
❦ Sift the remaining flour with the sugar, baking powder and salt into a large bowl. Stir in the egg, orange peel, butter and milk. Fold in the blueberries.
❦ Spoon the batter into a greased 12-muffin (patty) pan, filling each cup about two-thirds full. Bake until golden and firm, 20 to 25 minutes. Remove the pan from the oven and let stand for 5 minutes before unmolding the muffins.

MAKES ABOUT 12 MUFFINS

STICKY BUNS

BLUEBERRY MUFFINS

PUMPKIN ROLLS (right)
AND PARKER HOUSE ROLLS (center)

New Hampshire

PUMPKIN ROLLS

The Indians first taught New Englanders how to use pumpkin and other squashes in cakes and breads, which were made only with cornmeal at the time. The tradition, however, carried forward, and dinner rolls flavored with squash are commonly part of the Thanksgiving feast.

1½ teaspoons dry yeast
1 teaspoon sugar
¼ cup (2 fl oz/60 ml) lukewarm water
3 cups (12 oz/375 g) all-purpose (plain) flour (approximately)
3½ tablespoons (1 ¾ oz/55 g) unsalted butter
2 tablespoons light brown sugar
¼ teaspoon salt
1 cup (8 oz/250 g) pumpkin puree (page 32)
1 egg, lightly beaten
¼ cup (2 fl oz/60 ml) maple syrup
¼ teaspoon ground cinnamon
1 cup (4 oz/75 g) whole wheat (wholemeal) flour

❦ Combine the yeast, sugar and water in a large bowl; let stand for 5 minutes. Stir in ½ cup (2 oz/60 g) of the all-purpose flour; cover and let rise in a warm place for 1 hour.
❦ Melt 2 tablespoons of the butter and pour into a bowl. Beat in the brown sugar, salt, pumpkin, egg, maple syrup and cinnamon. Add to the yeast mixture and beat until smooth. Add the whole wheat flour and enough all-purpose flour, about 2½ cups (10 oz/310 g), to make a stiff dough. Knead briefly in the bowl. Cover and let rise in a warm place for 2 hours.
❦ Punch the dough down and transfer to a floured board. Knead briefly and roll out about ½ in (1 cm) thick. Cut into 1-in (2.5-cm) circles. Place the circles on baking sheets dusted with flour. Cover with flour-rubbed dish towels and let rise for 1 hour.
❦ Preheat the oven to 425°F (220°C). Melt the remaining 1½ tablespoons butter and brush on the tops of the rolls. Bake for 15 minutes.

MAKES ABOUT 24 ROLLS

Massachusetts

PARKER HOUSE ROLLS

The Parker House was one of the best-known restaurants in Boston in the mid-1800s. These yeast rolls were reportedly invented when the chef at the Parker House, in a fit of pique, threw some pieces of dough on a baking sheet, baked them and created an American phenomenon.

1 package (¼ oz/7 g) dry yeast
2 tablespoons sugar
½ cup (4 fl oz/375 ml) warm water
1½ cups (12 fl oz/375 ml) milk
1 tablespoon salt
½ cup (4 oz/125 g) unsalted butter, melted
6 cups (1½ lb/750 g) all-purpose (plain) flour (approximately)

❦ Combine the yeast with 1 tablespoon of the sugar and the water in the large bowl of an electric mixer. Let stand until bubbly, about 5 minutes. Scald the milk, cool to lukewarm and add to the bowl along with the remaining 1 tablespoon sugar, salt and half the butter. On low speed, add 1½ cups (6 oz/185 g) flour. Beat at medium speed for 3 minutes. On low speed, add the remaining flour, 1 cup (4 oz/125 g) at a time, until a soft dough is formed. Turn out on a lightly floured board and knead until smooth and elastic, 8 to 10 minutes. Transfer the dough to a greased bowl, turning to coat, cover and let stand in a warm place until doubled in volume, about 1 hour.
❦ Punch down the dough and turn out on a floured board. Let rest for 5 minutes. Roll out the dough ½ in (1 cm) thick and cut into 3-in (7.5-cm) rounds. Make a crease at the middle of each round with the back of a knife. Brush lightly with the remaining melted butter. Fold the dough over and gently press the edges together. Place the rolls 2 in (5 cm) apart on ungreased baking sheets. Cover with flour-rubbed dish towels and let rise in a warm place for 35 minutes.
❦ Preheat the oven to 425°F (220°C). Bake until golden brown, 12 to 15 minutes.

MAKES ABOUT 24 ROLLS

South Carolina

SPOON BREAD

Spoon bread is similar to a soufflé, and has often been called a cornmeal custard. The center of a spoon bread should be moist but not uncooked, and is generally eaten with a spoon, hence its name.

2⅓ cups (19 fl oz/580 ml) light (single) cream or half & half
  (half cream and half milk)
¼ cup (2 oz/60 g) unsalted butter
3 teaspoons sugar
1 tablespoon honey
½ teaspoon salt
1 cup (5 oz/155 g) white cornmeal
4 eggs, separated
1 teaspoon baking powder
pinch of ground white pepper

❦ Preheat the oven to 375°F (190°C). Combine the cream, butter, sugar, honey and salt in a saucepan. Cook, stirring occasionally, over low heat until the butter has melted. Slowly whisk in the cornmeal. Cook, stirring constantly, until thick.
❦ Transfer the cornmeal mixture to a large bowl. Add the egg yolks, one at a time, beating well after each addition. Add the baking powder and white pepper.
❦ Beat the egg whites until stiff. Fold into the cornmeal mixture. Transfer to a greased 2-qt (2-l) soufflé dish and bake until puffed and golden, about 35 minutes.

SERVES 6

California

SOURDOUGH BREAD

Although sourdough breads and biscuits once were found all across the country, they are generally associated with California. This is partly because "sourdough" was so important in the Gold Rush days, but mostly it is because that state, and San Francisco in particular, has kept the tradition alive and well. A traveler can even pick up a loaf at the airport on the way out of town.

1 cup (8 fl oz/250 ml) sourdough starter (recipe follows)
2 cups (16 fl oz/500 ml) lukewarm water

6 cups (1½ lb/750 g) all-purpose (plain) flour
1 package (¼ oz/7 g) dry yeast
1 tablespoon salt
cornmeal
1 egg yolk mixed with 1 tablespoon water

❦ The night before baking the bread, combine the sourdough starter with 1 cup (8 fl oz/250 ml) water and 2 cups (8 oz/250 g) flour in a large bowl. Cover tightly with plastic wrap and let stand at room temperature overnight.

❦ The next day, dissolve the yeast in the remaining 1 cup (8 fl oz/250 ml) water in a small bowl. Let stand for 5 minutes then stir into the sourdough mixture. Beat in the salt and enough flour to make a soft dough.

Vermont

CORNBREAD

Cornbread, the mainstay of early American life, is lightened these days with the aid of flour and baking powder or baking soda or both. Buttermilk is traditionally used in the batter in all regions, and in Vermont a little maple syrup finds its way into the mixture as well. Cornbread is best made in a cast-iron skillet, but an 8-in (20-cm) square pan is fine.

1½ cups (8 oz/250 g) yellow cornmeal
½ cup (2 oz/60 g) all-purpose (plain) flour
1 tablespoon baking powder
½ teaspoon baking soda (bicarbonate of soda)
1 teaspoon salt
1½ cups (12 fl oz/375 ml) buttermilk
1 egg, lightly beaten
¼ cup (2 oz/60 g) warm bacon drippings
3 tablespoons maple syrup
1 tablespoon unsalted butter, melted

❦ Preheat the oven to 425°F (220°C). Combine the cornmeal, flour, baking powder, baking soda and salt in a large mixing bowl. Stir in the buttermilk, egg, 3 tablespoons of the drippings, and the maple syrup. Mix well.

❦ Heat the remaining 1 tablespoon bacon drippings in a 9-in (23-cm) cast-iron skillet over medium heat. Pour the batter into the skillet and brush with melted butter. Bake until golden, 15 to 20 minutes. Serve warm.

SERVES 6

Oklahoma

CORN STICKS

Corn sticks can be heavy and uninteresting if not properly made. They should be light, airy morsels of cornbread, made in a cast-iron mold that gives them a crisp crust. Whether corn sticks are white or yellow is strictly a regional affair. Yellow cornmeal is preferred in most of the country, while the South still clings to white.

½ cup (3 oz/90 g) yellow cornmeal
½ cup (2 oz/60 g) all-purpose (plain) flour
2 tablespoons sugar
1½ teaspoons baking powder
½ teaspoon salt
1 cup (8 fl oz/250 ml) cream
1 egg yolk, lightly beaten
2 tablespoons (1 oz/30 g) unsalted butter, melted
2 egg whites

❦ Preheat the oven to 425°F (220°C). Combine the cornmeal with the flour, sugar, baking powder and salt in a large bowl. Stir in the cream, egg yolk and butter. Beat the egg whites until stiff and fold into the batter.

❦ Spoon the batter evenly into a greased corn stick mold. Bake until firm and golden, about 15 minutes. Serve hot.

MAKES 18 TO 20 SMALL CORN STICKS

CORNBREAD (top left)
AND CORN STICKS (right)

Kentucky

GRITS SOUFFLÉ

Southerners often call this dish a grits casserole, but it is in fact a soufflé. As for all regional recipes, there are many variations to be found in the South. In Tennessee folks are not averse to throwing finely chopped smoked ham into the mixture.

2½ tablespoons (1½ oz/50 g) unsalted butter
¼ cup (1 oz/30 g) freshly grated Parmesan cheese
2 green (spring) onions, finely chopped
2 garlic cloves, minced
1 cup (8 fl oz/250 ml) water
1 cup (8 fl oz/250 ml) milk
½ teaspoon salt
½ cup (3 oz/90 g) hominy grits
4 eggs, separated
dash of hot red pepper (Tabasco) sauce
¼ cup (2 fl oz/60 ml) cream
½ cup (2 oz/60 g) grated Cheddar cheese
salt and freshly ground pepper

❧ Preheat the oven to 400°F (200°C). Rub a 1-qt (1-l) soufflé dish with ½ tablespoon of the butter and sprinkle with 1 tablespoon of the Parmesan cheese. Set aside in a cool place.

❧ Melt 1 tablespoon of the butter in a small sauté pan over low heat. Add the green onions and garlic; cook for 5 minutes. Remove from the heat.

❧ Combine the water, milk and salt in a saucepan. Heat to boiling, whisk in the grits and reduce the heat. Cook, stirring constantly, until thick, 5 to 8 minutes. Add the remaining 1 tablespoon butter. Reduce the heat to low and beat in the egg yolks, one at a time, beating well after each addition. Transfer to a large bowl and beat in the pepper sauce, cream, Cheddar cheese, 2 tablespoons of the Parmesan cheese and salt and pepper to taste.

❧ Beat the egg whites until stiff. Fold into the grits. Transfer to the prepared soufflé dish and sprinkle the top with the remaining 1 tablespoon Parmesan cheese. Bake until puffed and golden, 30 to 35 minutes. Serve immediately.

SERVES 4 TO 6

Georgia

FANCY DINNER GRITS

Grits are ground dried hominy. To make hominy, the Indians soaked corn in water mixed with wood ashes. After a day's soaking, the bleached kernels puffed up and the hulls burst. The hominy was then washed well and dried whole for winter's use or ground and used for porridge. Early settlers called the porridge "groats," which Southerners mispronounced as "grits," and the name stuck. Grits are traditionally served at breakfast, in which case omit the garlic and cheese.

1 tablespoon unsalted butter
1 garlic clove, minced
1 cup (8 fl oz/250 ml) cream
1 cup (8 fl oz/250 ml) water or stock (see glossary)
½ cup (3 oz/90 g) hominy grits
salt and ground white pepper to taste
½ cup (2 oz/60 g) freshly grated Parmesan, Jarlsberg,
   Monterey Jack or mild melting cheese (optional)

❧ Melt the butter in a saucepan over low heat. Add the garlic; cook for 2 minutes. Add the cream and water or stock. Heat to boiling, reduce the heat and whisk in the grits. Cook, covered, stirring frequently, over low heat until tender and creamy, 12 to 15 minutes. Add salt and pepper to taste and, if desired, the cheese.

SERVES 4

GRITS SOUFFLÉ (top) AND FANCY DINNER GRITS (bottom)

PENNSYLVANIA DUTCH EGG NOODLES

The German noodle that so many dishes like "potpie" (page 46) depend on is really very easy to make. The noodles may be dried and stored in airtight containers, or cooked fresh in boiling water for 2 to 3 minutes and tossed in butter and sprinkled with poppy seeds.

1¼ cups (5 oz/155 g) all-purpose (plain) flour (approximately)
½ teaspoon salt
2 eggs, lightly beaten

❧ Combine the flour with the salt in a large bowl. Add the eggs and stir with a fork until a soft dough is formed. Scrape the dough out onto a well-floured board and knead, adding more flour if needed, for 10 minutes. Cover loosely with a flour-rubbed dish towel. Let stand for 30 minutes.

❧ Roll out the dough as thin as possible and cut into 4-in (10-cm) squares for potpie or in long strips for regular noodles. Place on lightly greased wax paper and refrigerate until ready to use (or dry and store in an airtight container).

MAKES ABOUT ½ LB (250 G)

Texas

CHUCKWAGON BEANS

Baked beans appear at almost every Texas cookout and, more often than not, are labeled "chuckwagon" beans. Although Texas-style beans these days are cooked in the oven with myriad flavorings added for good measure, the original chuckwagon beans of cattle drive days were cooked simply in a large kettle set overnight over low embers. If salt pork was in short supply, it wasn't unheard-of to flavor the beans with a rattlesnake or two.

1 lb (500 g) dried pink (pinto, *borletto* or kidney) beans
2 tablespoons (1 oz/30 g) unsalted butter
1 onion, chopped
1 large garlic clove, minced
1 can (12 fl oz/375 ml) beer (lager)
¼ cup (2 fl oz/60 ml) Worcestershire sauce
¼ cup (2 oz/60 g) brown sugar
2 tablespoons Dijon mustard
1 tablespoon sweet paprika
2 tablespoons mild ground chilies (or mild chili powder)
1 teaspoon dried red pepper flakes, crushed
pinch of dried thyme
3 cups (24 fl oz/750 ml) tomato juice (approximately)
2 oz (60 g) salt pork or bacon, cut into strips
salt and freshly ground pepper

❦ Soak the beans overnight in cold water to cover. Or place the beans in a large pot, cover with cold water and boil for 2 minutes. Remove from the heat and let stand, covered, for 1 hour. Drain.

❦ Preheat the oven to 300°F (150°C). Melt the butter in a large heavy saucepan over medium-low heat. Add the onion; cook for 1 minute. Add the garlic; cook 4 minutes longer. Stir in the beer, Worcestershire sauce, brown sugar, mustard, paprika, ground chilies, red pepper flakes, thyme and ½ cup (4 fl oz/125 ml) tomato juice. Heat to boiling, reduce the heat and simmer, uncovered, for 15 minutes. Stir in the drained beans.

❦ Transfer the beans to a greased bean (tight-lidded) pot. Place the salt pork on top and drizzle with 1½ cups (12 fl oz/375 ml) tomato juice. Cover and bake for 2 hours. Reduce the heat to 275°F (135°C) and continue to bake, adding more tomato juice as needed to prevent drying out, until the beans are tender, about 5 hours longer. Add salt and pepper to taste.

SERVES 6 TO 8

Massachusetts

BOSTON BAKED BEANS

The earliest baked bean recipes on record consisted of nothing but beans, salt pork, water and, on occasion, ground pepper "to render the beans less unhealthy." Molasses entered the picture around the 1850s. Today there are as many versions of this classic dish as there are pot stirrers. The recipe below includes rum, which early New Englanders were known to drink with gusto.

1 lb (500 g) dried navy (Boston or pearl haricot) beans,
    pea beans, Great Northern beans or white haricot beans
1 large onion, chopped
2 tablespoons dark brown sugar
¼ cup (2 fl oz/60 ml) molasses
1 tablespoon dry mustard
½ cup dark (4 fl oz/125 ml) rum
1½ cups (12 fl oz/325 ml) water (approximately)
4 oz (125 g) salt pork or bacon
salt and freshly ground pepper

❦ Soak the beans overnight in cold water to cover. Or place them in a large pot, cover with cold water and boil for 2 minutes. Remove from the heat and let stand, covered, for 1 hour. Drain.

❦ Preheat the oven to 300°F (150°C). Combine the beans with the onion in a greased bean (tight-lidded) pot. Combine the sugar, molasses, mustard, rum and water in a bowl. Pour over the beans. Cut the salt pork into 3 pieces and place on top of the beans. Cover and bake for 2 hours. Reduce the heat to 275°F (135°C) and continue to bake, adding more water as needed to prevent drying out, until the beans are tender, about 2 hours longer.

❦ Remove the salt pork and cut into pieces. Stir back into beans and add salt and pepper to taste.

SERVES 6 TO 8

Massachusetts

BOSTON BROWN BREAD

For generations in New England, Boston brown bread was inevitably served with baked beans. Flavored with rye flour and molasses, the bread is steamed, not baked, and usually made in round loaves with the aid of coffee cans. Raisins appear in many old recipes, but are considered an option rather than a rule.

½ cup (2 oz/60 g) rye flour
½ cup (2 oz/60 g) whole wheat (wholemeal) flour
½ cup (3 oz/90 g) cornmeal
1 teaspoon baking soda (bicarbonate of soda)
½ teaspoon salt
⅓ cup (3 fl oz/80 ml) molasses
1 cup (8 fl oz/250 ml) sour milk or buttermilk
½ cup (3 oz/90 g) seedless raisins (optional)

❦ Combine the rye and whole wheat flour with the cornmeal, baking soda and salt in a large bowl. Stir in the molasses, sour milk and raisins.

❦ Grease a coffee can or a 1-qt (1-l) pudding mold. Spoon in the dough. Cover the can securely with aluminum foil or a lid. Place in a large pot and add boiling water to come halfway up the side of the can or mold. Cover the pot and steam for 2 hours.

❦ Unmold the bread and serve hot. The hot bread is so moist, it is generally cut into slices with a string, but a sharp serrated knife will do just as well.

MAKES 1 LOAF

WILD RICE PILAF

1 lb (500 g) dried red kidney beans
2 bacon strips, chopped
1 large onion, chopped
1 large garlic clove, minced
1 cup (6 oz/185 g) chopped smoked ham
1 celery stalk, chopped
2 small hot red (chili) peppers, seeded, deveined and chopped
1 bay leaf
½ teaspoon ground allspice
4 cups (1 qt/1 l) boiling water or stock (see glossary)
1½ lb (750 g) smoked sausage (Wurst, Kabana or kielbasa),
   cut into 3-in (7.5-cm) lengths
salt and freshly ground pepper
hot cooked rice

❦ Place the beans in a large pot and cover with 2 qt (2 l) water. Heat to boiling and boil, uncovered, for 20 minutes. Drain.

❦ Sauté the bacon in a large heavy pot or Dutch oven over medium heat until crisp. Add the onion, garlic, ham and celery. Cook, stirring occasionally, for 10 minutes. Add the peppers, bay leaf and allspice. Reduce the heat and stir in the boiling water or stock and the drained beans. Simmer, covered, stirring occasionally, for 45 minutes.

❦ Remove ½ cup (4 fl oz/125 ml) of the beans to a bowl and mash with a fork. Stir back into the beans. Add the sausage. Simmer, uncovered, until the beans are tender and the mixture has thickened, about 45 minutes longer. Discard the bay leaf and add salt and pepper to taste. Serve with hot cooked rice.

SERVES 6 TO 8

Minnesota

WILD RICE PILAF

Pilaf (pilau) is basically steamed rice made with chicken, fish or vegetables. The dish comes from Persia and is common throughout the Middle East. In America pilaf is often served as a side dish, without the chicken, fish or vegetables. The following recipe is made with wild rice. Midwesterners generally add nuts to their pilafs, using indigenous black walnuts when they can find them. Almonds or pecans may be used instead.

1 cup (5 oz/155 g) wild rice
1 tablespoon unsalted butter
1 small onion, minced
½ cup (4 fl oz/125 ml) dry white wine
2½ cups (20 fl oz/625 ml) water or chicken stock
   (approximately) (see glossary)
salt and freshly ground pepper
½ cup (2 oz/60 g) toasted chopped nuts

❦ Rinse the wild rice under cold water and drain.

❦ Melt the butter in a heavy saucepan over medium-low heat. Add the onion; cook, covered, for 5 minutes. Stir in the rice, wine and 2 cups (16 fl oz/500 ml) of the water. Heat to boiling, reduce the heat and simmer, covered, adding more water if needed, until the rice is tender, 40 to 60 minutes. (If the rice is too wet at this point, uncover and raise the heat slightly.) Add salt and pepper to taste. Toss in the nuts.

SERVES 4

Louisiana

RED BEANS AND SAUSAGES

In the Cajun country of Louisiana, beans and rice have long been staples that are inexpensive and filling. Rice is now an important food crop in Louisiana, and beans, of course, were grown there long before the Spanish explored the area. The boucheries offer an overwhelming selection of smoked sausages, like the local chaurice (chorizo), which inevitably end up in such dishes as the one that follows. Any good smoked sausage may be used.

Louisiana

DIRTY RICE

Louisiana is home to "popcorn" rice, an aromatic long-grain rice that travels by various names around the country. The soil has much to do with the taste of the rice, and in Louisiana it does indeed have the aroma of popcorn when cooked. This classic rice dish, so called because of the dark roux and sautéed ingredients, may be used as a stuffing for poultry.

3 tablespoons vegetable oil
2 tablespoons all-purpose (plain) flour
½ lb (250 g) chicken gizzards, ground (minced)
½ lb (250 g) lean boneless pork, ground (minced)
2 onions, chopped
1 celery stalk, chopped
1 small green bell pepper (capsicum), seeded and chopped
2 garlic cloves, minced
1 tablespoon unsalted butter
¼ lb (125 g) chicken livers
3 green (spring) onions, chopped
1½ cups (12 fl oz/375 ml) chicken stock (see glossary)
1 teaspoon salt
¼ teaspoon freshly ground pepper
¼ teaspoon hot red pepper (Tabasco) sauce
2 cups hot cooked long-grain rice (4 oz/125 g uncooked)
4 tablespoons chopped fresh parsley

❦ Whisk 2 tablespoons of the oil with the flour in a small heavy saucepan. Cook, stirring frequently, over low heat until the roux is the color of dark mahogany, about 45 minutes. Do not let burn.

❦ Meanwhile, heat the remaining 1 tablespoon oil in a large heavy pot or Dutch oven over medium-low heat. Add the gizzards and pork. Cook, stirring occasionally, until brown, about 10 minutes. Add the onions, celery, pepper and garlic, scraping the bottom and sides of the pot. Cook, stirring occasionally, 20 minutes longer.

❦ Melt the butter in a small skillet over medium heat. Add the chicken livers and green onions. Cook, stirring constantly, until

DIRTY RICE (top) AND RED BEANS AND SAUSAGES (bottom)

the livers are no longer pink inside, about 5 minutes. Remove from the heat; let cool slightly and finely chop.

❧ Add the liver mixture to the gizzard-pork mixture. Add the roux, stock, salt, pepper and hot pepper sauce. Heat to boiling, reduce the heat and simmer, covered, over low heat for 45 minutes. Uncover and cook 20 minutes longer. Stir in just enough rice to make a moist mixture. Toss in the parsley and use as a stuffing or serve as a side dish.

SERVES 6 TO 8

161

South Carolina

HOPPING JOHN

Hopping John is a staple of African Americans in Gullah country, the low-lying coastal areas and islands of South Carolina. It is considered good luck to eat the dish on New Year's Day. Black-eyed peas, sometimes called cow beans in the South, are indeed beans, not peas.

1 package (10 oz/315 g) frozen black-eyed peas (beans) or ½ cup (4 oz/125 g) dried black-eyed peas
2 bacon strips
1 small onion, chopped
1 garlic clove, minced
1 cup hot cooked rice (2 oz/60 g uncooked)
2 tablespoons red wine vinegar
salt and freshly ground pepper
2 tablespoons chopped fresh chives
chopped fresh parsley

Cook the frozen peas in boiling salted water until tender, about 20 minutes. (Or soak the dried peas in water to cover overnight; drain. Cover with cold water; heat to boiling, reduce the heat and simmer for 1 hour.) Drain, reserving ¼ cup (2 fl oz/60 ml) liquid.

Sauté the bacon in a large heavy skillet until crisp. Drain on paper towels, crumble and reserve.

Add the onion to the skillet and cook over medium-low heat for 1 minute. Add the garlic; cook 3 minutes longer. Stir in the peas and rice. Cook, stirring constantly, until warmed through. Add the vinegar and enough reserved liquid to moisten the mixture. Cook for 5 minutes. Add salt and pepper to taste. Sprinkle with the bacon, chives and parsley.

SERVES 4

HOPPING JOHN

JAMBALAYA

Louisiana

JAMBALAYA

Jambalaya is not only the most famous Creole-Cajun dish, it is one of the most famous of all American dishes. The word is believed to stem from the Spanish for ham, jamón. There are many variations, but ham is almost always present, as are shrimp. Chicken, oysters or crawfish are often added as well.

2 *chaurices* or *chorizos* (Spanish sausages) or spicy smoked
    sausage (½ lb/250 g or more)
2 tablespoons (1 oz/30 g) unsalted butter
1 large onion, chopped
2 garlic cloves, minced
1 large green bell pepper (capsicum), seeded and chopped
1 large red bell pepper (capsicum), seeded and chopped
2 large tomatoes, seeded and chopped
pinch of sugar
1 teaspoon chopped fresh thyme or ½ teaspoon dried thyme
1 teaspoon chili powder
¼ teaspoon cayenne pepper
1 cup (5 oz/155 g) long-grain rice

1 cup (6 oz/85 g) chopped smoked ham
1½ cups (12 fl oz/375 ml) chicken stock (approximately)
    (see glossary)
1 lb (500 g) small shrimp (green prawns), shelled and deveined
3 tablespoons chopped fresh parsley

❦ Sauté the sausages in a greased heavy pot or Dutch oven over medium heat until well browned. Transfer to a plate.

❦ Discard all the drippings from the pot and add the butter. Add the onions and cook over medium-low heat for 2 minutes, scraping bottom and sides of the pot. Add the garlic; cook 3 minutes longer. Add the bell peppers, tomatoes, sugar, thyme, chili powder and cayenne pepper. Reduce the heat to low and cook, covered, for 15 minutes.

❦ Cut the sausages into slices and add to the pot along with the rice and ham, stirring to coat with the vegetables. Add the stock. Heat to boiling, reduce the heat and simmer, covered, until the rice is tender, about 30 minutes. Stir in the shrimp and cook, covered, until the shrimp turn pink, about 5 minutes longer. (Uncover if the mixture is too wet and stir over low heat to evaporate.) Toss in the parsley before serving.

SERVES 4

BAKED HOMINY (top) AND
SOUTHWESTERN BEAN BAKE (bottom)

Arizona

SOUTHWESTERN BEAN BAKE

Beans are an integral part of everyday fare in the Southwest, and there are numerous ways to prepare them. The following recipe may be made with leftover frijoles if you are lucky enough to have some on hand.

½ lb (250 g) dried pinto (*borlotto* or kidney) beans
3 bacon strips, chopped
1 large onion, finely chopped
1 garlic clove, minced
1 small hot green (chili) pepper, seeded, deveined and minced
1 can (4 oz/125 g) mild green chilies, chopped
2 tablespoons mild ground chilies (or mild chili powder)
4 tablespoons chopped fresh cilantro (coriander/Chinese parsley)
1 teaspoon salt
¼ cup (2 fl oz/60 ml) beef stock (see glossary)
¼ lb (125 g) Monterey Jack (mild melting) cheese

❦ Soak the beans overnight in cold water to cover. Or place the beans in a large pot, cover with cold water and boil for 2 minutes. Remove from the heat and let stand, covered, for 1 hour. Drain.

❦ Wipe out the pot and return the beans to it. Cover with cold water. Heat to boiling, reduce the heat and simmer until the beans are tender, 1 to 1½ hours. Drain.

❦ Preheat the oven to 400°F (200°C). Sauté the bacon in a heavy skillet over medium heat until crisp. Add the onion; cook for 1 minute. Add the garlic and hot pepper; cook 4 minutes longer. Stir in the chilies, cilantro, salt and stock. Remove from the heat and stir in the cheese. Transfer the beans to a baking dish and bake for 20 minutes.

SERVES 6

New Mexico

BAKED HOMINY

The techniques for making hominy also developed in the Southwest, where hominy is eaten whole more than in grits form. While hominy can be purchased frozen in the Southwest, in most areas of the country it is available only in cans. It is sometimes possible to find dried hominy in health food stores, generally labeled posole, but it must be soaked overnight and boiled before use.

2 tablespoons vegetable oil
1 onion, chopped
1 garlic clove, minced
1 large tomato, peeled, seeded and chopped
pinch of sugar
½ teaspoon chopped fresh thyme or ¼ teaspoon dried thyme
1 teaspoon tomato paste
2 small hot green peppers, seeded, deveined and minced
1 can (4 oz/125 g) mild green chilies, drained and chopped
1 can (29 oz/900 g) whole hominy, rinsed and drained
½ teaspoon salt
¼ teaspoon freshly ground pepper
2 cups (8 oz/250 g) grated Monterey Jack (mild melting) cheese

❦ Preheat the oven to 375°F (190°C). Heat the oil in a large heavy skillet over medium-low heat. Add the onion; cook for 1 minute. Add the garlic; cook 4 minutes longer. Stir in the tomato, sugar, thyme and tomato paste. Cook for 5 minutes. Add the hot peppers and green chilies; cook 5 minutes longer. Stir in the hominy, salt and pepper. Remove from the heat.

❦ Stir 1½ cups (6 oz/185 g) cheese into the hominy mixture and transfer to a greased baking dish. Sprinkle the top with the remaining cheese. Place in the oven and immediately reduce the heat to 350°F (180°C). Bake for 45 minutes. Let stand for 5 minutes before serving.

SERVES 4 TO 6

West Virginia

COUSH-COUSH

Coush-coush (couche-couche, cous-cous) is the fancy name for cornmeal mush. A particular southern favorite, the dish is basically just cornbread broken into pieces and either cooked with milk or cream, or served plain in bowls of milk, clabbered (clotted) cream or buttermilk. The name may very well derive from couscous, as the dish does have a similar texture when properly cooked.

2 cups (11 oz/345 g) yellow cornmeal
1 tablespoon baking powder
1 teaspoon salt
2 teaspoons sugar
1 egg, lightly beaten
1½ cups (12 fl oz/375 ml) milk (or 1 cup milk and ½ cup buttermilk)
½ cup (4 oz/125 g) unsalted butter
2 tablespoons cream

❦ Combine the cornmeal with the baking powder, salt and sugar in a bowl. Stir in the egg and 1 cup (8 fl oz/250 ml) milk.

❦ Melt the butter in a large cast-iron skillet over medium-high heat. Spread the cornmeal mixture evenly over the bottom of the skillet. Cook until the top is puffed and the underside is dark brown, 5 to 8 minutes. Break the mixture into small pieces with a spatula and stir until all the browned pieces are well distributed. Reduce the heat to medium.

❦ Stir the remaining ½ cup (4 fl oz/125 ml) milk and the cream into the cornmeal mixture. Cook, stirring frequently, for 15 minutes. Mound the mixture slightly and serve from the skillet.

SERVES 4 TO 6

Tennessee

HUSH PUPPIES

Hush puppies inevitably accompany fried catfish in the South. According to the legend, at a great outdoor fish fry, some cook fried up a batch of sticky batter to keep the dogs from barking. As he tossed the treat to the hounds, he cooed, "Hush, puppies."

⅔ cup (4 oz/125 g) white cornmeal
⅓ cup (1½ oz/45 g) cake or soft wheat flour or ¼ cup
   (1 oz/30 g) all-purpose (plain) flour and 1 tablespoon
   cornstarch (cornflour)
1 teaspoon baking powder
½ teaspoon salt
2 tablespoons grated onion
1 egg, lightly beaten
⅓ cup (3 fl oz/80 ml) warm milk (approximately)
oil for frying

❦ Combine the cornmeal, flour, baking powder and salt in a large bowl. Stir in the onion, egg and enough milk to form a soft, sticky dough.
❦ Heat the oil in a deep heavy saucepan until hot (about 370°F/190°C). Scoop the batter up by the tablespoonful and carefully drop in the hot oil. Fry until golden brown on both sides, about 3 minutes. Drain on paper towels and serve immediately.

SERVES 4

Texas

REFRIED BEANS

Refried beans are not "twice fried," as the name implies; they are twice cooked. First they are boiled, then fried and mashed in a skillet until creamy in texture and slightly crispy around the edges. A standard menu item in every Tex-Mex restaurant, refried beans are served either as a side dish or as a first course topped with salsa and cheese and gobbled up with crunchy tostadas (corn chips).

2 to 3 tablespoons bacon drippings or lard
1 small onion, finely chopped
¼ teaspoon ground oregano
3 cups cooked pinto (*borlotto* or kidney) beans with their liquid
   (about ½ lb/250 g dried)
salt and freshly ground pepper

❦ Heat the bacon drippings or lard in a large heavy skillet over medium heat. Add the onion; cook for 4 minutes. Stir in the oregano. Stir in the beans and mash with a potato masher to the desired texture (but not completely smooth). Thin with the reserved cooking liquid. The beans should be creamy in texture. Add salt and pepper to taste.

SERVES 4   *Photograph pages 166 – 167*

HUSH PUPPIES (top) AND COUSH-COUSH (bottom)

Texas

FLOUR TORTILLAS

Although it is rather difficult to make corn tortillas, it is fairly simple to make flour tortillas, which are integral to southwestern cuisine. Moreover, the flour tortillas in supermarkets have a tendency to be on the thick, dry side, so it is better to make them at home.

4 cups (1 lb/500 g) all-purpose (plain) flour
½ cup (4 oz/125 g) solid cold vegetable shortening
   (vegetable lard)
2 teaspoons salt
1 cup (8 fl oz/250 ml) warm water (115°F /45°C)

❦ Sift the flour into a large bowl. Cut in the shortening until the texture of coarse crumbs.

❦ Dissolve the salt in the warm water. Add the flour mixture in a steady stream while working together with your fingers. (The warm water causes a rapid swelling of the flour particles, giving the tortillas a chewy texture.) Knead the ingredients in the bowl until a solid mass is formed. Transfer to a lightly floured board and knead for 3 minutes. Cover with a flour-rubbed dish towel and let stand for 1 hour. Knead the dough for 1 minute. Cover and let stand 10 minutes longer.

❦ Pinch off 1½-in (4-cm) pieces from the dough and roll into 7-in (18-cm) circles. Roll from the center outward, being careful not to taper the edges by rolling over them. Stack the tortillas on top of each other.

❦ Heat a cast-iron skillet until very hot. Cook the tortillas, one at a time, for 20 seconds on the first side, 10 seconds on the second. The tortillas should be white, with light brown spots. Wipe out the skillet occasionally with paper towels. As the tortillas are cooked, stack on a plate and cover with a dish towel. Reheat, covered loosely with foil, in a low oven before serving.

MAKES 20 TORTILLAS

New Mexico

FRIJOLES

Frijoles are just boiled beans that are served in their cooking liquid, which is slightly thickened by mashing some of the cooked beans and stirring them back into the pot. A pot of beans is often made only to be used for refried beans later. The following recipe will serve four for dinner, with enough beans for four refried portions the following day.

1 lb (500 g) dried pinto (*borlotto* or kidney) beans, picked over
⅓ cup (2 oz/60 g) diced salt pork or bacon
1 small onion, chopped
2 garlic cloves, minced
½ teaspoon ground cumin
salt and freshly ground pepper

❦ Soak the beans overnight in cold water to cover. Or place the beans in a large pot, cover with cold water and boil for 2 minutes. Remove from the heat and let stand, covered, for 1 hour. Drain.

❦ Place the beans in a large heavy pot or Dutch oven. Add the salt pork, onion, garlic and cumin. Add water to cover by 2 in (5 cm). Heat to boiling, reduce the heat and simmer, covered, stirring occasionally, for about 3 hours or until very tender. Toward the end of the cooking time, keep the water level with the top of the beans.

❦ To serve the beans as frijoles, remove 1 cup (8 fl oz/250 ml) liquid and beans. Mash and stir back into the remaining beans and liquid. Add salt and pepper to taste. Or reserve half the beans and half the liquid for refried beans the next day.

SERVES 8

FLOUR TORTILLAS (top), REFRIED BEANS (left, recipe page 165) AND FRIJOLES (right)

THE MOUNTAIN STATES

THE MOUNTAIN STATES

In the western mountains, a land teeming with wildlife, the Indians quite naturally lived on game. Deer, elk, moose, bears, bighorn sheep, beavers and other small animals were easy to hunt. Large, sparkling lakes and icy cold rivers provided some of the best fishing in the country. The Indians who lived on the eastern slope of the Rocky Mountains hunted buffalo as well. The Cheyennes of the Algonquian family roamed the eastern territories of Colorado; the Sioux and the Crows of the Siouan family inhabited eastern Wyoming and Montana. The Blackfeet, also Algonquians, controlled western Montana. The tribes between the Rockies and the Sierra Nevada were nomads of the Uto-Aztecan family. They included the Shoshones, Snakes, Kiowas and Utes. The Nez Percé of Washington could also be found in Idaho. This region was the last stronghold of the Indians. Much of the land was owned by the tribes under treaty with the U.S. government, a fact simply ignored by trappers and gold diggers. The Indians' frustrations and outrage eventually led to Custer's undoing in Montana.

The first explorers of the mountainous West were the Spanish, whose presence in the southern portions of the region is still felt today. Then came the fur trappers, the famous mountain men of the West. They lived much the same as the Indians, and many even lived among the Indians and took Indian wives. It was these men who were destined to lead the wagon trains across the plains along the Oregon Trail.

The eastern section of the mountain states includes the western edge of the Great Plains. Huge numbers of buffalo grazed right up to the foothills of the mountains. Meriwether Lewis wrote of the "tremendous roaring" of buffalo bulls near Great Falls, Montana. Trappers stocked up on buffalo meat, mostly in the form of jerky, pemmican and sausage, before heading into the

ITS STREETS LINED WITH LOVELY VICTORIAN-STYLE BUILDINGS, TELLURIDE, COLORADO, IS A FORMER MINING TOWN THAT HAS BECOME A POPULAR ROCKY MOUNTAIN SKI RESORT.

PREVIOUS PAGES: SUNRISE OVER THE DELICATE PINK, RED AND WHITE LIMESTONE TOWERS AND NARROW ROCK-LINED ALLEYWAYS OF BRYCE CANYON IN SOUTHERN UTAH.
PHOTO: JAMES H. CARMICHAEL, JR/THE IMAGE BANK

171

mountains, and as settlements sprang up along the Rockies, buffalo became an important source of meat.

The Oregon Trail brought many settlers through Wyoming's South Pass and into Nevada and Idaho, but few stayed to settle the harsh land. Surprisingly, the Indians did not give the wagon trains much trouble, other than annoying them with incessant begging and minor pilfering. Possibly the reason was that the trains were well organized and traveled in great numbers. Those left behind, however, often met their doom, and farther north it was a different story.

The mountain region was rich in furs and beaver. Before the Northwest was ceded to the United States, English trappers based in Canada fought for control of the area with Americans who were moving in from the south. The Blackfeet, feeling the pinch, eventually fought them both. Once the region was under U.S. control, government-backed mountain recruits moved in on the Indians once and for all. Indian tribes, though not happy about the situation, agreed to stay on their own vast lands if the white man was kept off. Unfortunately, cries of gold rang out in Colorado and Nevada in 1859 and once again the rush was on, quickly followed by another rush when silver was discovered too. The miners also pushed farther and farther into Idaho, Wyoming and Montana, not only leaving settlements behind but leaving the Indians with less and less land as well. The mountain region was the scene of Indian battles well into the 1880s, but even after the Indians were beaten, peace in the area was not yet at hand.

With the Indians under control, the vast open public spaces of the mountains were deemed suitable for grazing cattle. Great herds were brought up from Texas, but then farmers moved in and sheepherders followed. Barbed-wire fences went up, keeping grazing cattle from water sources, and barbed-wire fences came down—with force. Cattle ranchers hated sheepherders, charging that the sheep were destroying grazing lands. Things got bloody. On top of this, beet farmers in eastern Colorado, as well as farmers from all over the West, began diverting huge amounts of water from the rivers for irrigation purposes. When the Arkansas River in wheat-growing Kansas began to shrink, things started getting out of hand once more. The government did not help matters any when, in a move to lure settlers to the West, it started giving away land with more water rights than there was water. For instance, in 1898 there were claims issued for 1,590,450 second-feet of the Boise River in Idaho. The river flowed at only 8,750 second-feet. Farmers took to guarding their floodgates with shotguns. This was also the time when rustlers and outlaws roamed the region. Life was indeed a bit wild in the Wild West.

The mountain territories had been divided into states by 1896 and admitted to the Union. The last was Utah, admitted in that year. Nevada had been admitted in 1864 during the Civil War, followed by Colorado in 1876, Montana in 1889 and Wyoming in 1890. Some of the region—Montana, Wyoming and parts of eastern Colorado—had come under U.S. control with the Louisiana Purchase. Most of Colorado and Utah and Nevada was ceded by Mexico in 1848.

The West, with its rocky peaks and dry plains, may not seem a likely place for agricultural pursuits, but irrigation has made the area blossom. Colorado, in addition to beef and lamb, produces sugar beets, potatoes, onions, barley and an impressive amount of spring wheat, cantaloupes and peaches. Montana, also a major producer of beef and lamb, is the nation's third largest wheat-

MONTANA IS PART OF THE ROCKY MOUNTAIN REGION THAT HAS A LANDSCAPE AND CLIMATE SIMILAR TO THE GREAT PLAINS. THIS VAST, SPARSELY POPULATED STATE IS DESERVEDLY KNOWN AS "BIG SKY COUNTRY."

MICHAEL MELFORD/THE IMAGE BANK

producing state, after North Dakota and Kansas. Montana, too, grows sugar beets, barley, oats and potatoes. Wyoming, the unlikely home of the suffragette movement, remains a state best known for game hunting. Beef and lamb are its biggest agricultural pursuits. Utah has a long history of inadequate water resources but manages to produce beef, dairy products, turkeys, wheat and barley. Nevada has a limited amount of agriculture, with lamb the most important product. Idaho has beef and lamb as well, but the potato, of course, is its main agricultural crop. A lesser-known crop of Idaho is hops, used in making beer.

Due to a Spanish influence, the cuisine of the southern regions of Colorado, Utah and Nevada has much in common with the cooking of the Southwest. In the north and high mountains, game is still frequently eaten. Much of the cookery in the area, however, is similar to that of the Midwest and Great Plains. These states are, after all, extensions of the move westward. Beef has always been the mainstay of western diets. There are those who say that the beef raised in the mountain states is the best in the world. Some of the finest lamb in the world is also raised there, but it is, in the main, unappreciated in this region, except in Idaho and Nevada, where the Basques have settled.

The Basques originally came from the area that straddles the present Spanish-French border where the Bay of Biscay meets the western part of the Pyrenees. The Basque culture is thought to go back seventy thousand years. Basques were among the leading groups of most of the Spanish expeditions to the New World. When the Spanish empire began to collapse, the Basques stayed home. In the 1850s, spurred by economic and political instability, Basque migration, largely of peasant stock, resumed. Most went to Argentina, where they brought their sheepherding skills. When Argentina

NEAR THE TOWN OF COLORADO SPRINGS, PIKE'S PEAK RISES MORE THAN 14,000 FEET FROM THE FOOTHILLS AND PRAIRIES BELOW, ITS RED GRANITE SUMMIT SOMETIMES COVERED BY CLOUDS.

SOUTHERN UTAH IS HOME TO LAKES AND PARKLANDS AS WELL AS DESERTS. THE MOUNTAINS IN DIXIE NATIONAL FOREST ARE DOTTED WITH BEAUTIFUL ASPENS WHOSE FINGERLIKE WHITE TRUNKS DISAPPEAR INTO A GOLDEN PUFF OF LEAVES.

closed its doors to them, they headed to the western United States, where they were welcomed with open arms by the sheep granges, and with rifles by cattle ranchers. Basques can be found today throughout the mountain states and are still being recruited abroad by western range associations. Even though they are spread far and wide over the area, a strong social culture exists, which has helped them keep their identity in modern America.

One major problem cooks face in the West is the elevation. The dry, thinner air (lower air pressure, actually) brings about evaporation more quickly than a denser, more humid air mass. This phenomenon is what causes a fresh slice of unwrapped bread to turn stale quickly (in contrast to lower elevations where bread will absorb moisture). Because of this rapid evaporation, water will boil at a lower temperature. Any cook who lives at a high elevation knows that baking becomes very tricky at elevations above 3,500 feet. Cakes rise higher, for one thing, so leavening must be reduced. The normal reduction, according to the Department of Agriculture, is by one-third at 3,500 feet, one-half at 5,000 feet and two-thirds above 5,000 feet. Reducing the amount of sugar in a recipe allows more room for liquid, which helps with the evaporation problem. Eggs should be beaten less than at lower altitudes. Cakes at high altitudes are generally baked twenty-five degrees higher to set the sides quickly.

The mountain states have always attracted a variety of settlers, and modern-day "settlers" are still coming, drawn by the beauty of the mountains and a casual way of life. One can still get steak and eggs for breakfast with a side of hash browns made from Idaho potatoes, or a Denver omelette with onions and peppers tucked between two slices of toast. Game is a specialty of many restaurants, and there is no better place to eat trout than in the mountain states. There is also no better eating than slicing into a roast leg of lamb that has been doused with buttermilk, or a two-inch-thick steak grilled over an open fire.

SALADS AND VEGETABLES

CATHERINE KARNOW

PRESIDENT THOMAS JEFFERSON HELPED POPULARIZE MANY OF THE TYPES OF
VEGETABLES PERCHED ON THIS NEW ENGLAND FARMER'S TRANSPORTABLE STALL.

SALADS AND VEGETABLES

When the Spaniards came to the Americas looking for gold and other riches, little did they realize that the plants they took back to the Old World would revolutionize the eating habits of the masses. But not every vegetable the conquistadors found to the south, like the potato and tomato, had yet found its way to North America. Corn, first cultivated by the Maya, Aztec and Inca Indians about eight thousand years ago, had spread throughout the continents, as had squash and the common bean. Lima beans had reached the Caribbean and may have been in Florida, although no one is certain. The same holds true for the sweet potato. It was cultivated by the early Virginia colonists, but there is some question about whether it was already present. Likewise the peanut, although there is reason to believe that the southern Indian tribes were harvesting peanuts before the English arrived. Peppers, another major find in the New World, may have found their way to the Southwest before the Spaniards arrived, but again no one is sure. All these vegetables originated in Central or South America. Peculiarly original to North America are Jerusalem artichokes (sunchokes), the dandelion and, of course, wild rice. Fiddlehead ferns, mushrooms and many wild roots and greens also flourished here, but they could be found elsewhere in the Americas, as well as the world.

Both the white potato and the tomato were introduced into North America via Europe. And both, just as in Europe, took a long time to be accepted. Okra, so important in the South today, originally came from

Africa. Some historians believe that the vegetable was first taken from Africa to Spain by the invading Moors of the eighth century and was introduced to the West Indies shortly after Columbus made his discovery. Since most of the slave trade came through the West Indies, the Africans must have been astounded, if not the tiniest bit grateful, to recognize a staple indigenous to their homeland. From the West Indies okra made its way to the southern United States.

Each group of settlers brought with them the familiar vegetable seeds of home. Root vegetables were quickly cultivated in those days before canning and freezing, when preserving was a matter of real concern, if not life and death. Almost all early American homes were built with root cellars, where hardy vegetables could be stored for winter's use. Like the Indians, the settlers dried vegetables, and they pickled them in barrels as well.

One person who had a lasting effect on American cuisine and imported seeds of all kinds from Europe was Thomas Jefferson, the third president. Jefferson, often called the first American gourmet, was fascinated with agricultural pursuits. He was one of the first planters here to grow the white (Irish) potato and the tomato. He also helped to popularize asparagus, broccoli, Brussels sprouts, cauliflower, cucumbers and eggplant (aubergine), among others.

As was the tradition of the times, vegetables were cooked to death. Not until the first half of this century was it discovered that the vitamins in vegetables were destroyed during long periods of cooking. Nutritionists

A FAMILY OF SCARECROWS STANDS GUARD OVER
A CAREFULLY TENDED VEGETABLE GARDEN.

THE HAYMARKET IN BOSTON, MASSACHUSETTS, IS AN OPEN-AIR MARKET THAT
ATTRACTS BOTH BUDGET-CONSCIOUS SHOPPERS AND SIGHTSEERS TO ITS
COLORFUL STALLS ON WEEKENDS.

began recommending that vegetables be cooked only until crisp-tender. It took a while for this information to sink in, but when it did, Americans began to discover the joy of vegetables. Today gourmet grocers are doing a booming business, and, more important, large cities have opened their parks and hearts to local farmers. "Green markets" set up in city centers not only guarantee urban dwellers a good supply of fresh farm produce but also give small farmers new economic hope.

It was Columbus, on his second trip, who brought the first lettuce seeds to this part of the world. Later on, Spanish missionaries would plant it in California. Green salad has never played a major role in American dinners. When it is served, it is generally plopped down before the main course and, as likely as not, will have tomatoes, onions and "what not" in it as well. This custom may have been borrowed from the Italian notion for *antipasto* or simply started by restaurant chefs trying to keep their patrons occupied until the meal was served. True European-style green salads, made of greens only and served with or after the main course, have yet to become a general trend. This is not to say that top-rate restaurants or Americans with sophisticated palates do not appreciate the integrity of these salads. It is simply that "salad," in this country, has always meant chicken, potato, cabbage and, more recently, main-course salads such as Caesar or chef's salad. Some prime examples of recipes from America's salad and vegetable larder follow.

177

Wisconsin

WILTED GREEN SALAD

Wilted salads, doused with warm bacon dressings, were once common in German American homes. Spinach may be substituted for the lettuce.

2 heads of Boston lettuce or 1 head each of Boston and
    Romaine (Cos)
4 eggs
¼ cup (2 fl oz/60 ml) water
¼ cup (2 fl oz/60 ml) red wine vinegar
salt and freshly ground pepper
¼ cup (2 oz/60 g) bacon drippings
dash of lemon juice

❦ Separate the lettuce leaves. Wash well and and pat dry. Tear the leaves into pieces and place in a large bowl.

❦ Beat the eggs in a bowl until frothy. Beat in the water, vinegar and salt and pepper to taste.

❦ Heat the bacon drippings in a small saucepan over low heat until hot. Remove from the heat and slowly whisk in the egg mixture. Return to low heat and cook, stirring constantly, until the sauce thickens, 1 or 2 minutes. Pour over the lettuce, sprinkle with lemon juice, toss well and serve immediately.

SERVES 4 TO 6

WILTED GREEN SALAD

New York

CORN SALAD

The next recipe is from Long Island's South Fork, where the corn is sweet and the tomatoes sweeter. It is particularly good with grilled foods.

6 large ears (cobs) of corn
1 large green bell pepper (capsicum), seeded and chopped
1 celery stalk, chopped
6 green (spring) onions, chopped
1 large ripe tomato, chopped
½ cup (4 fl oz/125 ml) mayonnaise
¼ cup (2 fl oz/60 ml) sour cream
¼ cup (2 fl oz/60 ml) beef stock
2 tablespoons red wine vinegar
salt and freshly ground pepper
chopped fresh parsley (optional)

❦ Cook the corn in boiling salted water for 3 minutes. Rinse under cold running water and drain. Cut the kernels from the cobs and place in a bowl. Add the bell pepper, celery, green onions and tomato. Toss to mix.

❦ Whisk the mayonnaise with the sour cream in a bowl until smooth. Whisk in the beef stock and vinegar. Pour over the corn mixture. Toss well and add salt and pepper to taste. Sprinkle with parsley. Serve well chilled.

SERVES 6

CORN SALAD

MIDWESTERN COLE SLAW (top) AND
OLD-FASHIONED COLE SLAW (bottom)

Connecticut

OLD-FASHIONED COLE SLAW

The Dutch are usually credited with the invention of cole slaw, but both the Dutch and the Germans were eating cabbage salads long before settling here. The Dutch called their salad koolsla *(cabbage salad), but the word* cole *is actually Old English for the German* kohl, *which means "cabbage." A mayonnaise-based dressing is the standard upholstery for this salad.*

1½ lb (750 g) green cabbage, shredded
1 large carrot, grated
½ green bell pepper (capsicum), seeded and finely chopped
1 small onion, finely chopped
1 cup (8 fl oz/250 ml) mayonnaise
¼ cup (2 fl oz/60 ml) sour cream
2½ teaspoons Dijon mustard
⅛ teaspoon dried red pepper (chili) flakes, crushed
3 to 4 tablespoons strong beef stock (see glossary)
salt and freshly ground pepper
3 bacon strips, fried crisp and crumbled
chopped fresh parsley

❧ Combine the cabbage with the carrot, bell pepper and onion in a large bowl.

❧ Whisk the mayonnaise with the sour cream in a bowl. Whisk in the mustard and red pepper flakes. Thin with beef stock. Pour over the cabbage mixture and toss well. Add salt and pepper to taste. Sprinkle with the bacon and parsley and serve at room temperature.

SERVES 6 TO 8

California

WARM GOAT CHEESE AND SPINACH SALAD

A fairly recent California inspiration, warm goat cheese salads have taken the country by storm. This rendering is inspired by Wolfgang Puck of Spago in Los Angeles. Romaine (Cos) lettuce may be substituted for the spinach.

½ lb (250 g) fresh goat cheese (*chèvre*)
¾ cup (6 fl oz/180 ml) olive oil
1 teaspoon chopped fresh thyme
1 lb (500 g) fresh (English) spinach, washed and stems removed
1 teaspoon Dijon mustard
1 teaspoon chopped fresh tarragon
1½ tablespoons red wine vinegar
1 egg yolk
salt and freshly ground pepper
3 bacon strips, fried crisp and crumbled

❧ Cut the goat cheese into 8 pieces and place in a shallow bowl. Drizzle on ¼ cup (2 fl oz/60 ml) of the oil and sprinkle with the thyme. Refrigerate, covered, overnight.

❧ Pat the spinach dry and tear the large leaves into pieces. Place in a large bowl.

❧ Whisk the mustard with the tarragon, vinegar and egg yolk in a bowl until smooth. Slowly whisk in the remaining ½ cup (4 fl oz/125 ml) oil. Add salt and pepper to taste. Pour over the spinach and toss well.

❧ Heat 2 tablespoons of the oil from the cheese in a heavy skillet over medium heat. Sauté the cheese pieces for 30 seconds on each side. Place over the spinach leaves and sprinkle with the bacon. Toss at the table.

Oklahoma

MIDWESTERN COLE SLAW

Lettice Bryan, a pioneer in American cooking, published a recipe for cole slaw sluiced with cider vinegar in 1839. It became a hit in both the Midwest and the South, where it is served to this day.

1 lb (500 g) green or red cabbage, shredded and chopped
½ green bell pepper (capsicum), finely chopped
3 tablespoons finely chopped onion
1 cup (8 fl oz/60 ml) cider vinegar
⅔ cup (5 oz/155 g) sugar
½ teaspoon celery seed
½ teaspoon dry mustard
¼ cup (2 fl oz/60 ml) water
chopped fresh parsley (optional)

❧ Combine the cabbage with the bell pepper and onion in a large bowl.

❧ Combine the vinegar with the sugar, celery seed and mustard in a saucepan. Heat, stirring frequently, to boiling. Reduce the heat and simmer until thick, about 15 minutes. Remove from the heat and whisk in the water. Immediately pour over the cabbage mixture and toss well. Refrigerate, covered, for 6 to 8 hours.

❧ Drain some of the liquid from the slaw before serving (it will still be quite wet). Sprinkle with parsley.

SERVES 4 TO 6

SERVES 4   *Photograph pages 174 – 175*

North Carolina

SHRIMP AND RICE SALAD

It was not until 1917 that frozen shrimp began making their way inland. Until that time only people who lived near the coast could enjoy the delicacy that has become America's most eaten shellfish. Homemakers in the Carolinas, where shrimp and rice have always been readily available, put the two together in both hot and cold dishes.

2 cups cooked rice (5 oz/155 g uncooked)
1 shallot (small onion), minced
2 small cucumbers, peeled, seeded and finely chopped
½ lb (8 oz/250 g) cooked shrimp (prawns), shelled, deveined
    and halved
1 teaspoon very fine julienne strips of lemon peel
1 small garlic clove, minced
½ teaspoon salt
1 teaspoon Dijon mustard
juice of 1 lemon
2 teaspoons red wine vinegar
⅓ cup (3 fl oz/80 ml) olive oil
freshly ground pepper
4 tablespoons chopped fresh parsley

❧ Combine the rice, shallot, cucumbers, shrimp and lemon peel in a bowl. Toss until well mixed.
❧ Mash the garlic with the salt in a small bowl. Whisk in the mustard, lemon juice, vinegar and oil. Pour over the salad and toss gently to mix. Add more oil if needed. Add pepper to taste. Toss in the parsley and serve slightly chilled.

SERVES 4   *Photograph pages 174 – 175*

New York

WALDORF SALAD

The original salad, created by Oscar Tschirky of the Waldorf-Astoria Hotel at the end of the nineteenth century, used only apples, celery and mayonnaise. The salad quickly became a standard item at hotels all over America, and by 1928 walnuts had been added. If you use homemade mayonnaise, there is no need to thin it with milk.

3 firm red apples
1 tablespoon lemon juice
2 celery stalks, sliced
½ cup (2 oz/60 g) coarsely chopped walnuts
½ cup (4 fl oz/125 ml) mayonnaise
2 to 3 tablespoons milk

❧ Core the apples and cut into slices or cubes. Place in a bowl and sprinkle with lemon juice. Toss to mix. Add the celery and walnuts. Toss once more.
❧ Whisk the mayonnaise with enough milk to thin and pour over the salad. Toss well and serve on lettuce leaves.

SERVES 4

WALDORF SALAD (UNTOSSED)

New Jersey

Asparagus in Ambush

Asparagus in Ambush, adapted from an old English recipe, was the rage at upper-crust tables in the eighteenth and nineteenth centuries. The dish consists of asparagus in egg sauce hidden inside toasted hollow dinner rolls. It is still an entertaining way to serve asparagus as a first course.

1 lb (500 g) asparagus
6 firm dinner rolls
2 tablespoons (1 oz/30 g) unsalted butter
2 tablespoons all-purpose (plain) flour
1½ cups (12 fl oz/375 ml) milk
2 egg yolks
1 teaspoon lemon juice
salt and freshly ground pepper

❦ Preheat the oven to 250°F (120°C). Break the tough ends off the asparagus and peel the stems. Cut into 1-in (2.5-cm) pieces. Cook in boiling salted water until crisp-tender, 3 to 5 minutes. Rinse under cold running water and drain.

❦ Trim a thin slice off the top of each roll. Scoop out the inside, leaving a shell ¼ in (5 mm) thick. Bake the rolls and their covers until crisp, about 15 minutes.

❦ Meanwhile, melt the butter in a saucepan over medium-low heat. Whisk in the flour. Cook, stirring constantly, for 2 minutes. Whisk in the milk. Heat, stirring constantly, to boiling. Reduce the heat and simmer, uncovered, until slightly thickened, about 4 minutes. Remove from the heat.

❦ Beat the egg yolks in a bowl and whisk in ¼ cup (2 fl oz/60 ml) of the hot sauce. Stir this mixture back into the sauce. Return to low heat and cook 2 minutes longer. Do not let boil. Whisk in the lemon juice and add salt and pepper to taste. Stir in the asparagus and heat until warmed through. Spoon into the hot roll shells, place the covers on top and serve immediately.

SERVES 6

Missouri

Chow-Chow

Chow-chow is a vegetable relish that is "put up" at harvest time when an excess of vegetables is on hand. The word is thought to stem from the Chinese who came over to work on the railroads and may be a derivation of the word choy, *which is Cantonese for "vegetables."*

1 large head of green cabbage, chopped (about 4 cups)
1 lb (500 g) chopped green tomatoes
1 lb (500 g) chopped ripe tomatoes
1½ to 2 cups (3½ oz/100 g) cauliflower florets
1 large green bell pepper (capsicum), seeded and chopped
2 or 3 teaspoons crushed dried red pepper (chili) flakes
1 cup (6 oz/185 g) packed dark brown sugar
2 onions, chopped (about 1 cup)
1 garlic clove, minced
½ cup (2 oz/60 g) corn kernels
1½ teaspoons ground ginger
¾ teaspoon ground cinnamon
¾ teaspoon ground cloves
1 tablespoon ground turmeric
¾ teaspoon curry powder
¾ teaspoon celery seed
1½ teaspoons coarse salt
1 tablespoon cornstarch (cornflour)
1 tablespoon dry mustard
1 cup (8 fl oz/250 ml) cider vinegar

❦ Combine all the ingredients from the cabbage through the salt in a large heavy pot or Dutch oven.

❦ Mix the cornstarch with the mustard and vinegar in a bowl until smooth. Add to vegetable mixture. Heat to boiling, reduce the heat and simmer, uncovered, stirring frequently, for 1 hour. Pour into sterilized jars and seal. Store in a cool place.

MAKES 4 PT (2 L)

Georgia

PAN-FRIED SUMMER SQUASH

This recipe for squash is typical of old southern recipes in that the squash cooks for a long time. It is important to keep the heat low so that the slices of squash retain their shape during cooking.

1½ lb (750 g) yellow summer squash (vegetable marrow),
    sliced
1 onion, thinly sliced
½ teaspoon salt
¼ teaspoon freshly ground pepper
⅛ teaspoon ground mace
1 cup (8 fl oz/250 ml) hot chicken stock (see glossary)
6 tablespoons (3 oz/90 g) bacon drippings

❧ Combine the squash with the onion in a large skillet and sprinkle with the salt, pepper and mace. Add the hot chicken stock and heat quickly to boiling. Boil, uncovered, stirring frequently, until all the liquid has evaporated, about 10 minutes.

❧ Stir the bacon drippings into the squash. Cook, uncovered, stirring occasionally, over low heat for 30 minutes.

SERVES 4 TO 6

Alabama

FRIED OKRA

Not just for gumbos, okra can be served in a variety of ways. It is wonderful barely blanched and served with Hollandaise sauce, served raw in a salad with sliced tomatoes, or fried, a traditional method in the South.

⅓ cup (1½ oz/50 g) all-purpose (plain) flour
⅓ cup (2 oz/60 g) white cornmeal
1 teaspoon salt
1½ lb (750 g) okra, cut into ¼-in (5-mm) slices
oil for frying

❧ Combine the flour, cornmeal and salt in a large shallow bowl. Add the okra and toss until well coated.

❧ Heat 1 in (2.5 cm) of oil in a large skillet until hot but not smoking. Fry the okra in batches until golden and crisp. Drain lightly on paper towels.

SERVES 4

Massachusetts

SUCCOTASH

Another native American original is the combination of corn and beans that the Narraganset Indians called misickquatash. *The Indians made it with corn and kidney beans cooked in bear fat. Lima beans are generally used today and cooked in butter or bacon drippings.*

1 tablespoon unsalted butter, vegetable oil
    or bacon drippings
1½ cups cooked corn kernels (½ lb/250 g uncooked)
1½ cups cooked lima (or butter) beans (½ lb/250 g uncooked)
¼ cup (2 fl oz/60 ml) cream
salt and freshly ground pepper

❧ Melt the butter in a large skillet over medium-low heat. Add the corn, lima beans and cream. Cook, stirring constantly, until warmed through; do not let boil. Add salt and pepper to taste.

SERVES 4

CORN ON THE COB

Iowa

CORN ON THE COB

Iowa is famous for corn, but this is one American original that belongs to every corner of the country. There are several ways to cook corn. Many corn lovers argue that cooking corn in boiling water, as the Indians did, is still the best way. Serve at least two ears (cobs) per person, but have extra in the pot, just in case.

❧ Method 1: Husk and desilk the ears and place in boiling water to which you have added 1 tablespoon sugar. When the water returns to the boil, cover and boil for 1 minute. Remove from the heat. The corn can rest up to 5 minutes before serving.

❧ Method 2: Husk and desilk the ears and rub each lightly with softened butter. Sprinkle with water and wrap tightly in aluminum foil. Bake in a 350°F (180°C) oven for 20 minutes.

❧ Method 3: Peel the husks back and desilk the ears. Rub the ears with butter and push the husks back together. Tie with string and soak in water for 30 minutes. Cook, turning once, on an outdoor grill for 15 minutes.

CHICKEN SALAD

Delaware

CHICKEN SALAD

There are many variations of chicken salad, but most are made with poached or leftover roast chicken, celery and mayonnaise. White grapes often stand in for the celery on the West Coast.

3 to 3½ cups (1 lb/500 g) diced cooked chicken
3 celery stalks, finely chopped
2 small shallots (small onions), minced
¼ cup (1 oz/30 g) toasted slivered almonds
1 tablespoon grated lemon peel
1 cup (8 fl oz/250 ml) mayonnaise
3 tablespoons light (single) cream or half & half
   (half cream and half milk)
2 teaspoons Dijon mustard
salt and freshly ground pepper
pimiento (canned sweet pepper) strips
chopped fresh parsley
lettuce leaves

❦ Combine the chicken, celery, shallots, almonds and lemon peel in a large bowl. Toss gently to mix.

❦ Whisk the mayonnaise with the light cream in a bowl. Beat in the mustard. Pour over the chicken mixture and toss gently to mix. Add salt and pepper to taste. Garnish with pimiento strips and chopped parsley. Serve on lettuce leaves.

SERVES 4

Arizona

GRAPEFRUIT SALAD

Fruit salads are peculiarly American, although they seem to be catching on around the globe. Many southwesterners enjoy growing citrus trees in their yards and have invented recipes to use the fruit.

2 large grapefruit
1 red onion, thinly sliced and separated into rings
peel of 1 orange, cut in fine julienne strips
1 garlic clove, minced
½ teaspoon coarse salt
1 teaspoon Dijon mustard
juice of 1 lemon
½ cup (4 fl oz/125 ml) olive oil
juice of 1 orange or about ¼ cup (2 fl oz/60 ml)
freshly ground pepper
leaves from 1 bunch of watercress (about ½ cup)

❦ Peel the grapefruit and remove all the white pith. Cut each grapefruit crosswise into slices ¼ in (5 mm) thick, or divide into segments. Cut each segment apart and place in a serving bowl. (There should be about 3 cups.) Place the onions over the top and sprinkle with the orange peel.

❦ Mash the garlic with the salt in a bowl. Slowly whisk in the mustard, lemon juice, olive oil and orange juice. Pour over the salad and sprinkle with pepper. Chill thoroughly and garnish with watercress leaves before serving.

SERVES 6

SARATOGA CHIPS (top) AND
COUNTRY-STYLE GREEN BEANS (bottom)

SUE FISHER KING

Iowa

COUNTRY-STYLE GREEN BEANS

Some say it was the Spanish, others say the French, who first appreciated the American bean in its fresh, young stage. No matter, the next recipe is pure Heartland, USA.

1 lb (500 g) green beans, trimmed and cut French-style
   (in long thin strips)
2 tablespoons (1 oz/30 g) unsalted butter
¼ cup (1½ oz/45 g) diced smoked ham
1 small onion, chopped
½ teaspoon beef bouillon powder (or ¼ stock cube)
1 small tomato, peeled, seeded and chopped
salt and freshly ground pepper
2 tablespoons chopped parsley (optional)

❧ Cook the beans in boiling salted water until almost tender, about 3 minutes. Rinse under cold running water and drain.

❧ Melt the butter in a large saucepan over medium-low heat. Add the ham and onion and sprinkle with the bouillon powder. Cook, stirring occasionally, for 5 minutes. Toss in the beans and tomato. Cook, tossing constantly, until warmed through, about 3 minutes. Add salt and pepper to taste. Sprinkle with parsley.

SERVES 4

New York

SARATOGA CHIPS

The invention of potato chips is attributed to George Crum, chef at the Moon's Lake House in Saratoga, New York, in 1853 who, in a rage over a dissatisfied customer's demand for a thinner chip, sliced his potatoes paper thin, fried them to a crisp, and startled everyone.

2 baking potatoes
oil for frying
salt

❧ Peel the potatoes and slice paper thin with a vegetable slicer. Soak in cold water for 2 hours.

❧ Heat oil in a deep fryer until hot (380°–390°F/195°C). Drain the potatoes and pat dry. Fry until crisp. Drain on paper towels. Sprinkle with salt.

SERVES 3 OR 4

CAESAR SALAD

California

CAESAR SALAD

Caesar salad was first concocted by an Italian immigrant named Caesar Cardini at his restaurant, Caesar's Place, in Tijuana, Mexico. A hit with the Hollywood crowd who crossed the border for good times, the salad soon appeared on the menu at Chasen's in Los Angeles and has since become an American classic.

3 garlic cloves
⅓ cup (3 fl oz/80 ml) plus ¼ cup (2 fl oz/60 ml) olive oil
    (approximately)
2 cups ½-in (1-cm) stale bread cubes (about 2 slices)
2 heads of Romaine (Cos) lettuce
½ teaspoon salt
juice of 1 lemon
½ teaspoon Worcestershire sauce
2 eggs, boiled for 1 minute
⅓ cup (1 ½ oz/50 g) freshly grated Parmesan cheese
6 anchovy fillets, cut into pieces

❦ Preheat the oven to 350°F (180°C). Mash 1 garlic clove with ⅓ cup oil. Lightly brush the bread cubes with this mixture (adding more oil if necessary) and bake, turning occasionally, until browned on all sides, about 15 minutes. Set aside.

❦ Separate the lettuce leaves, wash well and pat dry. Tear into pieces and place in a bowl.

❦ Mash the remaining 2 garlic cloves with the salt in a small bowl. Stir in the remaining ¼ cup oil, the lemon juice and Worcestershire sauce. Pour over the lettuce leaves. Scoop out the eggs from the shell and add to the salad. Sprinkle with the cheese and toss gently to mix. Place the anchovies and croutons on top and serve on chilled plates.

SERVES 4

GRILLED TUNA SALAD

California

GRILLED TUNA SALAD

Although tuna is found on both coasts, the Pacific yields the majority of the world's catch. While most Americans are still eating tuna from a can, fresh tuna is catching on, thanks to inventive chefs and food writers — and, most importantly, to a new way of looking at the backyard grill as useful for something other than hot dogs and hamburgers. Grilled tuna that has been marinated in lemon juice and garlic replaces the canned variety in the next recipe.

1 cup (5 to 6 oz/170 g) flaked grilled tuna (page 78)
2 anchovy fillets, chopped
1 small celery stalk, finely chopped
1 small shallot (small onion), minced
2 tablespoons lemon juice
3 tablespoons olive oil
salt and freshly ground pepper
1 tablespoon chopped parsley
lettuce leaves

❦ Combine the tuna, anchovies, celery and shallot in a bowl. Mix the lemon juice and olive oil together and pour over the tuna mixture. Add salt and pepper to taste. Toss in the parsley. Chill thoroughly before serving on lettuce leaves.

SERVES 2 OR 3

Missouri

CLASSIC POTATO SALAD

The Teutonic countries, particularly Germany, are credited with the invention of a cooked potato salat tossed with vinegar and oil. It may have been the French, however, who first doused potatoes with mayonnaise instead.

2 lb (1 kg) baking potatoes (about 4 medium)
1 celery stalk, finely chopped
1 large dill pickle (pickled cucumber), about 3 in (7.5 cm) long, chopped
6 hard-cooked (hard-boiled) eggs, peeled and roughly chopped
1 large garlic clove, minced
½ teaspoon salt
2 teaspoons Dijon mustard
1 teaspoon sweet paprika
⅛ teaspoon cayenne pepper (optional)
2 tablespoons lemon juice
¼ cup (2 fl oz/60 ml) olive oil
⅔ cup (5 fl oz/160 ml) mayonnaise
chopped fresh parsley (optional)

❦ Cook the potatoes, unpeeled, in boiling water until just barely tender, about 20 minutes. Rinse under cold running water and drain. Let cool.
❦ Peel the potatoes and cut in half lengthwise. Cut each half into slices ¼ in (5 mm) thick. Combine the potatoes with the celery, pickle and eggs in a large bowl.
❦ Mash the garlic with the salt in a small bowl. Whisk in the mustard, paprika, cayenne pepper, lemon juice, oil and mayonnaise. Pour over the potato mixture and toss gently to mix. Sprinkle with parsley and serve at room temperature or slightly chilled.

SERVES 4 TO 6

Maine

OLD NEW ENGLAND POTATO SALAD

Hot egg dressings were popular in America's early days and eventually wound up on bowls of cooked potatoes. The following is the traditional New England rendering. Because the salad is rich, one small potato per person is generally adequate.

1½ lb (750 g) baking potatoes (about 4 small)
2 tablespoons finely chopped green bell pepper (capsicum)
¼ cup sliced radishes (about 4)
1 shallot (small onion), minced
1 tablespoon lemon juice
3 eggs
3 tablespoons water
3 tablespoons red wine vinegar
½ teaspoon salt
⅛ teaspoon freshly ground pepper
pinch of cayenne pepper
¼ cup (2 oz/60 g) unsalted butter
chopped fresh parsley (optional)

❦ Cook the potatoes, unpeeled, in boiling water until just barely tender, 15 to 20 minutes. Rinse under cold running water and drain. Let cool.
❦ Peel the potatoes and cut in half lengthwise. Cut each half into slices ¼ in (5 mm) thick. Combine the potatoes with the bell pepper, radishes and shallot in a large bowl. Sprinkle with the lemon juice.
❦ Beat the eggs with the water, vinegar, salt, black pepper and cayenne pepper in a bowl until light.
❦ Melt the butter in a saucepan over medium-low heat. Remove from the heat and whisk in the egg mixture. Return to low heat and cook, whisking constantly, until the mixture thickens, about 3 minutes. Do not let boil. Pour over the potato mixture and toss gently to mix. Sprinkle with parsley and serve immediately.

SERVES 4

CLASSIC POTATO SALAD (top) AND
OLD NEW ENGLAND POTATO SALAD (bottom)

SWEET-AND-SOUR CABBAGE

Pennsylvania

SWEET-AND-SOUR CABBAGE

Sweet and sour is a favorite combination of the Pennsylvania Dutch.
Sweet-and-sour cabbage is usually served with roast duck or goose.

3 tablespoons (1½ oz/50 g) unsalted butter
1 small onion, finely chopped
1 apple, peeled, cored and chopped
1 small head of cabbage, coarsely chopped
1 teaspoon sugar
2 to 3 tablespoons cider vinegar
salt and freshly ground pepper

❦ Melt the butter in a large saucepan over medium-low heat. Add the onion and apple. Cook, stirring occasionally, for 5 minutes. Stir in the cabbage, sugar and 2 tablespoons of the vinegar. Cook, tossing occasionally, over medium heat until cabbage is tender but slightly crunchy, about 10 minutes. Add more vinegar if needed and salt and pepper to taste.

SERVES 4

Indiana

SAUTÉED PARSNIPS

Root vegetables were extremely important in the days before rapid shipping and modern farming virtually guaranteed a year-round supply of vegetables. Parsnips were introduced in Virginia but played a more important role in the survival of the northern plains settlers.

1 lb (500 g) parsnips, halved lengthwise (or small whole parsnips)
2 tablespoons (1 oz/30 g) unsalted butter
2 tablespoons dark brown sugar
2 tablespoons cider vinegar
salt and freshly ground pepper
chopped fresh parsley (optional)

❦ Cook the parsnips in boiling salted water until just tender, 5 or 6 minutes. Drain. Cut each parsnip into slices ¼ in (5 mm) thick.

❦ Melt the butter in a large skillet over medium heat. Add the parsnips and cook until lightly browned, about 4 minutes. Sprinkle with the brown sugar and turn over. Cook until very tender, about 4 minutes longer. Remove from the heat and sprinkle with the vinegar and salt and pepper to taste. Sprinkle with parsley before serving.

SERVES 4

Massachusetts

HARVARD BEETS

The origin of Harvard beets is somewhat cloudy. It may be that the deep crimson color of the beets is similar to the color of the Harvard football team jerseys. According to another story, the dish was invented in the seventeenth century in an English tavern called Harwood. Harwood beets became Harvard beets when a regular patron, a Russian immigrant, could not pronounce the name correctly.

3 lb (1.5 kg) beets (beetroot), trimmed
½ cup (4 oz/125 g) sugar
¼ cup (2 fl oz/60 ml) cider vinegar
¼ cup (2 fl oz/60 ml) water
1 teaspoon cornstarch (cornflour)
3 tablespoons (1½ oz/50 g) unsalted butter
salt and freshly ground pepper

❦ Place the beets in a saucepan and cover with cold water. Heat slowly to boiling, reduce the heat and simmer, uncovered, until barely tender, about 35 minutes. Rinse under cold water and drain. Peel, dice and set aside.

❦ Combine the sugar, vinegar, water and cornstarch in a saucepan. Boil, stirring frequently, until thickened, 4 or 5 minutes. Stir in the beets and the butter. Add salt and pepper to taste.

SERVES 6

Louisiana

CREOLE CARROT AND TURNIP ESCABÈCHE

The term escabèche *is usually applied to fish, but Louisiana cooks borrowed the word for a relish of marinated carrots and turnips. The flavors improve the longer the vegetables sit in the refrigerator.*

CREOLE CARROT AND TURNIP ESCABÈCHE (top),
HARVARD BEETS (center) AND SAUTÉED PARSNIPS (bottom)

2 lb (1 kg) carrots, cut into ¼-in (5-mm) slices
1 lb (500 g) white turnips, cut into ¼-in (5-mm) slices
½ cup (4 fl oz/125 ml) olive oil
½ cup (4 fl oz/125 ml) vegetable oil
⅓ cup (3 fl oz/80 ml) white vinegar
½ cup (2½ oz/75 g) chopped green olives
½ cup (2½ oz/75 g) chopped pimientos (or canned sweet peppers)
1 large garlic clove, minced
2 small onions, thinly sliced
¼ cup (2 fl oz/60 ml) vodka
salt and freshly ground pepper
chopped fresh parsley (optional)

❦ In separate saucepans, cook the carrots and turnips in boiling salted water until barely tender, 4 to 5 minutes. Rinse under cold running water and drain.

❦ Combine the oils, vinegar, olives, pimientos and garlic in a saucepan. Heat to boiling, reduce the heat and simmer, uncovered, for 5 minutes. Remove from the heat and let cool for 10 minutes.

❦ Combine the carrots, turnips and onions in a large heatproof bowl. Pour the marinade on top and stir in the vodka. Let cool completely. Add salt and pepper to taste. Refrigerate, covered, overnight; stir occasionally. Serve in the marinade, sprinkled with parsley.

SERVES 8

SWEET POTATO PONE (top)
AND GREENS WITH "POT LIKKER" (bottom)

Virginia

SWEET POTATO PONE

The word pone *is traditionally linked with corn because it derives from the Indian word* apone, *the name of a baked cake that was also called "ash cake." Today* pone *often refers to anything baked.*

2 eggs
2 cups (16 fl oz/500 ml) milk
1½ tablespoons vanilla extract (essence)
1 cup (8 oz/250 g) sugar
¼ teaspoon freshly grated nutmeg
½ teaspoon grated orange peel
3 small to medium sweet potatoes (about 1 lb/500 g), peeled
    and grated
6 tablespoons (3 oz/90 g) unsalted butter, melted

❦ Preheat the oven to 350°F (180°C). Beat the eggs in a large bowl until light. Beat in the remaining ingredients and pour into a buttered 2-qt (2-l) soufflé dish. Bake until firm and golden brown, about 2 hours. Let stand at least 20 minutes before serving, but serve while still warm.

SERVES 8

Mississippi

GREENS WITH "POT LIKKER"

In the American South greens are a way of life. They are cooked with salt pork or ham hocks for hours on end. The juices, or "pot likker," are served separately as a soup course.

3 lb (1.5 kg) collard or turnip greens (or silverbeet or spinach),
    stems removed
1 smoked ham hock or ¼ lb (125 g) salt pork
salt and freshly ground black pepper

❦ Wash the greens thoroughly in several changes of cold water. Cook in boiling salted water for 2 minutes. Rinse under cold running water and drain. (This step removes any bitterness in the leaves.)

❦ Place the greens in a large pot with the ham hock or salt pork. Cover with water and heat to boiling. Reduce the heat to low and cook, covered, for 2 hours. Add more water during the cooking if you plan to serve the "pot likker." Add salt and pepper to taste before serving.

SERVES 4

Wisconsin

GREEN BEANS AND POTATOES

This recipe has a German heritage. It is basically a hot potato salad dressed up with cooked green beans.

2 baking potatoes, unpeeled
½ lb (250 g) green beans, trimmed
3 bacon strips
1 onion, halved and sliced
¼ cup (2 fl oz/60 ml) red wine vinegar
2 tablespoons water
1 tablespoon unsalted butter
salt and freshly ground pepper

❦ Cook the potatoes in boiling salted water until just barely tender, about 15 minutes. Drain. Cut into slices ¼ in (5 mm) thick.

❦ Meanwhile, cook the beans in boiling salted water until crisp-tender, 1½ to 2 minutes. Rinse under cold running water and drain.

❦ Sauté the bacon in a large skillet until crisp. Drain on paper towels. Crumble and reserve.

❦ Add the onion to the bacon drippings and cook over medium heat until golden, about 5 minutes. Stir in the vinegar and water. Cook, stirring constantly, until thickened, about 3 minutes. Reduce the heat to medium-low and toss in the potatoes and green beans. Cook, tossing gently, for 5 minutes. Stir in the butter and bacon, and add salt and pepper to taste.

SERVES 4

Pennsylvania

CORN FRITTERS

The next recipe is an Amish specialty that is easy to prepare. The secret lies in the manner in which the corn is removed from the ears.

4 large ears (cobs) of corn
2 eggs, separated
2 tablespoons all-purpose (plain) flour
1 tablespoon sugar
salt and freshly ground pepper
unsalted butter

❦ Cut the kernels from 2 ears of corn into a bowl. Using a sharp knife, cut the kernels from the remaining ears to only half their depth. Then, with the back of the knife, scrape up and down each cob to remove all the pulp and "milk." Add to the bowl. The mixture will resemble scrambled eggs.

❦ Beat the egg yolks in a large bowl until light. Beat in the flour, sugar and salt and pepper to taste. Stir in the corn.

❦ Beat the egg whites in a large bowl until stiff. Fold into the corn mixture.

❦ Heat a griddle over medium heat and grease it lightly with butter. Drop the batter by small spoonfuls onto the hot griddle and cook until golden, about 30 seconds on each side. Transfer the cooked fritters to a lightly buttered serving platter and keep warm while cooking the remaining fritters.

SERVES 4

GREEN BEANS AND POTATOES (top) AND
CORN FRITTERS (bottom)

Rhode Island

BAKED ACORN SQUASH

The Indians baked acorn squash in hot coals until tender, a method still used by many outdoor cooks when grilling foods that require long, covered cooking.

2 acorn squash (or butternut/golden nugget squash)
4 teaspoons brown sugar
¼ cup (2 oz/60 g) unsalted butter

❦ Preheat the oven to 350°F (180°C). Cut the squash in half lengthwise. Scoop out the seeds. Trim a thin slice from the skin side of each half so that they lie flat.
❦ Place the squash halves in a shallow baking dish. Add 1 teaspoon sugar and 1 tablespoon butter to the center of each. Bake, basting occasionally with the sugar-butter mixture, until tender, 50 to 60 minutes.

SERVES 4

California

SCALLOPED POTATOES WITH PEPPERS

Scallop means to bake in a casserole with milk or sauce. While the dish is not indigenous to California, the notion of adding smoky peppers is indeed a southern California inspiration. These potatoes are wonderful at room temperature or even served cold.

1 large red bell pepper (capsicum)
4 baking potatoes (2 lb/1 kg), peeled and sliced
2 cups (16 fl oz/500 ml) milk
1½ cups (12 fl oz/375 ml) cream
1 large garlic clove, minced
1 small hot green (chili) pepper, seeded, deveined and minced
¾ teaspoon salt
½ teaspoon freshly ground white pepper
1 tablespoon unsalted butter, softened
¼ cup (1 oz/30 g) grated Gruyère cheese
¼ cup (1 oz/30 g) grated Parmesan cheese

❦ Roast the bell pepper over a gas flame or under a broiler (griller) until charred all over. Carefully wrap in paper towels and place in a plastic bag. Let cool. Rub off the skin, then seed and chop.
❦ Preheat the oven to 400°F (200°C). Combine the potatoes, milk, cream and garlic in a large heavy saucepan. Slowly heat to boiling. Remove from the heat and stir in the chopped roasted pepper, hot pepper, salt and white pepper.
❦ Rub a large gratin dish or shallow baking dish with the butter. Carefully pour the potato mixture into the dish. Sprinkle with the cheeses. Bake for 1 hour. Lower the temperature if the potatoes brown too quickly. Let stand at least 10 minutes before serving.

SERVES 6 TO 8

Colorado

DILL PICKLES

Great dill pickles depend on dill tops that have gone to seed. In the eighteenth century children were given dill seeds to chew on during church service to keep them quiet, and for that reason dill seeds are often called "meetin' seeds."

5 cups (1¼ qt/1.25 l) water
1 cup (8 fl oz/250 ml) cider vinegar
½ cup (4 oz/125 g) pickling salt
20 to 25 small cucumbers, rinsed
fresh dill tops gone to seed

❦ Combine the water, vinegar and salt in a saucepan. Heat to boiling, remove from the heat and let cool for 10 minutes.
❦ Pack the cucumbers into sterilized 1-pt (500-ml) jars. Add 3 dill tops with seeds to each jar. Pour the vinegar mixture into each jar to cover the cucumbers. Seal. Process in a hot-water bath for 10 minutes. Cool upside down. Let stand for 8 weeks before using.

MAKES ABOUT 6 PT (3 L)   *Photograph page 10*

Idaho

STUFFED BAKED POTATOES

Baking, of course, is the simplest (and some say best) way to cook a potato, but today baked potatoes have fallen victim to "fast food" status, stuffed with everything from broccoli to shrimp and reheated to order with dubious success. Needless to say, it is best to stuff a potato while it is still hot from the oven and the skin is crisp.

2 large baking potatoes
2 tablespoons (1 oz/30 g) unsalted butter
⅔ cup (3 oz/90 g) shredded sharp (mature) Cheddar cheese
¼ cup (2 fl oz/60 ml) sour cream
1 tablespoon chopped chives
salt and freshly ground pepper
3 bacon slices, fried crisp and crumbled

❦ Preheat the oven to 400°F (200°C). Wash and scrub the potatoes and prick once with a knife. Bake until the skins are very crisp and the potatoes are tender, about 1 hour 15 minutes.
❦ Carefully cut the potatoes in half lengthwise and scoop the centers into a bowl. Add the butter and mash until smooth. Fold in the cheese, sour cream and chives. Add salt and pepper to taste and toss in the bacon. Mound the mixture back into the potato shells and bake for another 15 minutes.

SERVES 4

STUFFED BAKED POTATOES

South Dakota

Fried Green Tomatoes

Fried green tomatoes are generally relegated to autumn, just before the first frost, when tomatoes are still on the vine. They need not be, however, since they are delicious at any time. Southern cooks use cornmeal instead of breadcrumbs for the coating.

3 firm green tomatoes
1 egg
⅓ cup (3 fl oz/80 ml) milk
dash of hot red pepper (Tabasco) sauce
½ cup (2 oz/60 g) fine dry breadcrumbs (approximately)
½ teaspoon salt
¼ teaspoon freshly ground pepper
4 to 6 tablespoons (2–3 oz/60–90 g) unsalted butter

❧ Cut the tomatoes crosswise into slices ½ in (1 cm) thick.
❧ Beat the egg with the milk and hot pepper sauce in a shallow bowl. Combine the breadcrumbs with the salt and pepper on a plate.
❧ Melt 2 tablespoons of the butter in a large skillet over medium heat. Dip the tomato slices in the milk mixture, shaking off any excess, then lightly coat with the crumbs. Fry a few slices at a time until golden, about 2 minutes on each side. Transfer to a heatproof serving dish and keep warm in a low oven. Continue to fry the tomatoes, adding more butter as needed.

SERVES 4

Louisiana

Maquechoux

Also known as "mock shoe" and "mark show," maquechoux means "false cabbage." No one seems to know why, as this Cajun dish of mixed vegetables has nothing to do with the texture of cabbage.

6 ears (cobs) of corn
2 bacon strips
1 large onion, chopped
1 large green bell pepper (capsicum), seeded and chopped
2 ripe tomatoes, seeded and chopped
1 teaspoon sugar
½ cup (4 fl oz/125 ml) light (single) cream or half & half (half cream and half milk)
½ teaspoon salt
¼ teaspoon freshly ground pepper

❧ Cut the kernels from 2 ears of corn into a bowl. Using a sharp knife, cut the kernels from the remaining ears to only half their depth. Then, with the back of the knife, scrape up and down each cob to remove all the pulp and "milk." Add to the bowl. The mixture will resemble scrambled eggs.
❧ Sauté the bacon in a large skillet until crisp. Drain on paper towels, crumble and set aside.
❧ Add the onion and bell pepper to the bacon drippings and cook for 5 minutes. Add the tomatoes and sprinkle with the sugar. Cook for 3 minutes. Stir in the corn and cream. Cook, stirring frequently, for 10 minutes. Add salt and pepper to taste and sprinkle with the bacon.

SERVES 6

New Hampshire

Sweet Zucchini Chips

Although native to the Americas, zucchini was favored more in Italy than on its own soil until the mid-twentieth century. That, of course, has changed, and now there is even a yearly festival in Harrisville, New Hampshire, which features a contest in zucchini carving.

4 zucchini (courgettes) (about 1½ lb/750 g), thinly sliced
2 small yellow (brown) onions, halved and thinly sliced
3 tablespoons salt
2 cups (16 fl oz/500 ml) white vinegar
1 cup (8 oz/250 g) sugar
1 teaspoon celery seed
1 teaspoon aniseed
2 teaspoons dry mustard

❧ Place the zucchini and onion slices in a large bowl. Sprinkle with the salt and add cold water to cover. Let stand for 1 hour.
❧ Combine the remaining ingredients in a large heavy saucepan. Heat to boiling and remove from the heat.
❧ Drain the zucchini and onions and add to the saucepan. Let stand for 1 hour.
❧ Place the pan over high heat and quickly heat to boiling. Boil for 2 minutes. Pour into sterilized jars and seal. Process in a hot-water bath for 10 minutes. Let cool and store in a cool place at least 4 weeks before serving.

MAKES 3 PT (1.5 L)   *Photograph page 10*

Minnesota

Green Bean Pickles

The pickling process was discovered by the Dutch way back in the fifteenth century, but home canning really took off in 1858 when a tinsmith named John L. Mason invented the screw-top lid for glass jars.

1½ to 2 lb (750 g to 1 kg) green beans, trimmed
2 cups (16 fl oz/500 ml) cider vinegar
⅓ cup (3 oz/90 g) sugar
1½ tablespoons pickling spices, tied in cheesecloth
1 tablespoon whole black peppercorns
1 bay leaf
1 garlic clove
1 large onion, chopped
1 small red bell pepper (capsicum), seeded and chopped
3 large dill sprigs

❧ Cook the beans in boiling salted water for 1 minute. Rinse under cold running water and drain.
❧ Place the vinegar, sugar, pickling spices, peppercorns, bay leaf and garlic in a saucepan. Heat to boiling, reduce the heat and simmer, uncovered, for 10 minutes. Discard the spices. Add the onion and bell pepper; cook 10 minutes longer. Discard the bay leaf and garlic.
❧ Pack the beans upright in 3 sterilized 1-pt (500-ml) jars. Using a slotted spoon, divide the onion and peppers among the jars. Place a sprig of dill in each jar. Pour in the hot liquid up to ½ in (1 cm) from the top. Seal the jars and process in a hot-water bath for 15 minutes.

MAKES 3 PT (1.5 L)   *Photograph page 10*

MAQUECHOUX (top right) AND FRIED GREEN TOMATOES

The Far West

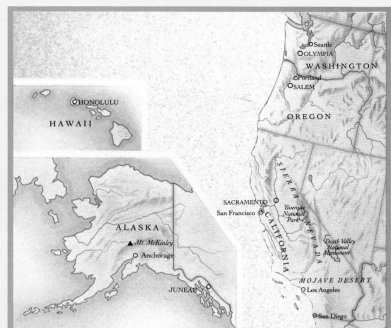

THE FAR WEST

❦

Salmon was the most important food of the Chinook Indians in the Northwest. When salmon made their annual migration upstream, the rivers were so alive with fish that all one had to do was stand at any rise in the river and simply club the fish as they leaped up the rapids. Great numbers of fish were also caught in nets made from grapevines. The Indians held salmon in great esteem because they believed the fish were actually "spirit people," sent from some mystical place under the sea to feed those living on the shores. According to ritual, the first seasonal salmon a fisherman caught had to be placed on the riverbank with its head pointed upstream, then a few apologies and prayers said over the fish. This act ensured that other fish would follow. If the first catch was not so duly honored, it would warn the rest to stay away. Herring also made annual visits to the rivers of the Northwest, and both herring and salmon roe were considered delicacies. To collect them, the Indians wove trays of branches and submerged them in the shallow waters where the fish were likely to lay their eggs. Oysters, clams and crabs gave the Indians variety in their diet, as did game animals and birds of all kinds.

The land was so blessed with wild fruits, berries and roots that the natives made no attempt at agriculture. Instead, they spent three months of the year gathering the wild foods that kept them well fed year round. Much like Indians elsewhere, they made jerky, but they used strips of salmon rather than game. They also made a form of pemmican out of the fish, adding their favorite seasoning, the juniper berry. Fresh salmon were planked and slowly smoked next to smoldering coals or cooked with seawater into tasty stews. Hot stones were added to the pot to cook the stews. The pots were made of wood, which were woven underwater so tightly that they were leakproof.

With leisure time on their hands, the Indians were free

SAN FRANCISCO IS ONE OF AMERICA'S MOST COSMOPOLITAN CITIES. ITS UNMISTAKABLE SKYLINE PROVIDES THE PERFECT BACKDROP TO A ROW OF QUAINT VICTORIAN HOMES.

PREVIOUS PAGES: THE WHITMAN COUNTY GROWERS GRANARY AND SILO IN THE WHEAT-GROWING AREA OF PALOUSE, EASTERN WASHINGTON.
PHOTO: BRUCE HANDS

203

THE FISHING COMMUNITY OF SITKA IS PART OF A LOOSE NETWORK OF ISLANDS AND INLETS ALONG THE COAST OF SOUTHEASTERN ALASKA. THE AREA IS SURROUNDED BY DEEP VALLEYS AND RUGGED, DENSELY FORESTED MOUNTAINS THAT SOAR AS HIGH AS 10,000 FEET.

to follow artistic pursuits. The men were masters at carving huge totems and ceremonial masks. The women were excellent weavers and made magnificent robes and blankets. Inland, the Wallawalla, Nez Percé and Yakima tribes dwelt in lush river valleys. Freshwater fish, small game and roots made up their diet. The camas (lily bulb) was eaten roasted or pounded into meal. Bitterroot, wild carrots, sunflower seeds, pine nuts and wild berries were eaten as well, but again no plants were cultivated.

Farther south in parts of California and Nevada, the Indians were the most primitive of all American tribes. The Digger Indians (Shoshones) grubbed roots and ate small game when they could find it. They also lived on insects and thought nothing of enjoying a feast of toasted caterpillars, a habit the first mountain men found slightly repulsive. Their homes consisted of simple lean-tos. In central and southern California, the Miwok, Maidu, Pomo and Hupa tribes of the Penutian family, often called the "Nut Eaters," existed mostly on acorns. Since acorns are toxic, the seeds had to be ground and then washed over and over in hot water. Hot water was obtained by heating spring water with hot stones in baskets lined with animal skins. The acorn meal was then dried and used very much like cornmeal and ground hominy.

The Spanish had come to the West Coast still looking for the fabled treasure cities of Cibola and El Dorado. In their wake they left missionaries and fruit groves, including peaches, apricots, apples and plums. They also planted figs, olives and oranges. Large *rancheros* consisting of hundreds of thousands of acres existed, but southern California was relatively poor and remained so long after the north boomed during the Gold Rush era.

By 1846 pioneers were pouring into the Northwest by the thousands along the Oregon Trail. To avoid war, the British ceded the whole area to the United States the same year. After the Mexican-American War, with California safely under American rule, prospectors flocked to the state in search of gold. After a bitter fight over the prohibition of slavery, California was admitted to the Union in 1850. Oregon was settled more slowly, entering the Union in 1859. Washington Territory, which included Idaho, rapidly expanded in population after the Civil War. Washington was admitted as a state in 1889; Idaho, a year later. Alaska and Hawaii were finally admitted in 1959.

Alaska was the first territorial acquisition by the United States outside its boundaries. Congress, however, was not too sure about the purchase promoted by Secretary of State William Seward. Seward was an expansionist and an extremist. He believed that the United States should take over the entire North American continent, moving the capital to Mexico City. Thankfully, saner minds prevailed, but in the end "Seward's Folly," as the 1867 purchase was dubbed, paid off many times over in natural resources alone. Alaska is a land of diverse climates. The panhandle, where Juneau is located, has the same average temperature as Washington, D.C., because of the warm Japan Current off the coast. The Matanuska Valley (about fifty miles from Anchorage) grows almost two-thirds of Alaska's produce. Even though the growing season is brief, the almost perpetual summer daylight ensures quick-growing fruits and vegetables that achieve incredible size. Then, too, Alaskans depend on the rich supply of fish and game that they are blessed with.

Hawaii was originally valuable as a base for American whaling fleets and as a trading link to the Far East. When American sugar planters began having great success with sugar cane, free trade with Hawaii was established. Since Americans virtually controlled the islands anyway, the United States government, crushing native resistance, simply annexed Hawaii in 1898. Needless to say, the strategic location of the islands was of tremendous importance during World War II. The food of Hawaii has been greatly influenced by Polynesian and Oriental settlers. Foods that we generally attribute to Hawaii, like pineapple, pomelo and mango, were all introduced. The coconut, however, is a genuine native. Pork has long been the favorite meat of the islands, and luaus are still a major dining experience.

The rich soil of the Northwest beckoned to the pioneers who had to travel the two thousand miles from Independence, Missouri, to Fort Vancouver over the Oregon Trail. The route became well marked not only by wagon wheel tracks but by furniture and tools that were abandoned as both oxen and people weakened considerably en route. Settlers on their way to California also had to follow the Oregon Trail for much of the way, but it was gold, not dirt, that attracted them. After gold was discovered at Sutter's mill in 1848, gold fever struck so many Americans and foreigners that only the length of the journey to California stopped a major stampede of prospectors and speculators. As it was, supplies were deleted so quickly that flour went from twenty-four dollars a barrel to eight hundred dollars a barrel in about a month. Sourdough bread became the staple not only for those along the trail but for those who had struck it rich. One *had* to be rich to afford the flour. Eggs often sold for more than three dollars each. Most prospectors lived on salt pork alone, and even that was in short supply much of the time. When the money began flowing freely, San Francisco grew by leaps and bounds. Fancy restaurants with imported chefs virtually sprang up overnight.

The cooking of the Northwest today still revolves around much that is wild in the woods or swims in the sea. It is a lush land where residents can harvest their own seafood and pick mushrooms, wild asparagus and greens in the forests. One of the most fertile areas in the country, the Northwest produces fruits, vegetables and wheat. The delectable fresh salmon, tiny Olympia oysters and Dungeness crabs are world-famous bounties of the sea. The Northwest is becoming an important wine-producing region as well, but to most people the Northwest means apples. Over 30 percent of apples found in American supermarkets are grown there.

California produces some of the finest wines in the country. The Napa and Sonoma Valley vineyards are world-renowned. Fresh fish and shellfish are abundant in Pacific waters, but agriculture is California's lifeblood. Irrigation of California's central valley literally changed the way all Americans eat. Since the climate is suitable for year-round farming, fresh (normally seasonal) fruits and vegetables are now found on American dining tables year round as well. Hardy produce was developed for shipping long distances, and experiments by men like Luther Burbank, one of the world's greatest horticulturists, produced countless varieties of fruits, vegetables and nuts. There are those, of course, who would argue that California's agribusinesses have turned West Coast produce into bland-tasting goods with long shelf life their only virtue. But then it is these critics who have rallied to support small local farmers.

California chefs have always been in the forefront of "what's new" in American cuisine and, in fact, were the first to take it upon themselves to search for the freshest and best-tasting produce available. They have also raised "grilling" to dizzying new heights. Their dishes in the past may have been somewhat bizarre hit-or-miss affairs, but California chefs were the first to experiment with a lighter style of cookery based on American classics and incorporating French techniques. California cuisine is coming of age.

HIGH IN THE SIERRA NEVADA, EMERALD BAY IS ONE OF THE MOST SCENIC INLETS AT LAKE TAHOE, THE LARGEST ALPINE LAKE IN NORTH AMERICA.

REG MORRISON

DESSERTS AND CAKES

THE FIRST FRUIT GROVES WERE PLANTED IN THE FAR WEST BY THE SPANISH, WHO GREW PEACHES, APRICOTS, APPLES AND PLUMS. FRUIT DESSERTS SUCH AS BAKED APPLES (FROM OREGON) AND PEACH UPSIDE-DOWN CAKE (FROM CALIFORNIA) BECAME POPULAR.

DESSERTS AND CAKES

Americans have always been fond of sweet endings. It has even been noted that in early cookbooks recipes for sweets outnumbered recipes for savories by more than two to one. Cobblers, slumps, buckles, grunts, pandowdies and brown Bettys are just a few of the desserts that can be called "more American than apple pie" (apple pie being English). Not to mention brownies, mud cakes, funeral pies, icebox pies, chocolate chip cookies, nut fudge, peanut brittle and many more too numerous to list here.

During colonial times most desserts were made with fruit. America was rich with wild fruits and nuts of all kinds. Apple orchards sprung up in the North, and out of New England came many of the apple recipes we use today. The South became famous for sweet, juicy peaches that grew in profusion there. And although the sweet dessert "pye" did not originate here, the pie as we know it, baked in a shallow dish, did. In the nineteenth century pies were made so frequently that they even had their own little houses. Called "pie safes," these cabinets had several cooling shelves and sported screen or perforated tin doors that protected the contents from unwelcome flying visitors. In colder climates pies were often made in great numbers and placed in an outdoor shed where they froze solid, ready for a midwinter's meal. Fruits, particularly apples, were sliced and dried and then reconstituted for use by overnight soaking in cold water. With the invention of refrigeration came silky, smooth-on-the-tongue chiffon pies.

Most of the aforementioned fruit desserts are still a part of everyday family life, but their somewhat wacky names have been interchanged so frequently that there is mass confusion over what the original concepts were. It seems that apple pandowdy, named for its somewhat dowdy appearance, was originally a dessert of sliced apples baked under a thick biscuit crust. The crust was broken into the pie before serving. A variation calls for breaking the crust into the pie as it cooks, resulting in a pudding-pie effect. Still other recipes call for sliced bread and are very much akin to bread puddings. Slumps are similar deep-dish pies with biscuit crusts that are sometimes turned upside down onto a plate before being served. When fruit is topped with a pastry of oats and brown sugar and not upended (as in Iowa), the dessert becomes a crisp. A brown Betty is a layered affair of fruit and buttered crumbs. A cobbler is a fruit pie baked either deep-dish style under a thick crust or, as out west, with the fruit on top of a soft dough, resulting in a moist, cakey dessert. A grunt and a buckle are virtually the same—steamed dishes of berries or other fruit. A grunt is steamed under a soft biscuit dough that "grunts" as it steams. A buckle is steamed under a cake batter that "buckles" as it cools. These two desserts date back to colonial times, but are seldom eaten today.

Many of the first cakes were of the English pound cake variety. Baking was a tricky affair. Even with fireplace brick ovens, timing and heat control were matters of guesswork. Although some yeast was used in baking cakes, the most common method of getting a cake to stand tall was with beaten eggs. In the eighteenth century it was not uncommon for a housewife to use as many as twenty eggs in one cake! Worse yet, she had to beat those eggs from three to five hours to ensure lightness in the finished product. The nineteenth century changed the baker's life forever. The first practical freestanding wood stove was invented and baking powder was introduced. As a result, by the later part of the century, layer cakes had established a place for themselves in American cuisine.

Puddings were not new to the colonists, although recipes did require major readjustment because the ingredients for traditional English puddings were not available on these shores. The earliest puddings were made of cornmeal sweetened with maple syrup, honey or molasses. In those days cornmeal puddings were either called "hasty puddings" because of the quickness of preparation or simply referred to as "Indian puddings," for the "Indian meal" that went into them. When wheat and rice flourished, so did bread puddings and rice puddings of all kinds. Sugar, however, was not a common sweetener until the late 1800s, when white refined sugar became affordable to most of the general public.

Our forefathers, or more accurately our foremothers, brought English teacakes, Scottish shortbread and Scandinavian *spritz* recipes with them. The earliest renditions were spicy morsels, notably of cinnamon and ginger. Spices helped to cover the taste of the animal fats that most housewives were forced to use in place of butter. The Dutch brought *koetje* recipes with them. These "little cakes" were so popular with the settlers that the English bastardization of *koetje*, "cookie," became the standard name of all such snacks by the end of the seventeenth century. The most famous American cookie, of course, is the chocolate chip, which was not invented until 1930. The standard cookie of that time was the butter drop do, said to have been invented way back in the 1700s at an inn along the "King's Path" that ran

CATHERINE KARNOW

DURING COLONIAL TIMES MOST DESSERTS WERE MADE WITH FRUIT. APPLE ORCHARDS SPRANG UP IN THE NORTH AND THEY ARE STILL THERE TODAY. THESE APPLES ARE FROM A SMALL ORCHARD IN NEW YORK STATE.

between New York and Philadelphia, and chocolate versions were common by the 1930s. As the story goes, Mrs. Ruth Wakefield of the Toll House Inn in Whitman, Massachusetts, one day set about making her usual batch of chocolate cookies. Instead of melting the chocolate as she was accustomed to doing, she just chopped it and stirred it into the batter, fully expecting the two to meld together in the oven. They did not, and a legend was born.

BROWNIES ARE CREDITED WITH HAVING BEEN INVENTED IN MAINE, AND THIS BAKERY IN CAMDEN IS SURE TO HAVE A FRESHLY BAKED SUPPLY.

BRUCE HANDS

APPLE BROWN BETTY

APPLE BROWN BETTY

The origin of Apple Brown Betty is unknown, but we do know the dessert appeared on kitchen tables sometime in the mid-1800s. Half a cup of raisins is sometimes added these days, even though they are not traditional. Whipped cream or ice cream on the side, however, is mandatory.

3 cups (6 oz/185 g) fresh breadcrumbs
½ cup (4 oz/125 g) unsalted butter, melted
2 lb (1 kg) tart apples (about 4 large)
juice of 1 lemon
¾ cup (4 oz/125 g) packed dark brown sugar
1 teaspoon ground cinnamon
⅓ cup (3 fl oz/80 ml) apple cider (nonalcoholic), apple juice, or water

❧ Preheat the oven to 350°F (180°C). Combine the breadcrumbs and butter in a bowl. Mix well.

❧ Peel, core and slice the apples into a bowl. Sprinkle with lemon juice as you cut them. Add the sugar and cinnamon. Toss well.

❧ Spread one-third of the crumbs over the bottom of a 1½- to 2-qt (1.5- to 2-l) casserole dish, about 2 in (5 cm) deep. Arrange half the apples on top. Add another third of the crumbs and the remaining apples. Spread the remaining crumbs over the top. Drizzle with the apple cider. Bake for 1 hour. Serve while still warm.

SERVES 6

Oregon

BAKED APPLES

Baked apples, redolent of cinnamon and brown sugar, have always been popular with American diners. This version, dusted with ground nuts, comes from the apple-growing Northwest. One may vary the filling by adding a little currant jelly, chopped cooked dried apricots or even a bit of mincemeat to each cavity.

½ cup (2 oz/60 g) walnut halves
¼ cup (2 oz/60 g) sugar
½ teaspoon ground cinnamon
4 baking apples
1 lemon, halved
¼ cup (2 oz/60 g) unsalted butter, melted, plus 2 tablespoons, cut into pieces
¼ cup (2 oz/60 g) packed dark brown sugar
¼ cup (1 oz/30 g) raisins (or sultanas)
4 small cinnamon sticks
apple juice
cream

❧ Preheat the oven to 375°F (190°C). Place the walnuts, sugar and cinnamon in a food processor and process until finely ground. Transfer to a bowl.

❧ Core and peel the apples. Sprinkle the insides with lemon juice. Rub the outsides well with lemon juice.

❧ Brush the apples with the melted butter. Press the walnut mixture evenly onto the apples. Transfer to a shallow baking dish.

❧ Combine the brown sugar with the cut-up butter in a small bowl. Work with a fork to mix. Add the raisins and mix with your fingers. Fill the apples with this mixture. Tuck a cinnamon stick into the top of each. Drizzle any remaining melted butter over the tops.

❧ Pour ¼ in (5 mm) apple juice into the dish. Bake the apples until tender, about 1 hour. Let cool on a rack for 15 minutes.

❧ Transfer the apples to individual shallow bowls. Spoon the juices around the apples and serve while still warm, or at room temperature, with cream on the side.

SERVES 4

Texas

TEXAS-STYLE PEACH COBBLER

For a period of about ten years beginning in 1840, a huge number of German immigrants headed for Texas, mostly to the hill country around Fredericksburg. In most parts of the West, a cobbler is a deep-dish fruit pie, usually laden with a heavy crust. This version, slightly upside down in its method, is of German-Texan extraction.

1 cup (4 oz/125 g) all-purpose (plain) flour
¾ cup (3 oz/90 g) sugar
2 teaspoons baking powder
½ cup (4 oz/125 g) unsalted butter
1 cup (8 fl oz/250 ml) milk
6 to 8 fresh peaches, peeled and sliced
1 teaspoon ground cinnamon
vanilla ice cream or sweetened whipped cream

❧ Preheat the oven to 350°F (180°C). Combine the flour with ½ cup (2 oz/60 g) of the sugar and the baking powder. Cut ¼ cup (2 oz/60 g) of the butter into pieces and add to the flour mixture. Cut in until the texture of coarse crumbs. Stir in the milk until the batter is smooth; set aside.

❧ Place the remaining butter in a 9-in (23-cm) square or 10-in (25-cm) round baking dish. Place in the oven until the butter melts, 5 to 6 minutes. Swirl the butter over the bottom and sides, then pour the batter evenly into the dish. Arrange the peach slices, slightly overlapping, on top of the batter, in rows if the dish is square, in circles if it is round.

❧ Combine the remaining sugar with the cinnamon; sprinkle over the peaches. Place the dish on a baking sheet and bake until golden brown, about 45 minutes. Serve warm with ice cream or whipped cream.

SERVES 6 TO 8

BAKED APPLES (left) AND TEXAS-STYLE PEACH COBBLER (right)

PEACH UPSIDE-DOWN CAKE

California

PEACH UPSIDE-DOWN CAKE

Upside-down cakes started appearing on dining room tables around the turn of this century. The following comes from California, the largest peach-producing state, where sliced almonds, another California crop, are often added to give the top more crunch.

4 fresh peaches
½ cup (2 oz/60 g) sliced almonds
1 cup (8 oz/250 g) unsalted butter, softened
1 cup (5½ oz/170 g) dark brown sugar
½ cup (4 oz/125 g) sugar
2 eggs
½ teaspoon vanilla extract (essence)
1½ cups (6 oz/185 g) all-purpose (plain) flour
1½ teaspoons baking powder
½ teaspoon salt
¼ cup (2 fl oz/60 ml) cream
¼ cup (2 fl oz/60 ml) orange juice
whipped cream or sour cream

❧ Preheat the oven to 350°F (180°C). Place the peaches in boiling water for 1 to 2 minutes to loosen their skins; remove the skins and cut the peaches into ¼-in (5-cm) slices.
❧ Spread the almonds on a baking sheet. Toast in the oven until brown, about 10 minutes.
❧ Melt ¼ cup (2 oz/60 g) of the butter and pour into a 9-in (23-cm) round (preferably nonstick) cake pan. Tilt the pan to coat the bottom and sides. Sprinkle the bottom and sides with ¾ cup (4 oz/125 g) of the brown sugar. Spread half the almonds over the bottom and arrange the peach slices over the bottom and around the sides in a decorative pattern. Sprinkle with the remaining brown sugar and remaining almonds. Let stand in a cool place.

❧ Beat the remaining butter with the sugar in the large bowl of an electric mixer until light and fluffy. Add the eggs, one at a time, beating thoroughly after each addition. Beat in the vanilla.
❧ Sift the flour with the baking powder and salt. Combine the cream and orange juice. Add the flour mixture to the butter-sugar mixture in 3 parts, alternating with the liquid.
❧ Spoon the batter carefully over the peaches in the cake pan. Bake until a toothpick inserted in the center comes out clean, 35 to 40 minutes. Let cool on a wire rack for 10 minutes before inverting onto a serving platter. Serve slightly warm with the whipped cream.

SERVES 8

New York

NEW YORK CHEESECAKE

Cheesecakes have been around for a long time. Italian-style cheesecakes are made with ricotta cheese, but the New York version (of Jewish heritage) uses cream cheese. The most famous of all New York cheesecakes was the one made at Lindy's restaurant in New York City, which the following closely resembles.

FOR THE PASTRY

1 cup (4 oz/125 g) sifted all-purpose (plain) flour
¼ cup (2 oz/60 g) sugar
1 teaspoon finely grated lemon peel
1 teaspoon finely grated orange peel
½ cup (4 oz/125 g) cold unsalted butter
1 egg yolk
¼ teaspoon vanilla extract (essence)

FOR THE FILLING

2½ lb (1.25 kg) cream cheese
1¾ cups (14 oz/440 g) sugar
3 tablespoons all-purpose (plain) flour
1½ teaspoons finely grated lemon peel
1½ teaspoons finely grated orange peel
¼ teaspoon vanilla extract (essence)
5 eggs plus 2 egg yolks
¼ cup (2 fl oz/60 ml) cream

❧ To prepare the pastry, combine the flour with the sugar, lemon peel and orange peel in a large bowl. Cut in the butter until the texture of coarse crumbs. Stir in the egg yolk and vanilla to form a soft dough. Chill for at least 1 hour.
❧ Preheat the oven to 400°F (200°C). Roll out the pastry on a floured board to ⅛ in (3 mm) thick. Cut out a 9-in (23-cm) circle; refrigerate the trimmings. Place the circle of dough over the bottom of a greased 9-in (23-cm) springform pan. (If the pastry is too soft to roll, refrigerate it longer or pat half over the bottom of the pan with your fingers.) Bake the pastry until golden, about 20 minutes. Let cool on wire rack.
❧ To prepare the filling, beat the cream cheese with the sugar, flour, lemon peel, orange peel and vanilla in the large bowl of an electric mixer. Add the eggs and egg yolks, one at a time, beating thoroughly after each addition. Stir in the cream.
❧ Increase the oven temperature to 550°F (290°C) or highest temperature of the oven. Grease the sides of the springform pan. Roll out the reserved pastry trimmings and cut into strips 2 in (5 cm) wide. Pat the strips into place against the sides of the pan, pressing an edge into the bottom crust. Fill immediately with the cream cheese mixture. Bake for 12 minutes. Reduce the oven temperature to 200°F (95°C); bake for 1 hour. Let the cake cool on wire rack. Refrigerate for at least 2 hours before serving.

SERVES 8 TO 10 *Photograph pages 206 – 207*

PHILADELPHIA ICE CREAM (left) AND RHUBARB PIE (right)

Colorado

RHUBARB PIE

In the 1800s rhubarb pie was so popular that rhubarb was often referred to as the "pie plant." It grows extremely well at higher elevations, as in Alaska and Colorado, and thrives to such a degree in Silverton, Colorado, that they celebrate every 4th of July with a rhubarb festival.

FOR THE PASTRY

2 cups (8 oz/250 g) all-purpose (plain) flour
2 teaspoons sugar
½ teaspoon salt
½ cup (4 oz/125 g) cold lard
¼ cup (2 oz/60 g) cold solid vegetable shortening
   (vegetable lard)
1 egg, lightly beaten
1½ teaspoons red wine vinegar
2 tablespoons cold water

FOR THE FILLING

2½ cups (10 oz/315 g) cubed fresh rhubarb (about 3 stalks)
½ teaspoon ground cinnamon
3 tablespoons all-purpose (plain) flour
¼ teaspoon grated lemon peel
pinch of grated orange peel
⅛ teaspoon salt
1¼ cups (10 oz/315 g) sugar
3 tablespoons (1½ oz/50 g) unsalted butter, melted
3 eggs, lightly beaten

❦ To make the pastry, combine the flour with the sugar and salt in a bowl. Cut in the lard and shortening until the texture of coarse crumbs. Add the beaten egg, vinegar and water, a tablespoon at a time, and mix gently with a fork to form a soft dough. Chill for 1 hour.
❦ Preheat the oven to 400°F (200°C). Roll out slightly more than half the pastry on a lightly floured board and line a deep 9-in (23-cm) pie pan or 10-in (25-cm) loose-bottom tart pan with the pastry. Cover the pastry with aluminum foil and weight with rice or beans. Bake for 10 minutes. Remove the foil and let cool.
❦ To make the filling, combine the rhubarb, cinnamon, flour, lemon peel, orange peel, salt, sugar and butter in a large bowl; mix well and let stand for 5 minutes. Turn into the prepared shell. Pour the eggs over the filling.
❦ Roll out the remaining pastry and cut into strips ½ in (1 cm) wide. Arrange over the pie in a lattice pattern, pressing the ends to the shell. Sprinkle lightly with a spoonful of sugar. Bake for 15 minutes. Reduce the oven temperature to 350°F (180°C) and bake 45 minutes longer. Let cool on a wire rack.

SERVES 8

Pennsylvania

PHILADELPHIA ICE CREAM

Ice cream is one of America's favorite foods, and judging by the myriad new ice cream products appearing in markets daily, it is bound to stay that way. Philadelphia became renowned for its rich, creamy ice creams. True American-style ice creams contain no egg custards.

2 cups (16 fl oz/500 ml) light (single) cream or half & half
   (half cream and half milk)
¾ to 1 cup (6–8 oz/180–250 g) sugar (according to taste)
2 cups (16 fl oz/500 ml) heavy (double) cream
2 teaspoons vanilla extract (essence)

❦ Combine the light cream with the sugar in a saucepan and stir over low heat just until the sugar dissolves. Do not let boil. Let cool and stir in the heavy cream and vanilla. Pour into the canister of an ice cream freezer and proceed according to the manufacturer's directions.

MAKES ABOUT 1½ QT (1.5 L)

and cold milk in a small bowl; stir into egg yolk mixture. Whisk in the hot milk. Cook over boiling water, stirring constantly, until thick enough to coat a spoon, about 30 minutes. Beat in the butter by bits. Beat in the vanilla. Let cool slightly, then cover with wax paper and refrigerate until cold.

❦ Preheat the oven to 400°F (200°C). Roll out three-fourths of the dough on a floured board into a large circle. Line a 9-in (23-cm) pie pan with the pastry (it is fragile, so patience is a must). The pastry should hang over the edge of the pan by about ½ in (1 cm). Spoon the custard into the shell.

❦ Roll out the remaining dough between 2 sheets of lightly floured wax paper to a 10-in (25-cm) circle (it will be paper-thin). Remove the top piece of wax paper. Invert the pastry onto the custard and gently remove the remaining paper. Carefully tuck the pastry inside the edge with a spoon. Fold the overhanging edge of the bottom pastry up over the top. Press the edges lightly with a fork. Bake until golden, 25 to 30 minutes. Let cool completely on a wire rack.

SERVES 8

Maine

ICEBOX BLUEBERRY PIE

Maine is blueberry country, and this open-faced icebox pie makes a refreshing dessert in blueberry season. Although icebox pies, which originated in the 1920s, often have a custard base, this one is pure and simple.

FOR THE PASTRY

1¼ cups (5 oz/155 g) all-purpose (plain) flour
¼ teaspoon salt
¼ cup (2 oz/60 g) cold unsalted butter
¼ cup (2 oz/60 g) solid vegetable shortening (vegetable lard)
½ teaspoon grated orange peel
2 to 3 tablespoons cold orange juice

FOR THE FILLING

¾ cup (6 oz/185 g) sugar
2½ tablespoons cornstarch (cornflour)
¼ teaspoon salt
⅔ cup (5 fl oz/160 ml) water
3 cups (12 oz/375 g) fresh blueberries, picked over
2 tablespoons (1 oz/30 g) unsalted butter
1½ tablespoons lemon juice
1½ tablespoons Grand Marnier liqueur
sweetened whipped cream (optional)

❦ To make the pastry, combine the flour with the salt in a large bowl. Cut in the butter and shortening and sprinkle with the orange peel. Blend until the texture of coarse crumbs. Add the orange juice, a tablespoon at a time, and mix gently with a fork to form a soft dough. Chill for 1 hour.

❦ Preheat the oven to 425°F (220°C). Roll out the pastry on a lightly floured board and line a 9-in (23-cm) pie pan with the pastry. Trim and flute the edges. Cover the pastry with aluminum foil and weight with rice or beans. Bake for 10 minutes. Remove the foil and bake 5 minutes longer. Let cool on a wire rack.

❦ To make the filling, combine the sugar with the cornstarch and salt in a saucepan. Add the water and 1 cup (4 oz/125 g) of the blueberries. Heat to boiling, stirring constantly; boil until very thick, about 15 minutes. Remove from the heat and stir in the butter, lemon juice and Grand Marnier. Let cool.

❦ Stir the remaining blueberries into the cooked blueberry mixture. Refrigerate for 1 hour. Spoon into the pastry shell and refrigerate at least 1 hour before serving. Garnish with whipped cream if desired.

SERVES 6 TO 8

Louisiana

CAJUN CUSTARD TART

Double-crusted custard tarts are a specialty of the Cajuns in Louisiana. This recipe has been handed down in the Bourque family in New Iberia from generation to generation for well over a hundred years.

FOR THE PASTRY

3 tablespoons (1½ oz/50 g) solid vegetable shortening
    (vegetable lard), softened
⅓ cup (3 oz/90 g) sugar
1 egg
2 tablespoons milk
2 teaspoons vanilla extract (essence)
1 teaspoon baking powder
1 to 1½ cups (6 oz/185 g) all-purpose (plain) flour

FOR THE FILLING

2 egg yolks
⅓ cup (3 oz/90 g) sugar
3 tablespoons cornstarch (cornflour)
1 teaspoon ground ginger
2 tablespoons cold milk
2 cups (16 fl oz/500 ml) hot milk
2 tablespoons (1 oz/30 g) cold unsalted butter
1 teaspoon vanilla extract (essence)

❦ To make the pastry, beat the shortening with the sugar in a large bowl until smooth. Beat in the egg until smooth, then the milk and vanilla. Stir in the baking powder and enough flour to make a stiff dough. Refrigerate for 4 hours or overnight.

❦ To make the filling, beat the egg yolks with the sugar in the top of a double boiler until light. Mix the cornstarch, ginger

Massachusetts

BOSTON CREAM PIE

Not a pie at all, Boston cream pie is really a plain butter cake filled with custard. According to food sleuth John Mariani, it dates back to early American history. When it is filled with chocolate custard, it is known as Parker House pie.

FOR THE CAKE

½ cup (4 oz/125 g) unsalted butter, softened
1¼ cups (10 oz/315 g) sugar
2 eggs, separated
1 teaspoon vanilla extract (essence)
2 cups (8 oz/250 g) sifted cake or soft wheat flour (or plain flour, substituting cornflour for 2½ tablespoons flour)
2 teaspoons baking powder
¼ teaspoon baking soda (bicarbonate of soda)
¼ teaspoon salt
¾ cup (6 fl oz/180 ml) milk

FOR THE CUSTARD

1 cup (8 fl oz/250 ml) light (single) cream or half & half (half cream and half milk)
⅓ cup (3 oz/90 g) sugar
3 tablespoons flour
pinch of salt
2 egg yolks
1 teaspoon vanilla extract (essence)
powdered (icing) sugar

❧ Preheat the oven to 350°F (180°C). To make the cake, beat the butter with the sugar in the large bowl of an electric mixer until light and fluffy. Add the egg yolks, one at a time, beating thoroughly after each addition. Beat in the vanilla.

❧ Sift the flour with the baking powder, baking soda and salt. Add to the batter in 3 parts, alternating with the milk. Beat the egg whites until stiff and fold into the batter.

❧ Pour the batter into 2 greased and floured 9-in (23-cm) round cake pans. Bake until a toothpick inserted in the center comes out clean, 25 to 30 minutes. Let cool before unmolding.

❧ To make the custard, scald the cream and remove from the heat. Combine the sugar, flour and salt in another saucepan. Add the hot cream and whisk until smooth. Cook over medium heat, stirring constantly, until very thick. Remove from the heat and beat in the egg yolks. Place over low heat and continue to cook, stirring constantly, for 4 minutes. Beat in the vanilla. Let cool, stirring occasionally. Cover and refrigerate until well chilled.

❧ Spread the custard over one of the cake layers. Place the other layer on top. Refrigerate until ready to serve. Dust with powdered sugar before serving.

SERVES 8 TO 10

Tennessee

STRAWBERRY SHORTCAKE

Shortcake gets it name from the "short" dough, generally made with lard, that is the basis of this dessert. Shortcake can be made in individual servings using any short biscuit dough, or, as was more typical in days gone by, it can be made in one large, stunning presentation. Fresh peaches may be used instead of strawberries.

2½ cups (10 oz/315 g) all-purpose (plain) flour
½ cup (4 oz/125 g) sugar
4 teaspoons baking powder
½ teaspoon salt
3 oz (90 g) cream cheese

STRAWBERRY SHORTCAKE

3 tablespoons (1½ oz/50 g) cold unsalted butter, plus 2 tablespoons, melted
1 egg, lightly beaten
2 tablespoons sour cream
1¾ cups (14 fl oz/430 ml) cream
1 qt (1 lb/500 g) fresh strawberries, cleaned and hulled (stemmed)
2 tablespoons Grand Marnier liqueur
1 tablespoon powdered (icing) sugar

❧ Preheat the oven to 450°F (230°C). Combine the flour with ¼ cup (2 oz/60 g) of the sugar, the baking powder and salt in a large bowl. Cut in the cream cheese and cold butter until the texture of coarse crumbs.

❧ Whisk the egg with the sour cream and ¾ cup (6 fl oz/180 ml) of the cream in a bowl. Stir into the flour mixture to form a soft dough. Divide the dough in half. Press out one half on a lightly floured board to an 8-in (20-cm) circle. Place in a greased 8-in (20-cm) cake pan. Smooth with your fingertips. Press out the second half and place on top of the dough already in the pan. Drizzle with the melted butter and bake for 20 minutes. Turn off the heat and, with the oven door ajar, leave the biscuit in the oven for 1 hour. Transfer to a rack. Split apart when cool. Transfer to a large serving platter.

❧ Lightly crush half the berries. Combine with the whole berries, ¼ cup (2 oz/60 g) sugar and the Grand Marnier. Cover and refrigerate.

❧ Just before serving, beat the remaining 1 cup (8 fl oz/250 ml) cream with the powdered sugar until stiff. Spoon slightly more than half the berries over the bottom shortcake layer. Place the other layer on top and spoon the remaining berries over the top. Cover with the whipped cream.

SERVES 8

Mississippi

MISSISSIPPI MUD CAKE

Craig Claiborne, who grew up in the Mississippi Delta, once remarked that he had never heard of this cake until he moved to the North and therefore assumes that it is a fairly recent devise. This black cake is rich and dense, just like the muddy banks of the Mississippi River.

unsweetened cocoa
1¼ cups (10 fl oz/310 ml) strong brewed coffee
¼ cup (2 fl oz/60 ml) bourbon
5 oz (155 g) unsweetened (bitter cooking) chocolate
1 cup (8 oz/250 g) unsalted butter, cut into pieces
2 cups (1 lb/500 g) sugar
2 cups (8 oz/250 g) all-purpose (plain) flour
1 teaspoon baking soda (bicarbonate of soda)
⅛ teaspoon salt
2 eggs, lightly beaten
1 teaspoon vanilla extract (essence)
powdered (icing) sugar
sweetened whipped cream (optional)

❧ Preheat the oven to 275°F (135°C). Butter a 9-in (23-cm) tube pan (3½ in/9 cm deep) and dust the bottom and sides with cocoa.

❧ Heat the coffee and bourbon in a heavy saucepan over low heat. Add the chocolate and butter. Cook, stirring constantly, until smooth. Remove from the heat and stir in the sugar. Let stand for 5 minutes. Transfer to the bowl of an electric mixer.

❧ Sift the flour with baking soda and salt. Beat into the chocolate mixture (on low speed) in 4 parts. Add the eggs and vanilla. Beat until smooth. Pour into the tube pan.

❧ Bake the cake until a toothpick inserted in the center comes out clean, about 1½ hours. Let cool completely on a wire rack before unmolding. Sprinkle with powdered sugar and serve with whipped cream if desired.

SERVES 10

Georgia

PECAN PIE

Pecans are native to North America and grow along the rivers of the lower Midwest and the South, extending into Texas. Georgia pecans are particularly prized for their flavor. These nuts were important not only to the Indians who lived in these areas, but to the settlers, who quickly learned to appreciate them. Pecan pie, of course, is one of the great southern desserts.

FOR THE PASTRY

1½ cups (6 oz/185 g) all-purpose (plain) flour
¼ teaspoon salt
6 tablespoons (3 oz/90 g) cold unsalted butter
2 tablespoons plus 1 teaspoon cold solid vegetable shortening (vegetable lard)
3 to 4 tablespoons cold water

MISSISSIPPI MUD CAKE (top) AND PECAN PIE (bottom)

VILLEROY & BOCH; CLAIRE'S ANTIQUE LINEN AND GIFTS

FOR THE FILLING

3 eggs
2 tablespoons (1 oz/30 g) unsalted butter, melted
2 tablespoons all-purpose (plain) flour
½ teaspoon vanilla extract (essence)
⅛ teaspoon salt
½ cup (4 oz/125 g) sugar
1½ cups (12 fl oz/375 ml) dark corn (or golden) syrup
1½ cups (6 oz/185 g) chopped pecans
½ cup (2 oz/60 g) unbroken pecan halves
sweetened whipped cream (optional)

❧To make the pastry, combine the flour with the salt in a large bowl. Cut in the butter and shortening until the texture of coarse crumbs. Add the water, a tablespoon at a time, and mix gently with a fork to form a soft dough. Do not overwork. Chill for 1 hour.

❧ Preheat the oven to 425°F (220°C). Roll out the pastry on a lightly floured board and line a 9-in (23-cm) pie pan with the pastry. Trim and flute the edges.

❧To make the filling, beat the eggs in a large bowl until light. Whisk in the butter, flour, vanilla, salt, sugar and corn syrup.

❧Sprinkle the chopped pecans over the bottom of the pastry shell. Gently pour the egg mixture over the pecans. Make a ring of unbroken pecan halves around the edge. Make another ring inside and continue until the surface is covered. Bake for 10 minutes. Reduce the oven temperature to 325°F (165°C) and bake 40 minutes longer. Let cool on a wire rack. Serve garnished with sweetened whipped cream if desired.

SERVES 8

California

CHOCOLATE BEETROOT CAKE

An old chocolate confection, this cake depends on pureed beets to keep it moist. The recipe was brought to California from the Midwest by covered wagon more than a century ago and is just as miraculous today as it was then.

3 oz (90 g) semisweet (plain) chocolate
1 cup (8 fl oz/250 ml) vegetable oil
1¾ cups (14 oz/435 g) sugar
3 eggs
2 cups (1 lb/500 g) pureed cooked or canned beets (beetroot)
1 teaspoon vanilla extract (essence)
2 cups (8 oz/250 g) sifted all-purpose (plain) flour
2 teaspoons baking soda (bicarbonate of soda)
¼ teaspoon salt
powdered (icing) sugar

❧ Preheat the oven to 375°F (190°C). Melt the chocolate with ¼ cup (2 fl oz/60 ml) of the oil in the top of a double boiler over hot water. Let cool slightly.

❧Beat the sugar with the eggs in the large bowl of an electric mixer until light and fluffy. Slowly beat in the remaining ¾ cup (6 fl oz/180 ml) oil, the beets, chocolate mixture and vanilla.

❧ Sift the flour with the baking soda and salt. Slowly stir into the batter. Pour the batter into a greased and floured 10-cup Bundt (ring-shaped) pan. Bake until a toothpick inserted in the center comes out clean, about 1 hour. Let cool on wire rack for 15 minutes before unmolding. Dust with powdered sugar.

SERVES 8

Massachusetts

FUDGE

It is said that fudge was first made in New England women's colleges before the turn of the century. The young ladies, it seems, used the excuse of candy making to stay up late, "fudging" a bit on their studies. Fudge is tricky to make, and so it is best to use a candy thermometer for good results.

unsalted butter
2 cups (1 lb/500 g) sugar
¾ cup (6 fl oz/180 ml) milk
2 oz (60 g) unsweetened (bitter cooking) chocolate
pinch of salt
1 teaspoon corn (or golden) syrup
1 teaspoon vanilla extract (essence)
½ cup (2 oz/60 g) roughly chopped pecans

❦ Generously butter an 8-in (20-cm) square cake pan. Set aside.
❦ Butter the sides of a 1½–2 qt (1.5–2 l) saucepan and add the sugar, milk, chocolate, salt and corn syrup to the pan. Attach a candy (sugar) thermometer. Place over medium heat and stir frequently until boiling. Reduce the heat slightly and gently boil, without stirring, until the thermometer reads 238°F (115°C), about 20 minutes. The mixture will form a soft ball if dropped into cold water.
❦ Remove the pan from the heat and dot with 2 tablespoons butter. Do not stir. Allow the mixture to cool to 165°F (75°C), about 20 minutes. Add the vanilla and beat vigorously until the fudge has lost its gloss. Stir in the nuts and immediately spread the fudge into the prepared pan. Let cool completely on a rack. Cut into 1½-in (4-cm) squares and store in an airtight container.

MAKES 25 PIECES

Massachusetts

CHOCOLATE CHIP COOKIES

When chocolate chip cookies were introduced about sixty years ago (for the story, see page 209), they were such a success that the Nestle Company began packaging chocolate chips in 1939. The original Toll House recipe was printed on the package, which is why these are often called Toll House cookies.

1 cup (4 oz/125 g) plus 2 tablespoons sifted all-purpose (plain) flour
½ teaspoon baking soda (bicarbonate of soda)
½ teaspoon salt
½ cup (4 oz/125 g) unsalted butter, softened
6 tablespoons (3 oz/90 g) sugar
6 tablespoons (3 oz/90 g) packed light brown sugar
½ teaspoon vanilla extract (essence)
¼ teaspoon water
1 egg
1 cup (6 oz/185 g) semisweet (plain) chocolate chips
½ cup (2 oz/60 g) chopped nuts

❦ Preheat the oven to 375°F (190°C). Sift the flour with the baking soda and salt.
❦ Beat the butter with the sugars, vanilla, water and egg in a large bowl until creamy. Stir in the flour mixture; mix thoroughly. Stir in the chocolate chips and nuts.
❦ Drop the cookie dough by tablespoons onto greased baking sheets. Bake for 10 to 12 minutes. Cool on the baking sheet for a few minutes before transferring to a wire rack to cool completely.

MAKES ABOUT 24 COOKIES

Maine

BROWNIES

One story about brownies credits a former librarian in Maine with the invention when she forgot to add baking powder to her chocolate cake. Undaunted by the flatness of her failure, she cut the pieces into squares and had an instant hit on her hands. The librarian, by the way, was named Brownie Schrumpf.

2 oz (60 g) unsweetened (bitter cooking) chocolate
½ cup (4 oz/125 g) unsalted butter, cut into pieces
2 eggs
1 cup (8 oz/250 g) sugar
1 teaspoon vanilla extract (essence)
½ cup (2 oz/60 g) all-purpose (plain) flour
pinch of salt
¼ cup (2 oz/60 g) sour cream
⅔ cup (3 oz/90 g) chopped walnuts

❦ Preheat the oven to 325°F (165°C). Melt the chocolate with the butter in the top of a double boiler over hot water. Let cool slightly.
❦ Beat the eggs with the sugar in a large bowl until light. Slowly beat in the chocolate mixture. Stir in the vanilla. Sift in the flour, 2 tablespoons at a time, mixing well after each addition. Stir in the salt, sour cream and walnuts.
❦ Pour the batter into a greased 8-in (20-cm) square cake pan. Bake until a toothpick inserted in the center comes out fairly clean, 25 to 30 minutes. The center should be slightly cakey. Let cool completely on a wire rack before cutting into bars.

MAKES ABOUT 20 BROWNIES

Missouri

ANGEL FOOD CAKE

Angel food cake depends solely on beaten egg whites for its airy texture. Although it has been around since the late 1800s, no one is quite sure who invented the recipe. Some say it comes from Pennsylvania Dutch country, while others claim it originated in the southern regions of Missouri.

1 cup (4 oz/125 g) sifted cake flour (or plain flour, substituting cornflour for 2 tablespoons flour)
1½ cups (12 oz/375 g) sugar
1¼ cups (10 fl oz/310 ml) egg whites (about 10 eggs), room temperature
1¼ teaspoons cream of tartar
¼ teaspoon salt
1 teaspoon vanilla extract (essence)
¼ teaspoon almond extract (essence)
powdered (icing) sugar

❦ Preheat the oven to 325°F (165°C). Sift the flour with ½ cup (4 oz/125 g) of the sugar 3 times.
❦ Beat the egg whites in the large bowl of an electric mixer until foamy. Add the cream of tartar and salt and beat until soft peaks form. Beat in the remaining 1 cup (8 oz/250 g) sugar on high speed, about 2 tablespoons at a time, beating well after each addition. Add the vanilla and almond extracts. The egg whites will be stiff and glossy.
❦ Sift about 4 tablespoons of the flour-sugar mixture over the egg whites and fold in until no flour shows. Repeat until all of it has been incorporated.
❦ Pour into an ungreased angel cake pan. Bake until a toothpick inserted in the center comes out clean, about 1 hour. Invert the pan and let the cake cool completely before unmolding. Dust with powdered sugar before serving.

SERVES 8 TO 10   *Photograph page 222*

CHOCOLATE CHIP COOKIES (top),
BROWNIES (left) AND FUDGE (right)

ANGEL FOOD CAKE (top left, recipe page 220), LACE COOKIES (bottom) AND BENNE WAFERS (on top of lace cookies and curled wafers, top right)

North Carolina

BENNE WAFERS

It is said that African slaves brought sesame seeds to this country for good luck. Since then, good cooks in the South use benne seeds (their original name) in everything, including the following regional cookie.

1 egg
½ teaspoon vanilla extract (essence)
6 tablespoons (3 oz/90 g) unsalted butter, melted
¾ cup (4 oz/125 g) light brown sugar
¼ cup (1 oz/30 g) all-purpose (plain) flour
½ cup (2 oz/60 g) chopped pecans
½ cup (2 oz/60 g) toasted white sesame seeds

❧ Preheat the oven to 400°F (200°C). Beat the egg with the vanilla in the bowl of an electric mixer. Slowly beat in the butter. Beat in the sugar on medium speed until light. Beat in the flour on low speed in 3 parts. Stir in the pecans and sesame seeds.
❧ Lightly grease a baking sheet lined with aluminum foil. Drop teaspoons of cookie batter onto the foil, placing them far apart. There should be only 6 cookies on each baking sheet, as they will spread. Bake until golden brown, 5 to 7 minutes. Remove the foil from the baking sheet. Let the cookies cool completely on the foil on a wire rack before peeling off the foil. Repeat until all the dough is used.

MAKES ABOUT 24 COOKIES

South Carolina

LACE COOKIES

Another southern specialty, lace cookies are the ultimate in oatmeal cookies. The batter is thin and the finished cookies have lacy edges.

1 egg
½ teaspoon vanilla extract (essence)
½ cup (4 oz/125 g) unsalted butter, melted
1 cup (5½ oz/170 g) light brown sugar
2 cups (6 oz/185 g) rolled oats
½ cup (2 oz/60 g) chopped walnuts

❧ Preheat the oven to 375°F (190°C). Beat the egg with the vanilla in the bowl of an electric mixer. Slowly beat in the butter. Beat in the sugar until light. Beat in the rolled oats on low speed. Stir in the walnuts.
❧ Lightly grease a baking sheet lined with aluminum foil. Drop the batter by generous teaspoons onto the foil, placing far apart. There should be only 6 cookies on each baking sheet. Spread the cookie dough flat; do not mound. Bake until golden brown, about 8 minutes. Remove the foil from the baking sheet. Let the cookies cool completely on the foil on a wire rack before peeling off the foil. Repeat until all the dough is used.

MAKES ABOUT 24 COOKIES

Rhode Island

INDIAN PUDDING

The first colonial versions of Indian pudding were most probably made with water, cornmeal, honey, suet and lots of ginger. The recipe evolved, however, as other ingredients became available. The amount of ginger in the following recipe makes the dessert reminiscent of pumpkin pie.

1 cup (8 fl oz/250 ml) water
½ cup (3 oz/90 g) yellow cornmeal
3 cups (24 fl oz/750 ml) cold milk
2 tablespoons (1 oz/30 g) unsalted butter
¼ teaspoon salt
½ cup (4 fl oz/125 ml) molasses (or treacle)
1 teaspoon ground ginger
1 egg, lightly beaten

❧ Preheat the oven to 325°F (165°C). Whisk the water with the cornmeal in a heavy saucepan until smooth. Place over medium-high heat and stir constantly until boiling. Whisk in the milk and reduce the heat to medium. Heat to boiling once more, stirring constantly, about 5 minutes. Reduce the heat to low. Gently simmer, stirring frequently, for 15 minutes. The mixture will be like a thick, creamy porridge. Whisk in the butter and salt and remove from the heat. Let stand, stirring occasionally, for 10 minutes.
❧ Whisk the molasses into the cornmeal mixture until well incorporated. Add the ginger and beaten egg. Transfer to a greased 1½- to 2-qt (1½- to 2-l) baking dish. Bake until firm, about 1½ hours. Let cool on a wire rack. The pudding will thicken as it cools. Serve with cream.

SERVES 8

Louisiana

NEW ORLEANS BREAD PUDDING

Bread pudding recipes came to this country with the English, but at first, of course, there was no bread for making them. Indian puddings of cornmeal had to suffice until flour became available. Bread puddings are now standard American fare. This one originated at Chez Helene, a

INDIAN PUDDING (top) AND NEW ORLEANS BREAD PUDDING (bottom)

soul food establishment in New Orleans. It is not the standard bread pudding served at diners around the country, but it is incredibly delicious and deserves a place in any book on regional cookery.

1 loaf of stale French or Italian-style bread (8–10 oz/250–300 g),
    torn into pieces
2½ cups (20 fl oz/625 ml) milk
1 cup (8 oz/250 g) unsalted butter, softened
2 cups (1 lb/500 g) sugar
1 can (13 fl oz/410 ml) evaporated milk
2 tablespoons freshly grated nutmeg
2 tablespoons vanilla extract (essence)
1 cup (5 oz/155 g) raisins (or sultanas)
hard sauce (recipe follows)

❧ Preheat the oven to 350°F (180°C). Combine the bread with the milk in a large bowl. Let stand for 10 minutes.
❧ Beat the butter with the sugar in a large bowl until light and fluffy. Beat in the evaporated milk, nutmeg and vanilla. Stir in the soaked bread and the raisins.

❧ Pour the mixture into a deep 3- to 4-qt (3- to 4-l) baking dish. Place the dish on a baking sheet and bake for 1 hour. Gently stir the mixture with a wooden spoon. Continue to bake until all the liquid is absorbed, about 1 hour longer. Serve while still warm with hard sauce.

SERVES 8 TO 10

HARD SAUCE

½ cup (4 oz/125 g) unsalted butter, softened
1 cup (6 oz/185 g) powdered (icing) sugar
3 tablespoons dark rum

❧ Beat the butter with the sugar in a large bowl until light and fluffy. Beat in the rum. Cover and refrigerate. Remove from the refrigerator at least 30 minutes before serving, to allow the sauce to soften.

MAKES ABOUT 2 CUPS (1 PT/500 ML)

OLD-FASHIONED CHOCOLATE LAYER CAKE

Illinois

OLD-FASHIONED CHOCOLATE LAYER CAKE

Chocolate layer cakes began appearing in cookbooks in the 1880s. At first they were regarded with suspicion by the general populace. Not because of the chocolate in the cakes, but because the baking sodas and powders used for leavening were still new and highly mistrusted.

FOR THE CAKE

4 oz (125 g) semisweet (plain) chocolate
1¼ cups (10 fl oz/310 ml) milk
2 cups (10 oz/315 ml) light brown sugar
1 teaspoon vanilla extract (essence)
3 eggs, separated
2 cups (10 oz/315 g) sifted cake or soft wheat flour (or plain flour, substituting cornflour for 2½ tablespoons flour)
1 teaspoon baking soda (bicarbonate of soda)
½ teaspoon salt
½ cup (4 oz/125 g) unsalted butter, softened

FOR THE ICING

3 oz (90 g) unsweetened (bitter cooking) chocolate
1 can (14 oz/440 g) sweetened condensed milk
½ cup (4 oz/125 g) unsalted butter, cut into pieces
1 egg yolk, lightly beaten
1½ teaspoons vanilla extract (essence)

❦ Preheat the oven to 350°F (180°C). To make the cake, combine the chocolate, milk, brown sugar, vanilla and 1 egg yolk in the top of a double boiler. Cook, stirring over hot water until smooth. Remove from the heat and let cool.
❦ Sift the flour with the baking soda and salt.
❦ Beat the butter in the large bowl of an electric mixer until light. Add the remaining 2 egg yolks, one at a time, beating

thoroughly after each addition. Beat in the chocolate mixture in 3 parts, alternating with the flour mixture. Do not overbeat.
❦ Beat the egg whites until stiff; fold into the batter.
❦ Pour the batter into 2 greased and floured 9-in (23-cm) round cake pans. Bake until a toothpick inserted in the center comes out fairly clean, 25 to 30 minutes. Let cool on a wire rack before unmolding.
❦ To make the icing, melt the chocolate in the top of a double boiler over hot water. Stir in the condensed milk until smooth. Stir in the butter, bit by bit, until smooth. Whisk in the egg yolk and vanilla and cook until slightly thickened. Let cool slightly, then smooth over the bottom layer; place other layer on top, then ice the sides and top of the cake.

SERVES 8 TO 10

Pennsylvania

FUNERAL PIE

Raisin pie was once served at so many funeral suppers by the Pennsylvania Dutch that it became known as "funeral pie." Although the Amish still hold to this tradition, today many descendants of the Pennsylvania Dutch eat it on joyous occasions as well.

FOR THE PASTRY

2½ cups (10 oz/315 g) all-purpose (plain) flour
1 teaspoon sugar
½ teaspoon salt
½ cup (4 oz/125 g) cold unsalted butter
½ cup (4 oz/125 g) cold solid vegetable shortening (vegetable lard)
¼ cup (2 fl oz/60 ml) cold water

FOR THE FILLING

2 cups (10 oz/315 g) raisins
1 cup (8 fl oz/250 ml) orange juice
1 cup (8 fl oz/250 ml) water
1 teaspoon grated orange peel
¾ cup (6 oz/185 g) plus 1 tablespoon sugar
2 tablespoons cornstarch (cornflour)
¾ teaspoon ground allspice
⅛ teaspoon freshly grated nutmeg
1 tablespoon lemon juice
½ cup (2 oz/60 g) chopped walnuts
1 egg, beaten
whipped cream or vanilla ice cream

❦ To make the pastry, combine the flour with the sugar and salt in a bowl. Cut in the butter and shortening until the texture of coarse crumbs. Add the water, a tablespoon at a time, and mix gently with a fork to form a soft dough. Chill for 1 hour.
❦ Preheat the oven to 425°F (220°C). Roll out half the dough on a lightly floured board. Line a 9-in (23-cm) pie pan with the pastry.
❦ To make the filling, combine the raisins, orange juice, water and orange peel in a saucepan. Heat to boiling, reduce the heat and simmer for 5 minutes.
❦ Combine the ¾ cup (6 oz/185 g) sugar with the cornstarch, allspice and nutmeg. Stir slowly into the raisin mixture. Cook, stirring constantly, until thickened, about 2 minutes. Stir in the lemon juice and walnuts. Pour into the pastry shell.
❦ Roll out the remaining pastry and place over the pie. Seal, trim and flute the edges. Cut several slashes in the top pastry to release steam. Brush with beaten egg and sprinkle with the remaining 1 tablespoon sugar. Bake until golden, 20 to 25 minutes. Serve warm with whipped cream or vanilla ice cream.

SERVES 8

South Carolina

BAKED RICE PUDDING

A taste for rice pudding was brought here by the English, who were stirring up rice puddings long before the sixteenth century. Although generally made with leftovers, rice pudding is worth making anytime for its own merits. The following is an adaptation of an old Alice B. Toklas recipe. Half a cup of raisins may be added before baking.

8 egg yolks
1 cup (8 oz/250 g) sugar
5 tablespoons all-purpose (plain) flour
2 cups (16 fl oz/500 ml) milk, scalded
1 teaspoon vanilla extract (essence)
1½ cups cooked rice (3 oz/90 g uncooked)
3 egg whites
vanilla sauce (recipe follows)

❧ Preheat the oven to 350°F (180°C). Beat the egg yolks in the large bowl of an electric mixer until light and lemon-colored. Sift the sugar with the flour; gradually add to the yolks. Beat for 10 minutes. Slowly add the scalded milk.

❧ Transfer the mixture to the top of a double boiler. Cook, stirring constantly, over hot water until thick enough to coat a wooden spoon. Strain into a large bowl. Beat in the vanilla. Stir in the rice.

❧ Beat the egg whites until stiff but not dry; fold into the rice mixture. Pour into a greased 2-qt (2-l) soufflé dish. Bake for 25 to 30 minutes; the center should be slightly wet. Serve slightly warm or well chilled with vanilla sauce.

SERVES 8   *Photograph page 225*

VANILLA SAUCE

6 egg yolks
1 cup (8 oz/250 g) sugar
2¼ cups (18 fl oz/560 ml) milk, scalded
1 teaspoon vanilla extract (essence)
1 tablespoon kirsch liqueur
½ cup (4 fl oz/125 ml) cream, whipped

❧ Beat the yolks with the sugar in the top of a double boiler. Whisk in the milk. Cook, stirring constantly, over hot water until thick, about 30 minutes. Remove from the heat. Whisk in the vanilla. Let cool to room temperature.

❧ Stir the kirsch into the sauce. Fold in the cream. Refrigerate until chilled.

MAKES 3½ TO 4 CUPS (1 QT/1 L)

Georgia

PEANUT BRITTLE

Peanut brittle appeared in the South around the turn of the nineteenth century. Peanut stands were selling roasted peanuts by the 1860s, and it was not long before "brittle" (referring to the texture of this candy) made its way into southern hearts (and mouths) of all ages.

3 cups (1 lb/500 g) raw shelled peanuts
1½ teaspoons baking soda (bicarbonate of soda)
½ teaspoon salt
2 cups (1 lb/500 g) sugar
1 cup (8 fl oz/250 ml) light corn (or golden) syrup
½ cup (4 fl oz/125 ml) water
¼ cup (2 oz/60 g) unsalted butter

❧ Preheat the oven to 350°F (180°C). Spread the peanuts in a 10- by 5-in (25- by 13-cm) baking pan. Bake for 15 minutes. Transfer to a bowl and keep warm.

❧ Combine the baking soda and salt and set aside.

PEANUT BRITTLE (top) AND SWEET POTATO PIE (bottom)

❧ Combine the sugar, corn syrup and water in a saucepan. Heat to boiling; boil rapidly until the syrup begins to turn golden, 275°F (135°C) on a candy (sugar) thermometer. Add the nuts and continue to cook, stirring frequently, until the syrup is a clear gold color (295°F/145°C). Remove from the heat and quickly stir in the butter and the baking soda mixture. Immediately pour into the baking pan. Let cool for 2 hours before breaking into pieces.

MAKES ABOUT 2¼ LB (1.12 KG)

Virginia

SWEET POTATO PIE

Southerners have a long tradition of making sweet potato pies. The sweet potato has traveled under various names in the past, including Virginia potato, Indian potato, Tuckahoc, long potato and hog potato.

FOR THE PASTRY

1¼ cups (5 oz/155 g) all-purpose (plain) flour
¼ teaspoon salt
¼ cup (2 oz/60 g) cold unsalted butter
¼ cup (2 oz/60 g) cold solid vegetable shortening
    (vegetable lard)
2 to 3 tablespoons cold water

FOR THE FILLING

2 cups mashed cooked sweet potatoes (about 2 small potatoes)
2 eggs, beaten

1¼ cups (10 fl oz/310 ml) milk
¼ cup (2 oz/60 g) light brown sugar
½ cup (4 oz/125 g) sugar
¼ teaspoon salt
½ teaspoon ground cinnamon
½ teaspoon freshly grated nutmeg
pinch of ground cloves
2 tablespoons dark rum
¼ cup (2 oz/60 g) unsalted butter, melted

❦ To make the pastry, combine the flour with the salt in a large bowl. Cut in the butter and shortening until the texture of coarse crumbs. Add the water, a tablespoon at a time, and mix gently with a fork to form a soft dough. Chill for 1 hour.

❦ Preheat the oven to 425°F (220°C). Roll out the dough on a lightly floured board and line a 9-in (23-cm) pie pan with the pastry. Trim and flute the edges.

❦ To make the filling, place the potatoes in a large bowl and whisk in the remaining ingredients until smooth. Pour the filling into the pastry shell and bake for 10 minutes. Reduce the oven temperature to 300°F (150°C) and bake until firm, 45 to 60 minutes longer.

SERVES 6 TO 8

Vermont

New England Pumpkin Pie

Pumpkin pie is said to have been served at the second Thanksgiving in 1623 and has been that holiday's traditional dessert ever since. The egg whites are beaten separately in the following Vermont prescription, which lightens the pie considerably.

FOR THE PASTRY

2 cups (8 oz/250 g) all-purpose (plain) flour
2 teaspoons sugar

½ teaspoon salt
½ cup (4 oz/125 g) cold lard
¼ cup (2 oz/60 g) cold solid vegetable shortening (vegetable lard)
1 egg, lightly beaten
1½ teaspoons red wine vinegar
2 tablespoons cold water

FOR THE FILLING

1½ cups (¾ lb/375 g) pumpkin puree (page 32)
3 tablespoons (1½ oz/50 g) unsalted butter, melted
½ cup (4 oz/125 g) sugar
¼ cup (2 fl oz/60 ml) maple syrup
1 teaspoon ground cinnamon
½ teaspoon freshly grated nutmeg
¼ teaspoon ground cloves
3 eggs, separated
½ cup (4 fl oz/125 ml) milk
¼ cup (2 fl oz/60 ml) cream
sweetened whipped cream

❦ To make the pastry, combine the flour with the sugar and salt in a bowl. Cut in the lard and shortening until the texture of coarse crumbs. Add the beaten egg, vinegar and water, a tablespoon at a time, and mix gently with a fork to form a soft dough. Chill for 1 hour.

❦ Preheat the oven to 350°F (180°C). Roll out the dough on a lightly floured board and line a 10-in (25-cm) pie pan with the pastry. Trim and flute the edges.

❦ To make the filling, combine all the ingredients except the egg whites and whipped cream in a large bowl. Mix thoroughly.

❦ Beat the egg whites until stiff but not dry. Fold into the filling mixture. Pour into the pastry shell and bake until a toothpick inserted halfway between the center and edge of the pie comes out clean, about 50 minutes. Let cool on a wire rack. Serve with sweetened whipped cream.

SERVES 6 TO 8

NEW ENGLAND PUMPKIN PIE

New York

APPLE PIE

The apple was an important staple in the Northeast during the eighteenth and nineteenth centuries, when it was not uncommon to eat apple pie once a day, even for breakfast. The apple pie had been a part of English cuisine since Elizabethan times, so it is no surprise that apples were the first cultivated fruit crop to flourish in America.

FOR THE PASTRY

2 cups (8 oz/250 kg) all-purpose (plain) flour
¼ teaspoon sugar
½ teaspoon salt
pinch of ground cinnamon
½ cup (4 oz/125 g) cold unsalted butter
3 tablespoons cold solid vegetable shortening (vegetable lard)
5 tablespoons cold water (approximately)

FOR THE FILLING

2½ lb (1.25 g) green apples (about 5 large)
1½ tablespoons all-purpose (plain) flour
1 cup (8 oz/250 g) sugar
pinch of salt
1 tablespoon ground cinnamon
⅛ teaspoon freshly grated nutmeg

1 tablespoon lemon juice
finely grated peel of 1 lemon
½ teaspoon vanilla extract (essence)
1½ tablespoons (1 oz/30 g) unsalted butter, cut into pieces
1 egg, beaten

❦ To make the pastry, combine the flour with the sugar, salt and cinnamon in a medium bowl. Cut in the butter and shortening until the texture of coarse crumbs. Add the water, a tablespoon at a time, and mix gently with a fork to form a soft dough. Do not overwork. Chill for 1 hour.

❦ Preheat the oven to 450°F (230°C). To make the filling, peel, core and slice the apples into a large bowl. Sprinkle with the flour and add the sugar, salt, cinnamon, nutmeg, lemon juice, lemon peel and vanilla. Toss well.

❦ Roll out slightly more than half the pastry on a lightly floured board. Line a 9-in (23-cm) pie pan with the pastry. Fill with the apple mixture and dot with butter.

❦ Roll out the remaining pastry and place over the pie. Seal, trim and flute the edges. Cut several slashes in the top pastry to release steam. Brush with beaten egg. Place the pie on a baking sheet and bake for 15 minutes. Reduce the oven temperature to 350°F (180°C) and bake until the pastry is golden and the apples tender, about 50 minutes longer.

SERVES 8

APPLE PIE

New York

BOOZY CHIFFON PIE

Chiffon pies came into vogue at the beginning of this century and were especially popular during the Roaring Twenties. Chiffon pies are generally made with a cookie-crumb crust and filled with a light, gelatinous custard. The following, created by the late Bert Greene, is a spectacular example.

FOR THE CRUST

1½ cups (6 oz/185 g) chocolate wafer (digestive biscuits) crumbs
¼ cup (1½ oz/45 g) sifted powdered (icing) sugar
6 tablespoons (3 oz/90 g) unsalted butter, melted
1 teaspoon ground cinnamon
1 teaspoon instant coffee powder

FOR THE FILLING

1 envelope unflavored gelatin
½ cup (4 fl oz/125 ml) cold water
⅔ cup (5 oz/155 g) sugar
⅛ teaspoon salt
3 eggs, separated
¼ cup (2 fl oz/60 ml) cognac
¼ cup (2 fl oz/60 ml) crème de cacao
2 cups (16 fl oz/500 ml) cream, whipped
chocolate curls for garnish (see note on page 232)

❦ Preheat the oven to 300°F (150°C). To make the crust, combine the wafer crumbs, sugar, butter, cinnamon and coffee powder in a bowl; mix thoroughly. Grease a 9-in (23-cm) pie pan and press the crumb mixture over the bottom and sides. Bake for 15 minutes. Let cool on a wire rack.

❦ To make the filling, sprinkle the gelatin over the cold water in a saucepan. Add the sugar, salt and egg yolks. Cook over low heat, stirring constantly, until slightly thickened; do not let boil. Remove from the heat and stir in the cognac and crème de cacao. Refrigerate until the custard is partially set, about 30 minutes.

❦ Beat the egg whites until stiff but not dry. Whisk the custard to remove any lumps (if it is too thick, add a few drops of boiling water and whisk until smooth). Fold in the egg whites, then half of the whipped cream. Spread in the crust and refrigerate for 3 hours.

❦ Before serving, garnish with the remaining whipped cream and the chocolate curls.

SERVES 6 TO 8

Florida

KEY LIME PIE

Key lime pies made their debut in the Florida Keys in the late 1850s. Since fresh milk was unavailable on the islands, the introduction of canned milk was more than appreciated by the folks who lived there. The original pie was made in an ordinary pastry shell but today is more likely to be served in a graham cracker crust. It can be topped with a meringue, as in the following recipe, or served well chilled (some people even freeze it) with whipped cream.

FOR THE CRUST

1½ cups (6 oz/185 g) graham cracker (wholemeal or digestive biscuit) crumbs
⅓ cup (3 oz/90 g) sugar
⅓ cup (3 oz/90 g) unsalted butter, melted

BOOZY CHIFFON PIE (top) AND KEY LIME PIE (bottom)

FOR THE FILLING

4 egg yolks
1 can (14 fl oz/440 ml) sweetened condensed milk
½ cup (4 fl oz/125 ml) lime juice (approximately)
finely grated peel of 1 lime
dash of bitters

FOR THE MERINGUE

4 egg whites
¼ teaspoon cream of tartar
½ cup (4 oz/125 g) sugar

❦ Preheat the oven to 350°F (180°C). To make the crust, combine the crumbs with the sugar and butter in a bowl. Mix well and press over the bottom and sides of a greased 9-in (23-cm) pie pan. Bake for 8 to 10 minutes. Let cool on a wire rack.

❦ To make the filling, beat the egg yolks with the condensed milk in a large bowl until smooth. Beat in the lime juice, lime peel and bitters. Add more lime juice if needed—the filling should be quite tart. Pour into the pie shell and bake for 15 minutes. Let cool on a wire rack. Refrigerate.

❦ To make the meringue, beat the egg whites with the cream of tartar in the large bowl of an electric mixer until soft peaks form. Slowly beat in the sugar until the meringue is stiff and glossy. Spread over the pie, making sure that the meringue touches the edges of the crust to keep it from shrinking. Place the pie under a preheated broiler (griller) until the top is nicely browned, 1 to 2 minutes. Serve well chilled.

SERVES 6 TO 8

MIDWESTERN OATMEAL CAKE (top) AND
APPLESAUCE CAKE (bottom)

Ohio

MIDWESTERN OATMEAL CAKE

Jim Fobel is a young baker whose Old-Fashioned Baking Book *is full of good midwestern recipes that he inherited from a family of outstanding cooks. This recipe is fairly standard throughout the Midwest.*

FOR THE CAKE

1 cup (5 oz/155 g) rolled oats
1¼ cups (10 fl oz/310 ml) boiling water
1½ cups (6 oz/185 g) all-purpose (plain) flour
1 teaspoon ground cinnamon
½ teaspoon baking powder
½ teaspoon baking soda (bicarbonate of soda)
½ teaspoon salt
½ cup (4 oz/125 g) unsalted butter, softened
¾ cup (4 oz/125 g) firmly packed dark brown sugar
½ cup (4 oz/125 g) sugar
2 large eggs
1 teaspoon vanilla extract (essence)

FOR THE TOPPING

¼ cup (2 oz/60 g) unsalted butter
⅓ cup (3 fl oz/80 ml) evaporated milk
½ cup (3 oz/90 g) firmly packed dark brown sugar
½ cup (2 oz/60 g) rolled oats
½ cup (1½ oz/45 g) shredded (dessicated) sweetened coconut
½ cup (2 oz/60 g) chopped walnuts
½ cup (2 oz/60 g) chopped pecans

❧ Preheat the oven to 350°F (180°C). To make the cake, place the oats in a heatproof bowl and pour the boiling water over them. Stir until well mixed and let cool to lukewarm.

❧ Combine the flour, cinnamon, baking powder, baking soda and salt.

❧ Beat the butter in the large bowl of an electric mixer until light and fluffy. Slowly beat in the sugars. Then add the eggs, one at a time, beating thoroughly after each addition. Beat in the vanilla.

❧ On low speed, add the flour mixture to the butter mixture in 3 parts, alternating with the oatmeal. Beat only until mixed; do not overbeat.

❧ Pour the batter into a greased and floured 9-in (23-cm) springform pan. Place the pan in the center of the oven and bake until firm, 30 to 35 minutes. Let cool on a rack, then remove the sides of the pan. Transfer to a baking sheet.

❧ To make the topping, preheat the broiler (griller). Combine the butter and evaporated milk in a saucepan. Heat slowly to a simmer, stirring to melt the butter. Add the brown sugar and stir until dissolved. Remove the pan from the heat and stir in the oats, coconut, walnuts and pecans. Spoon over the top of the cake. Place the cake under the broiler until the topping is bubbling and golden brown, about 2 minutes. (Be careful: the topping burns easily.) Let the cake cool before serving.

SERVES 8 TO 10

Massachusetts

APPLESAUCE CAKE

In the old days apples went into just about every dish imaginable, so it is no surprise that applesauce found its way into a cake. The following cake from Marblehead is, quite simply, an applesauce-spiked spice cake. Homemade applesauce makes all the difference.

FOR THE CAKE

½ cup (3 oz/90 g) raisins
½ cup (3 oz/90 g) currants
½ cup (2 oz/60 g) chopped walnuts
1½ cups (6 oz/185 g) sifted all-purpose (plain) flour
½ cup (4 oz/125 g) unsalted butter, softened
1 cup (8 oz/250 g) sugar
1 egg
1 teaspoon baking soda (bicarbonate of soda)
½ teaspoon baking powder
½ teaspoon freshly grated nutmeg
½ teaspoon ground cloves
1 teaspoon ground cinnamon
1¼ cups (90 oz/280 g) thick applesauce (recipe follows)

FOR THE ICING

¼ cup (2 oz/60 g) unsalted butter, softened
1½ teaspoons vanilla extract (essence)
3 cups powdered (icing) sugar
3 to 4 tablespoons (2 fl oz/60 ml) cream

❧ Preheat the oven to 350°F (180°C). To make the cake, combine the raisins, currants and walnuts in a small bowl. Add ¼ cup (1 oz/30 g) of the flour and mix well. Set aside.

❧ Beat the butter in the large bowl of an electric mixer until light and fluffy. Slowly beat in the sugar, then the egg.

❧ Sift the remaining 1¼ cups (5 oz/155 g) flour with the baking soda, baking powder, nutmeg, cloves and cinnamon in a large bowl. Add to the batter in 3 parts, alternating with the applesauce. (If using commercial applesauce, add ¼ to ½ cup (1–2 oz/30–60 g) more flour to thicken the batter.) Stir in the raisin-nut mixture.

❧ Spoon the batter into a greased and floured 9-in (23-cm) springform pan. Bake until a toothpick inserted in the center comes out clean, about 50 minutes. Let cool in the pan on a wire rack. Remove the sides of the pan.

❧ To make the icing, beat the butter with vanilla in the large bowl of an electric mixer. Slowly add the powdered sugar.

CHERRY PIE

Continue to beat until light and mealy. Beat in just enough cream to make the icing of spreading consistency. Spread over the sides and top of the cake.

SERVES 8 TO 10

HOMEMADE APPLESAUCE

3 lb (1.5 kg) tart green apples (about 6 large or 9 medium)
½ teaspoon grated lemon peel
1 cup (5½ oz/170 g) dark brown sugar
2 teaspoons lemon juice
3 tablespoons dark rum
2 tablespoons (1 oz/30 g) unsalted butter

❧ Peel and core the apples; cut into slices ⅛ in (3 mm) thick. Place the apples and lemon peel in a large heavy saucepan. Cook, covered, over low heat, stirring occasionally, until very tender, about 30 minutes.

❧ Mash the apples and add the sugar, lemon juice, rum and butter. Cook, partially covered, over low heat, for 10 minutes. Increase the heat slightly if the applesauce seems too thin. Refrigerate, covered, until ready to use.

MAKES ABOUT 2 LB (1 KG)

Michigan

CHERRY PIE

Wild cherries were plentiful as pioneers pushed their way into the upper Midwest. The Indians had been using them for years, pounding them into their pemmican (a kind of meat cake). The settlers cultivated and crossbred the cherries with European varieties, and as a consequence, the eastern shores of Lake Michigan are abloom with the fruit every year.

FOR THE PASTRY

2½ cups (10 oz/315 g) all-purpose (plain) flour
1 teaspoon sugar
½ teaspoon salt
½ cup (4 oz/125 g) cold unsalted butter
½ cup (4 oz/125 g) cold solid vegetable shortening (vegetable lard)
¼ cup (2 fl oz/60 ml) cold water

FOR THE FILLING

4 cups (2 lb/1 kg) pitted fresh sweet cherries
1 cup (8 oz/250 g) sugar
1 tablespoon red wine vinegar
5 tablespoons all-purpose (plain) flour
1½ tablespoons (1 oz/30 g) unsalted butter

❧ To make the pastry, combine the flour with the sugar and salt in a bowl. Cut in the butter and shortening until the texture of coarse crumbs. Add the water, a tablespoon at a time, and mix gently with a fork to form a soft dough. Chill for 1 hour.

❧ Preheat the oven to 450°F (230°C). Combine the cherries, sugar and vinegar in a large bowl. Sift in the flour, 1 tablespoon at a time, stirring gently after each addition.

❧ Roll out slightly more than half the pastry on a lightly floured board. Line a 9-in (23-cm) pie pan with the pastry. Fill with the cherry mixture and dot with butter.

❧ Roll out the remaining pastry and place over the pie. Seal, trim and flute the edges. Cut several slashes in the top pastry to release steam. Place the pie on a baking sheet and bake for 15 minutes. Reduce the oven temperature to 350°F (180°C) and bake until the pastry is lightly browned, 30 to 35 minutes longer. Let cool on a wire rack.

SERVES 6 TO 8

CHOCOLATE ANGEL PIE

Oregon

CHOCOLATE ANGEL PIE

Angel pies are similar to icebox pies but usually have a meringue crust. This chocolate confection was created by cookbook author Rose Naftalin, who once owned a restaurant in Portland, where this pie was a major hit.

FOR THE MERINGUE SHELL

3 large egg whites
pinch of salt
¼ teaspoon cream of tartar
⅔ cup (5 oz/155 g) sugar
½ teaspoon vanilla extract (essence)
⅓ cup (1½ oz/45 g) finely chopped walnuts or pecans

FOR THE FILLING

5 oz (155 g) semisweet (plain) chocolate
¼ cup (2 fl oz/60 ml) hot milk
1 teaspoon vanilla extract (essence)
pinch of salt
1¾ cups (14 fl oz/440 ml) cream
2 tablespoons powdered (icing) sugar
chocolate curls*

🍂 Preheat the oven to 275°F (135°C). To make the meringue shell, beat the egg whites, salt and cream of tartar together in the large bowl of an electric mixer until soft peaks form. Gradually beat in the sugar until a very stiff meringue is formed. Beat in the vanilla.

🍂 Grease a 9-in (23-cm) glass pie pan. Spread the meringue over the bottom and sides, building up the sides as high as possible. Sprinkle the nuts over the bottom. Bake for 1 hour. (If after 10 minutes the sides start to sag, gently push back into place.) Turn off the oven and let the shell cool in the oven for 30 minutes. Then cool completely on a wire rack.

🍂 To make the filling, melt the chocolate in the top of a double boiler over hot water. Add the milk, vanilla and salt and stir until smooth. Let cool.

🍂 Whip 1 cup (8 fl oz/250 ml) of the cream until stiff and fold into the cooled chocolate. Spread evenly in the meringue shell. Refrigerate for 4 hours.

🍂 Before serving, whip the remaining cream with the powdered sugar; spread over the top of the pie. Decorate with chocolate curls. (May be refrigerated for up to 1½ hours.)

*To make chocolate curls, scrape a bar of chocolate with a vegetable peeler.

SERVES 6 TO 8

Colorado

DENVER RED CAKE

This cake supposedly originated at the Waldorf Astoria Hotel in New York at the turn of the century but migrated west with some silver-rich Coloradoan who paid $1,000 for the formula. Since then the cake has definitely belonged to the Mile High City.

FOR THE CAKE

½ cup (4 oz/125 g) unsalted butter, softened
1½ cups (12 oz/375 g) sugar
2 eggs
¼ cup (2 fl oz/60 ml) red food coloring
1 teaspoon vanilla extract (essence)
2 tablespoons unsweetened cocoa
1 teaspoon salt
1 cup (8 fl oz/250 ml) buttermilk
2¼ cups (9 oz/280 g) sifted cake or soft wheat flour (or 2 cups plain flour and 2½ tablespoons cornflour)
1 teaspoon baking soda (bicarbonate of soda)
1 teaspoon cider vinegar

FOR THE ICING

3 tablespoons all-purpose (plain) flour
1 cup (8 fl oz/250 ml) milk
1 cup (8 oz/250 g) unsalted butter, softened

1 cup (8 oz/250 g) sugar
1 teaspoon vanilla extract (essence)

❦ Preheat the oven to 350°F (180°C). To make the cake, beat the butter with the sugar in the large bowl of an electric mixer until light and fluffy. Add the eggs, one at a time, beating thoroughly after each addition.

❦ Stir the food coloring, vanilla and cocoa together to form a paste. Beat into the batter.

❦ Stir the salt into the buttermilk. Add to the batter in 3 parts, alternating with the flour.

❦ Stir the baking soda into the vinegar and add to the batter. Pour the batter into 2 greased and floured 9-in (23-cm) round cake pans. Bake until a toothpick inserted in the center comes out clean, about 30 minutes. Let cool on a wire rack.

❦ When the cake is completely cool, unmold the cake then cut each layer in half horizontally to form 4 layers.

❦ To make the icing, slowly whisk the flour with the milk in a saucepan until smooth. Cook, stirring frequently, over medium heat until thick, about 5 minutes. Let cool.

❦ Beat the butter with the sugar in the large bowl of an electric mixer until light and fluffy. Beat in the vanilla. Slowly beat in the cooled milk mixture. Spread the icing over the tops of 3 cake layers. Place one on top of the other and top with remaining layer. Ice the sides and top of the cake.

SERVES 8 TO 10

FILLAMENTO; ED HARDY

DENVER RED CAKE

BREAKFAST, BRUNCH AND SUNDAY SUPPERS

HAMBURGERS ARE SAID TO HAVE BEEN FIRST CREATED IN CONNECTICUT.

BREAKFAST, BRUNCH AND SUNDAY SUPPERS

WITH TODAY'S BUSY PACE, THE CLASSIC AMERICAN BREAKFAST OF EGGS, HASH BROWN POTATOES AND BACON IS MORE OFTEN A GLASS OF MILK AND SLICE OF TOAST OR A SIMPLE BUT NOURISHING BOWL OF CEREAL.

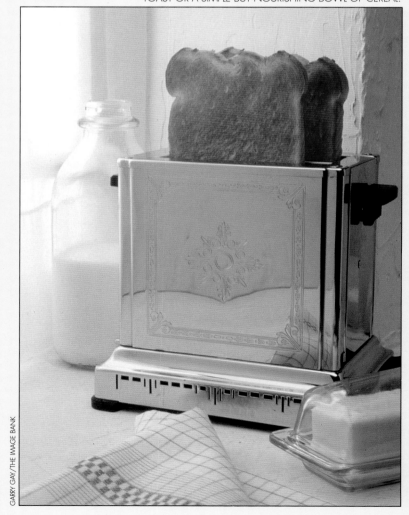

With the busy lives that most Americans lead these days, breakfast is likely to consist of nothing more than a bowlful of one of the hundred or so breakfast cereals on the market. (Ready-to-eat cereals, by the way, were first introduced in the middle of the nineteenth century.) Good old-fashioned *filling* breakfasts for the most part have been relegated to the weekends, when the family is together and time is a bit less precious. It was not always so.

The Indians started their days with cornmeal mush or cornbread, and the settlers naturally followed their example. Chicken eggs were not commonly available until the nineteenth century, but the eggs of the quail, duck, turkey, goose, grouse and pigeon filled in nicely. In the South turtle and crocodile eggs were a favored delicacy. Pork products, which have become synonymous with breakfast, were the most readily available meats, so it was inevitable that they became a breakfast staple. Later other dishes started appearing on the morning table, including soups, hash and apple pie in New England. Pancakes have always been popular around the country, as well as waffles and French toast. The classic American breakfast, however, comprises eggs, hash brown potatoes and a side of bacon, ham or sausage—that is, as noted, when Americans take time to eat breakfast in the first place. In the South grits usually stand in for hash browns, and homemade biscuits are served on the side with a tub of sweet butter and honey or homemade jam and jelly. There are a few other regional peculiarities. New Yorkers, for instance, eat lox and bagels: smoked salmon on bagels spread with cream cheese. Philadelphians eat fried scrapple: a sort of chilled cornmeal mush flavored with pork and cut into slices. Denverites eat Denver omelettes: eggs with peppers, ham and onion, also known as the western omelette. Everywhere out west, it seems, one can get "steak and eggs." In San Antonio and throughout the Southwest, breakfast means *huevos rancheros*: eggs served on tortillas and topped with a tomato salsa.

John Mariani, in *The Dictionary of American Food & Drink*, says that "brunch" was introduced way back in 1895, the word indicating a combination of breakfast and lunch. The practice did not really take hold, however, until the 1930s. Brunch is generally a weekend affair, and hundreds of restaurants in every major city serve brunch of one kind or another, usually accompanied by Bloody Marys. Standard brunch fare, not only in restaurants but at home as well, includes eggs Benedict, smoked salmon or other smoked fish, omelettes, soufflés and quiche, among other entrees.

Sunday suppers date back further, contrary to what one might think. Since colonial times supper has always been a light, informal meal. Dinner, the heavy meal of the day, was served at noon. Even today the majority of Americans still eat Sunday dinner at midday, usually after church services. Sunday suppers are casual, informal affairs, often eaten in front of the television set. The food served ranges from sandwiches or summertime hot dogs and hamburgers on the grill, to such classic American "family" foods as pizza, Sloppy Joes, macaroni and cheese or tuna-noodle casserole.

What follows is a collection of some of America's favorite breakfast and brunch foods, along with some of the more casual fare that the country is noted for.

BRUNCH IS GENERALLY A WEEKEND AFFAIR, A TIME TO QUIETLY ENJOY THE MORNING NEWSPAPER, OR SHARE A MEAL WITH FAMILY AND FRIENDS.

TASTY MORSELS OF FRENCH TOAST AT THE CAFE DU MONDE IN NEW ORLEANS, WHERE COOKING IS BASED ON CLASSIC FRENCH CUISINE.

TUNA-NOODLE CASSEROLE

Heat to boiling, reduce the heat and simmer until thickened, 3 or 4 minutes. Add the nutmeg, hot pepper sauce and salt and pepper to taste. Remove from the heat and set aside, stirring frequently to keep a skin from forming.

❧ Cook the noodles in boiling salted water until tender, about 4 minutes. Rinse briefly under cold running water and drain. Toss with the 1 teaspoon oil.

❧ Slice the mushroom caps and cut in half. Chop the stems. Heat the remaining 2 tablespoons oil in a heavy skillet over high heat and sauté the mushrooms until golden brown. Stir into the sauce.

❧ Flake the tuna and add to the sauce. Add the noodles and toss until thoroughly mixed. Transfer to a greased baking dish and sprinkle the potato chips or breadcrumbs over the top. Bake until bubbly, 20 to 25 minutes. Let stand for a few minutes before serving.

SERVES 4

Rhode Island

RED FLANNEL HASH

It has been claimed that red flannel hash developed out of the need to use up the leftovers from a New England boiled dinner. Those who disagree insist that the original contained nothing but bacon, potatoes and beets, the key ingredient. A standard item at diners across the country, red flannel hash is generally made from scratch. It is traditional to top it with poached eggs and serve bottled chili sauce on the side.

2 whole beets (beetroot) (about ½ lb/250 g), root ends
    trimmed but not peeled
2 baking potatoes, peeled
1 lb (500 g) cooked corned beef, cut into ½-in (1-cm) cubes
    (about 3 cups)
2 carrots, finely chopped
1 small green pepper (capsicum), seeded and finely chopped
1 large onion, finely chopped
1 small garlic clove, minced
3 tablespoons chopped fresh parsley
2 thick bacon strips, chopped
1 teaspoon Worcestershire sauce
1 teaspoon hot red pepper (Tabasco) sauce
¼ cup (2 fl oz/60 ml) tomato juice (approximately)
½ teaspoon salt
⅛ teaspoon freshly ground pepper
4 to 6 poached eggs

❧ Place the beets in a saucepan and cover with cold water. Heat to boiling, reduce the heat and simmer, uncovered, until barely tender, about 35 minutes. Rinse under cold water and drain. Rub the skins off and cut into ½-in (1-cm) cubes. Place in a large bowl.

❧ Cook the potatoes in boiling salted water for 10 minutes. Drain and cool slightly. Cut into ½-in (1-cm) cubes. Add the potatoes, corned beef, carrots, green pepper, onion, garlic and parsley to the beets. Mix well.

❧ Sauté the bacon in a 10-in (25-cm) cast-iron skillet until crisp. Transfer to the hash mixture and toss well. Transfer the hash to the skillet and press it down. Cook, uncovered, over medium heat for 6 minutes. Stir in the Worcestershire sauce, hot pepper sauce, tomato juice, salt and pepper. Toss well and press down in the pan once more. Cook over low heat without stirring for 25 to 30 minutes.

❧ Preheat the oven to 325°F (165°C). Using 2 large spatulas, turn the hash over in the skillet (or flip over into a second skillet). Transfer to the oven and bake until the potatoes are tender and the top is well browned, 20 to 25 minutes. Drizzle with more tomato juice if the mixture seems too dry. Serve from the skillet, topped with poached eggs.

SERVES 4 TO 6

Indiana

TUNA-NOODLE CASSEROLE

Most Americans growing up in the 1950s and 1960s ate a lot of tuna-noodle casserole, made, no doubt, with canned cream of mushroom soup. There is no cream of mushroom soup in the following recipe. There are, however, crumbled potato chips over the top, almost a requirement these days. Buttery breadcrumbs may be substituted.

¼ cup (2 fl oz/60 ml) plus 1 teaspoon olive oil
1 tablespoon minced shallot or onion
3 tablespoons all-purpose (plain) flour
1 cup (8 fl oz/250 ml) milk
1 cup (8 fl oz/250 ml) light (single) cream or half & half
    (half cream and half milk)
pinch of freshly grated nutmeg
dash of hot red pepper (Tabasco) sauce
salt and freshly ground pepper
2 cups (3 oz/90 g) small egg noodles
¼ lb (125 g) large white mushrooms
1 can (7 oz/220 g) tuna, drained
1 cup broken potato chips (or ½ cup fresh breadcrumbs mixed
    with 1 tablespoon melted butter)

❧ Preheat the oven to 350°F (180°C). Heat 2 tablespoons of the oil in a saucepan over medium-low heat. Add the shallot; cook for 2 minutes. Whisk in the flour; cook, stirring constantly, 2 minutes longer. Whisk in the milk and cream.

RED FLANNEL HASH (top) AND HASH BROWNS (bottom of plate)

Idaho

HASH BROWNS

Hash browns or home-fried potatoes are most often served with eggs for breakfast but are also served with steak for dinner. Often made with grated potatoes, hash browns most likely originated as a way to use up leftover cooked potatoes (similar to hash) and are best made with baked ones.

6 tablespoons (3 oz/90 g) unsalted butter or bacon drippings
    (approximately)
1 white onion, halved and sliced
3 medium to large cold baked potatoes, chopped

2 teaspoons Worcestershire sauce
dried red pepper (chili) flakes, crushed
salt and freshly ground pepper

❦ Melt the butter in a large cast-iron skillet over medium heat. Add the onion; cook for 1 minute. Stir in the potatoes and toss until well coated with butter. Sprinkle with the Worcestershire sauce and red pepper flakes to taste. Cook, tossing occasionally, until the potatoes are crisp, about 20 minutes, adding more butter if they become too dry. Reduce the heat if they brown too quickly. Add salt and pepper to taste.

SERVES 4

TAMALE PIE (left) AND CHILE CON QUESO (right)

Texas

TAMALE PIE

Tamales are a Mexican specialty of meat and cornmeal dough steamed inside corn husks. Tamale pie, however, is a meat sauce baked inside cornmeal mush. The pie is often served with salsa on the side.

¾ cup (4 oz/125 g) yellow cornmeal
1 cup (8 fl oz/250 ml) cold water
2 cups (16 fl oz/500 ml) boiling water
2 tablespoons (1 oz/30 g) unsalted butter
¼ lb (125 g) sausage meat
2 small onions, finely chopped (about ¾ cup)
1 large garlic clove, minced
2 tablespoons chili powder
¼ teaspoon ground cumin
¾ lb (375 g) ground (minced) beef
¼ teaspoon hot red pepper (Tabasco) sauce
1 celery stalk, chopped
1 small green Italian (mild chili) pepper, finely chopped
2 tomatoes, peeled, seeded and chopped (about 1½ cups)
2 ears (cobs) of corn
1 teaspoon salt
⅓ cup (2 oz/60 g) sliced pitted black olives
½ cup (2 oz/60 g) shredded Monterey Jack (or mild melting) cheese
¾ cup (3 oz/90g) shredded mild Cheddar cheese

❦ Gradually stir the cornmeal into the cold water. Stir this mixture into the boiling water in a heavy saucepan. Heat, stirring constantly, to boiling; reduce the heat. Add the butter and cook, covered, stirring occasionally, for 35 minutes.

❦ Meanwhile, sauté the sausage meat in a large skillet over medium heat until it begins to lose its pink color. Add the onion; cook for 1 minute. Add the garlic; cook 4 minutes longer. Stir in the chili powder and cumin. Add the ground beef and continue to cook until the beef loses its pink color, about 5 minutes. Stir in the hot pepper sauce, celery and green pepper and cook for 5 minutes. Add the tomatoes and cook, stirring occasionally, 5 minutes longer.

❦ Using a sharp knife, cut the corn kernels off each cob, but only to half their depth. Using the back of the knife, scrape the cobs to remove the remaining bits of kernel and milky residue. Add to the tomato-meat mixture. Cook for 10 minutes. Add salt to taste.

❦ Preheat the oven to 350°F (180°C). Lightly grease a 10-in (25-cm) round baking dish at least 2 in (5 cm) deep. Spread two-thirds of the cornmeal mixture over the bottom and sides. Spoon the meat filling evenly into the dish. Arrange the olive slices on top and sprinkle with the Monterey Jack cheese. Cover with the Cheddar cheese.

❦ Spoon the remaining cornmeal mixture evenly over the top of the pie to form a crust. (If the cornmeal has become too thick to spread, thin with a few drops of boiling water.) Bake until golden brown, about 45 minutes. Let stand for 10 minutes before serving.

SERVES 4 TO 6

Arizona

CHILE CON QUESO

Americans do love cheese. This recipe from the Southwest mixes melted cheese with peppers (chilies). Each diner places a large dab of chile con queso on the edge of a tortilla, rolls it up, and eats it with fingers only.

3 tablespoons olive oil
1 large onion, finely chopped
1 garlic clove, minced
1 small green bell pepper (capsicum) or poblano (mild chili)
   pepper, seeded and finely chopped
1 tablespoon chili powder
1 can (10 oz/315 g) mixed tomatoes and green chilies
2 tablespoons chopped canned jalapeño peppers (pickled chilies)
1 lb (500 g) Monterey Jack (or mild Cheddar) cheese
²⁄₃ cup (5 fl oz/160 ml) hot cream
18 to 20 warm flour tortillas (page 166)

❦ Preheat the oven to 200°F (95°C). Heat the oil in a large skillet over medium heat. Add the onion, garlic and bell pepper; cook for 5 minutes. Add the chili powder, mixed tomatoes and chilies, and jalapeño peppers; cook 5 minutes longer. Keep warm.
❦ Place the cheese in a large heatproof bowl. Heat in oven until just melted, about 10 minutes. (The cheese will turn stringy if overcooked.) Immediately remove from oven and stir in the hot cream and pepper mixture. Serve with tortillas.

SERVES 5 OR 6

New York

BASIC WAFFLES

The Dutch are often credited with the invention of the waffle, but the Germans also lay claim to it, as do the French. The Dutch, however, did introduce the waffle to the New World, and it was customary in New Amsterdam to give a bride a waffle iron engraved with her initials and the date of her wedding. Waffles were made with a yeast batter and baked over fires in those days, but today baking powder and the electric nonstick iron have simplified matters immensely.

1¾ cups (7 oz/315 g) sifted all-purpose (plain) flour
1 teaspoon baking soda (bicarbonate of soda)
½ teaspoon salt
2 tablespoons sugar
2 cups (16 fl oz/500 ml) buttermilk (approximately)
3 eggs, separated
6 tablespoons (3 oz/90 g) unsalted butter, melted

❦ Preheat the oven to 250°F (120°C). Sift the flour with the baking soda, salt and sugar in a large bowl. Slowly whisk in the buttermilk, egg yolks and butter. Add up to ½ cup (4 fl oz/125 ml) more buttermilk if the batter seems too thick.
❦ Beat the egg whites until stiff and fold into the batter.
❦ Heat a lightly greased waffle iron. Pour about ½ cup (4 fl oz/125 ml) batter into the iron (depending on its size) and bake until crisp. Transfer to a wire rack on a baking sheet and keep warm in the oven while making the remaining waffles.

MAKES ABOUT 10 LARGE WAFFLES

BASIC WAFFLES (right) AND FRENCH TOAST (left, recipe page 242)

Louisiana

FRENCH TOAST

Called pain perdu *("lost bread") in New Orleans, French toast has always been a staple of French-Creole cuisine. In most luncheonettes around the country, plain white bread is used, but French toast is best made with French or Italian bread cut on the diagonal. It is usually served with maple syrup, honey or a thin fruit sauce.*

1 cup (8 fl oz/250 ml) milk
⅓ cup (3 fl oz/80 ml) cream
2 eggs
1 teaspoon ground cinnamon
⅛ teaspoon freshly grated nutmeg
¼ cup (2 oz/60 g) sugar
1 loaf (about 1 lb/500 g) stale French bread,
    cut into 1½-in (4-cm) slices
½ cup (4 oz/125 g) unsalted butter (approximately)
powdered (icing) sugar
maple syrup

❧ Whisk the milk with the cream, eggs, cinnamon, nutmeg and sugar in a large bowl. Place the bread slices in the mixture until soaked but not mushy.
❧ Preheat the oven to 250°F (120°C). Melt half of the butter in a heavy skillet until foamy. Sauté the bread, 3 or 4 slices at a time, until golden brown on both sides, adding more butter as needed. The bread will puff up slightly. Transfer to a platter and dust with powdered sugar; keep warm in the oven until all the bread is sautéed. Dust once more with powdered sugar and serve with maple syrup.

SERVES 4   *Photograph page 241*

New York

EGGS BENEDICT

Eggs Benedict, English muffins topped with ham, poached eggs and Hollandaise sauce, was either created at Delmonico's (home of Lobster Newburg) for patrons named Benedict or invented by a Wall Street broker, one Lemuel Benedict. No matter, it is now a classic breakfast/brunch dish.

2 English muffins, halved, or 4 slices homemade bread
4 ham slices, ½ in (1 cm) thick
4 eggs
2 egg yolks
2 tablespoons lemon juice
¼ teaspoon Dijon mustard
½ cup (4 oz/125 g) unsalted butter, frozen
dash of hot red pepper (Tabasco) sauce
salt and freshly ground white pepper

❧ Preheat the oven to 250°F (120°C). Toast the muffins or bread until golden. Place on a lightly greased shallow baking dish.
❧ Sauté the ham in a lightly greased skillet over high heat until lightly browned. Place a piece of ham on each muffin and place the dish in the oven.
❧ Poach the eggs in simmering water. Place an egg on top of each piece of ham. Return the dish to the oven.
❧ Beat the egg yolks with the lemon juice in the top of a double boiler over simmering water. Stir in the mustard. Add the butter, 1 tablespoon at a time, stirring constantly until the sauce is smooth and thick. Add hot pepper sauce and salt and white pepper to taste. Spoon over each egg.

SERVES 2 TO 4   *Photograph pages 234 – 235*

MICHIGAN PASTIES

Michigan

MICHIGAN PASTIES

Pasties were a staple of the Cornish miners who immigrated to Michigan's upper peninsula in the 1800s. In fact, these meat turnovers are such a part of Michigan folklore that May 24 has been declared Michigan Pasty Day.

FOR THE PASTRY

1 cup (4 oz/125 g) plus 2 tablespoons all-purpose (plain) flour
1 teaspoon salt
4½ tablespoons (2½ oz/80 g) unsalted butter
4 to 5 tablespoons cold water

FOR THE FILLING

2 tablespoons olive oil
2 cups (about 1 lb/500 g) cubed boneless steak
1 onion, chopped
2 large carrots, chopped (about 1 cup)
1 rutabaga (yellow turnip or Swede), chopped (about 1 cup)
1 teaspoon beef bouillon (stock) powder or ½ stock cube
½ teaspoon salt
¼ teaspoon freshly ground pepper
2 tablespoons unsalted butter, melted

❧ First, make the pastry. Combine the flour with the salt in a bowl. Cut in the butter until the texture of coarse crumbs. Add enough water to make a soft dough. Chill for 1 hour.
❧ Meanwhile, make the filling. Heat the oil in a large skillet over high heat. Quickly sauté the meat, a few pieces at a time, until well browned. Transfer to a large bowl. Add the onion, carrots, rutabaga, bouillon powder, salt and pepper. Mix well.
❧ Preheat the oven to 450°F (230°C). Divide the dough in half. Roll each half into an 11-in (28-cm) circle. Line a 9-in (23-cm) pie plate with one circle, leaving ½ in (1 cm) hanging over the edge. On one side of the pastry, place half the filling. Fold the other half of the pastry over the filling; crimp the edges to seal. Cut a slit in the pastry to let steam escape. Repeat the procedure, laying the second pasty gently next to the first pasty in the pie plate.
❧ Bake the pasties for 15 minutes. Reduce the oven temperature to 350° F (180°C) and bake 45 minutes longer. If the pasties become too dark, cover with aluminum foil.
❧ Remove the pasties from the oven. Pour 1 tablespoon melted butter into each vent hole. Cover with a dish towel and let steam for 15 minutes before serving.

SERVES 4

DEVILED HAM (bottom left), DEVILED EGGS (center) AND CLUB SANDWICH (top right)

Arkansas

DEVILED HAM

Deviled ham was probably invented as a good way to use up leftover ham. The spicy seasonings also helped to keep the ham mixture fresh longer. Nowadays deviled ham is usually served as party fare.

½ lb (250 g) cooked ham, roughly chopped
1 canned jalapeño pepper (pickled chili), roughly chopped
3 tablespoons (1½ oz/50 g) unsalted butter, softened
1½ teaspoons Dijon mustard
salt and freshly ground pepper

❧ Place the ham, jalapeño pepper, butter and mustard in a food processor. Process, using the pulse switch, until a fine paste is formed. Add salt and pepper to taste. Serve on thin slices of French or Italian bread.

SERVES 4 TO 6

Delaware

DEVILED EGGS

"Deviled" applies to anything that contains hot, spicy seasonings, such as mustard and hot peppers. Deviled eggs have long been popular for casual dining, particularly when eating out-of-doors.

6 hard-cooked (hard-boiled) eggs
2 small plum (egg) tomatoes, seeded and finely chopped
3 tablespoons mayonnaise
2 teaspoons Dijon mustard
dash of hot red pepper (Tabasco) sauce
½ teaspoon chopped fresh basil
freshly ground pepper

❧ Peel the eggs and cut in half lengthwise. Scoop the yolks into a bowl and set the whites aside. Add the tomatoes, mayonnaise, mustard, hot pepper sauce and basil to the yolks. Mash together until smooth.
❧ Fill the egg whites with the mixture. Sprinkle with pepper. Serve at room temperature or slightly chilled.

SERVES 6

New York

CLUB SANDWICH

The club sandwich may have come by its name because it was first served in railway "club" cars or in fashionable country "club" dining rooms or in the back rooms of thriving casino "clubs." It does not really matter—this is one of America's most popular sandwiches.

3 slices of bread, toasted
mayonnaise
2 or 3 crisp lettuce leaves
4 thin slices of cooked chicken or turkey
salt and freshly ground pepper
3 or 4 thin slices of ripe tomato
3 or 4 slices of crisp-fried bacon

❧ Spread one side of each piece of toast with mayonnaise. Place the lettuce on one piece and top with the chicken or turkey. Sprinkle with salt and pepper. Cover with the second piece of toast. Top that with tomato and bacon (and more lettuce if you wish). Cover with the remaining piece of toast, mayonnaise side down. Insert toothpicks to keep the sandwich from falling apart and cut diagonally into quarters.

SERVES 1

New York

BUTTERMILK PANCAKES

The breakfast pancake (griddle cake, hotcake, flapjack) would seem to be a purely American invention. Not so. The pancake came from Holland, where pannekoeken *cooked in heavy skillets over open fires date back to the sixteenth century.*

3 eggs, separated
2 cups (16 fl oz/500 ml) buttermilk
2 cups (8 oz/250 g) all-purpose (plain) flour
1 teaspoon baking soda (bicarbonate of soda)
1 tablespoon sugar
¼ cup (2 oz/60 g) unsalted butter, melted, plus butter for
   serving
maple syrup

❦ Beat the egg yolks in a large bowl until light. Add the buttermilk and beat until smooth. Stir in the flour, baking soda and sugar until well mixed. Do not overbeat; the small lumps will disappear in the cooking. Stir in the melted butter.

❦ Beat the egg whites until stiff. Fold into the batter. Bake on a hot griddle, using about ⅓ cup (3 fl oz/80 ml) batter for each pancake, until bubbles form on the top and the underside is nicely browned. Turn the cakes over and brown the other side. Serve with plenty of butter and maple syrup.

MAKES ABOUT 12 4-IN (10-CM) PANCAKES

Alaska

OLD-FASHIONED BUCKWHEAT PANCAKES

Buckwheat pancakes were a favorite with gold miners in the mid-nineteenth century, not necessarily because they loved the taste of buckwheat, but because wheat flour was a rarity. These cakes are made with a yeast starter much like the sourdough starter of gold rush days.

2½ cups (20 fl oz/625 ml) milk
2 tablespoons molasses or treacle
1½ teaspoons dry yeast
1⅓ cups (6 oz/185 g) buckwheat flour
⅔ cup (3 oz/90 g) all-purpose (plain) flour
½ cup (2 oz/60 g) fine cornmeal
½ teaspoon salt
1 teaspoon sugar
1 teaspoon baking soda (bicarbonate of soda)
½ cup (4 fl oz/125 ml) lukewarm water
2 tablespoons unsalted butter, melted, plus butter for serving
2 egg yolks, lightly beaten
3 egg whites
maple syrup

❦ The night before serving, scald the milk and stir in the molasses. Let cool to lukewarm. Stir in the yeast; let stand for 10 minutes. Transfer to a large bowl. Add the buckwheat flour, all-purpose flour, cornmeal and salt and beat until smooth. Cover and let stand at room temperature overnight.

❦ The next morning, dissolve the sugar and baking soda in the lukewarm water. Stir into the batter along with the melted butter and egg yolks.

❦ Beat the egg whites until stiff. Fold into the batter. Bake on a hot griddle, using about ⅓ cup (3 fl oz/80 ml) batter for each pancake, until bubbles form on the top and the underside is nicely browned. Turn the cakes over and brown the other side. Serve with butter and maple syrup or honey thinned with warm water.

MAKES ABOUT 18 4-IN (10-CM) PANCAKES

WILLIAMS-SONOMA INC.

OLD-FASHIONED BUCKWHEAT PANCAKES (left) AND BUTTERMILK PANCAKES (right)

ULTIMATE CHICKEN HASH

Missouri

HAMBURGERS

Hamburg steak was originally pounded beefsteak that was quickly sautéed in a skillet and served on the rare side. Sometime in the early part of this century, perhaps at the 1904 Exposition in St. Louis, ground meat was substituted, and by 1912 Americans were eating "hamburgers" on soft buns. It is imperative not to overwork ground beef or the meat will toughen. For those who like their hamburgers well-done, use ground chuck to keep the meat from drying out; rarer burgers can be made with sirloin or round.

1⅓ lb (670 g) ground (minced) beef
1 tablespoon melted unsalted butter or heavy cream
salt and freshly ground pepper

❦ Place the ground beef on a plate and gently spread apart with 2 forks. Sprinkle with butter or cream. Lift the meat and fold it over on itself. Gently shape into 4 patties, ¾ to 1 in (2 to 2.5 cm) thick. Grill, broil or sauté over medium-high heat for 3 to 4 minutes on each side for rare, 5 to 6 minutes on each side for medium-rare. Add salt and pepper to taste before serving.

MAKES 4 HAMBURGERS

New York

ULTIMATE CHICKEN HASH

The following dish was invented by Louis Diat at the Ritz-Carlton Hotel in New York City. To be sure, the dish is of French origin, but it has become legendary in upscale hostelries across the country.

2 tablespoons (1 oz/30 g) unsalted butter
2 tablespoons plus 2 teaspoons all-purpose (plain) flour
1¼ cups (10 fl oz/310 ml) chicken stock (see glossary)
2 tablespoons dry sherry
salt
10 oz (315 g) cooked chicken, cut into 1-in (2.5-cm) cubes
    (about 2 cups)
1 small white onion, halved and thinly sliced
⅔ cup (5 fl oz/160 ml) light (single) cream or half & half
    (half cream and half milk)
¼ teaspoon freshly ground pepper
2 egg yolks
2 tablespoons freshly grated Parmesan cheese
chopped fresh parsley (optional)

❦ Melt 4 teaspoons of the butter in a heavy skillet over medium-low heat. Stir in 2 tablespoons flour and cook, stirring constantly, for 2 minutes. Whisk in the stock and cook until thick, about 5 minutes. Add the sherry and ¼ teaspoon salt. Stir in the chicken. Spoon the mixture into a greased shallow 1- to 1½-qt (1- to 1.5-l) serving dish and keep warm in a low oven.

❦ Melt the remaining 2 teaspoons butter in a small saucepan over medium-low heat. Add the onion; cook for 5 minutes. Stir in the remaining 2 teaspoons flour and cook, stirring constantly, for 2 minutes. Whisk in the cream, ¼ teaspoon salt and the pepper. Cook, stirring, until slightly thickened, about 4 minutes. Remove from the heat.

❦ Preheat the broiler (griller). Beat the egg yolks in a small bowl. Slowly whisk in ¼ cup (2 fl oz/60 ml) of the hot sauce. Beat this mixture back into the sauce. Cook, stirring constantly, over low heat until thickened, 2 to 4 minutes. Do not let boil. Stir in the cheese and spoon over the hash. Place under the broiler to lightly brown the top, about 1 minute. Sprinkle with parsley.

SERVES 4

Missouri

HOT DOGS

Frankfurters, the ubiquitous American pork sausage (now made with beef, chicken or even turkey), were supposedly brought to St. Louis by a German immigrant in the 1880s and first served on a roll at the Exposition in 1904. The term "hot dog" may have been coined in Coney Island, New York. In any case, hot dogs they are and always will be. Because they are precooked, hot dogs only need to be heated through. Serve them on warm buns and garnish with one or more of the following: mustard, ketchup, relish, sauerkraut, chili beans, cheese, hot peppers, pickles, tomatoes, onions or whatever suits your fancy.

❦ To simmer: Simmer, do not boil, in salted water for 5 minutes and drain.
❦ To fry: Film the bottom of a skillet with oil. Cut the dogs lengthwise down the middle but not all the way through. Sauté over medium heat for about 2 minutes on each side.
❦ To grill or broil: Place over hot coals or close to a broiler (griller) until well browned on all sides, 4 to 5 minutes.

HAMBURGERS (left) AND HOT DOGS (right)

FILLAMENTO

Texas

HUEVOS RANCHEROS

Served on corn tortillas and topped with salsa, huevos rancheros (ranch-style eggs) are the morning specialty of the Southwest. Many cooks today fry or scramble the eggs, but the original method calls for poaching them in the salsa. Serve with refried beans (page 165).

¼ lb (125 g) bacon, coarsely chopped
1 onion, chopped
2 large garlic cloves, thinly sliced
2 jalapeño or other hot (chili) peppers, seeded and minced
1 can (4 oz/125 g) mild green chilies, chopped
1 can (1 lb/12 oz/875 g) plum (egg) tomatoes
1 teaspoon chopped fresh basil or pinch of dried basil
⅛ teaspoon chopped fresh oregano or pinch of dried oregano
1 to 2 teaspoons chopped fresh cilantro
      (coriander/Chinese parsley)
½ teaspoon salt
¼ teaspoon freshly ground pepper

3 tablespoons (1½ oz/50 g) unsalted butter
3 tablespoons vegetable oil
4 to 6 corn tortillas
4 to 6 eggs

❦ Fry the bacon in a large heavy skillet over medium heat until almost crisp. Drain off all but 2 tablespoons drippings. Add the onion; cook for 1 minute. Add the garlic; cook 4 minutes longer. Stir in the hot peppers, chilies, tomatoes, basil, oregano, cilantro, salt and pepper. Cook, stirring occasionally, over low heat until fairly thick and smooth, about 1 hour. Keep warm.

❦ Heat the butter and oil in a large skillet over medium-high heat. Using tongs, place each tortilla in the hot oil for about 10 seconds to heat (longer if you prefer them crisp). Drain on paper towels.

❦ Carefully break each egg on top of tomato mixture. Cover and cook until poached, 3 to 5 minutes. To serve, place an egg on each tortilla and spoon the sauce over the top.

SERVES 4 TO 6

SLOPPY JOES

Montana

SLOPPY JOES

A hot sandwich of ground or chopped beef in a tomatoey sauce, the Sloppy Joe probably originated in the late 1950s or early 1960s—no one is quite sure. The name? They are sloppy to be sure, and according to some authorities, Joe is more than likely the quintessential American "good ol' Joe." Serve the mixture on toasted sandwich buns.

1 lb (500 g) ground (minced) beef
1 onion, finely chopped
½ green bell pepper (capsicum), finely chopped
2 large mushrooms, finely chopped
1 can (8 oz/250 g) tomato sauce (pureed tomatoes)
1 tablespoon Dijon mustard
1 tablespoon Worcestershire sauce
1 teaspoon tomato paste
salt and freshly ground pepper

❦ Heat a heavy skillet over high heat for about 30 seconds and add the ground beef. Break up the lumps, then add the onion. Cook, stirring frequently, until the meat begins to sizzle. Stir in the bell pepper, mushrooms, tomato sauce, mustard, Worcestershire sauce and tomato paste. Mix well. Heat to boiling; reduce the heat until the mixture just barely bubbles. Cook, stirring occasionally, for 1 hour. Add salt and pepper to taste before serving.

SERVES 3 OR 4

PLANTATION SKILLET CAKE

South Carolina

PLANTATION SKILLET CAKE

A favorite breakfast dish of South Carolinians, skillet cake is somewhat like Yorkshire pudding, baked in a cast-iron skillet until puffed and golden. It is usually served with applesauce and brown sugar.

¼ cup (2 oz/60 g) unsalted butter
3 eggs
¾ cup (6 fl oz/180 ml) milk
2 tablespoons orange juice
¾ cup (3 oz/90 g) all-purpose (plain) flour
pinch of freshly grated nutmeg
powdered (icing) sugar

❦ Preheat the oven to 425°F (220°C). Place the butter in a heavy 2-qt (2-l) pan or skillet not more than 3 in (7.5 cm) deep. Place in the oven until the butter melts.

❦ Meanwhile, beat the eggs in a large bowl until light. Beat in the milk, orange juice, flour and nutmeg until smooth.

❦ Swirl the melted butter over the bottom and sides of the pan. Pour in the batter and return to the oven. Bake until golden brown and puffed, about 25 minutes. Dust with powdered sugar and serve immediately.

SERVES 2 TO 4

North Dakota

MACARONI AND CHEESE

Mary Randolph, in The Virginia Housewife *(1831), printed what just might be the first recipe for a macaroni and cheese dish. Her recipe was simply boiled macaroni layered in a dish with butter and cheese, then baked. Toward the end of the nineteenth century, cooks began adding white sauce to the dish, and this ever-popular recipe has not changed much since then.*

1 cup (4 oz/125 g) elbow macaroni
3 tablespoons (1½ oz/50 g) unsalted butter
1 small shallot (small onion), minced
1 tablespoon all-purpose (plain) flour
½ cup (4 fl oz/125 ml) hot chicken stock (see glossary)
½ cup (4 fl oz/125 ml) hot cream
½ teaspoon salt
¼ teaspoon freshly ground pepper
dash of hot red pepper (Tabasco) sauce
1 egg, lightly beaten
1 cup (4 oz/125 g) shredded Cheddar cheese
½ cup (1 oz/30 g) fresh breadcrumbs

❦ Preheat the oven to 350°F (180°C). Cook the macaroni in boiling salted water until just tender, about 8 minutes. Rinse under cold running water and drain. Stir occasionally to keep from sticking together.

❦ Melt 2 tablespoons of the butter in a saucepan over medium-low heat. Add the shallot; cook for 5 minutes. Stir in the flour. Cook, stirring constantly, 2 minutes longer. Whisk in the stock and cream. Heat to boiling, boil for 1 minute and remove from the heat. Whisk in the salt, pepper and hot pepper sauce. When the sauce has stopped bubbling, whisk in the egg. Stir in the cheese and macaroni. Mix well and transfer to a greased baking dish.

❦ Melt the remaining 1 tablespoon butter in a small skillet. When it foams, stir in the breadcrumbs. Sprinkle over the macaroni and cheese. Bake for 30 minutes. Let stand for 5 minutes before serving.

SERVES 4

Illinois

CHICAGO DEEP-DISH PIZZA

Pizza may not be a totally American invention, but Americans certainly can take credit for popularizing it. Chicago-style deep-dish pizza, made in a pan or heavy skillet, was reportedly first made at the Numero Uno Pizzeria in that city.

FOR THE CRUST

1½ cups (12 fl oz/375 ml) milk
6 tablespoons (3 oz/90 g) unsalted butter
2 tablespoons plus 1 teaspoon dry yeast
¼ cup (2 fl oz/60 ml) lukewarm water
2 tablespoons sugar
1 teaspoon salt
⅓ cup (2 oz/60 g) yellow cornmeal
3 eggs, beaten
5 cups (1¼ lb/625 g) all-purpose (plain) flour (approximately)

FOR THE TOMATO SAUCE

2 tablespoons (1 oz/30 g) unsalted butter
1 onion, finely chopped
2 garlic cloves, minced
2½ lb (1.25 kg) canned plum (egg) tomatoes
½ cup (4 fl oz/125 ml) tomato sauce (pureed tomatoes)
2 teaspoons sugar
2 teaspoons chopped fresh basil or ½ teaspoon dried basil
¼ cup chopped Italian parsley
1 teaspoon dried oregano
2 teaspoons salt
½ teaspoon freshly ground pepper
¼ teaspoon freshly grated nutmeg
⅛ teaspoon ground allspice

FOR THE FINAL ASSEMBLY

1½ lb (750 g) mild Italian sausage (fennel-flavored sausage)
1½ lb (750 g) mozzarella cheese, half thinly sliced and half shredded
⅓ cup (1½ oz/45 g) freshly grated Parmesan cheese

❦ First, make the crust. Scald the milk in a saucepan over medium heat and add the butter by bits. When the butter melts, allow the mixture to cool to lukewarm.

❦ Combine the yeast, lukewarm water and sugar in a small bowl. Let stand for 10 minutes.

❦ Pour the lukewarm milk into a large bowl. Stir in the yeast mixture, salt, cornmeal, eggs and 3 cups (12 oz/375 g) of the

flour. Stir until smooth; add enough extra flour to make a sticky dough, about 1½ cups (6 oz/185 g). Scrape onto a floured board and knead for 15 minutes, adding more flour if needed. Place the dough in a lightly greased bowl, turning to coat. Cover with plastic wrap, then a heavy towel. Let rise in a warm place until doubled in volume, about 1½ hours.

❦ Punch down the dough. Cover and let rise until doubled in volume, about 1½ hours.

❦ Meanwhile, make the tomato sauce. Melt the butter in a heavy saucepan over medium-low heat. Add the onion; cook for 1 minute. Add the garlic; cook 4 minutes longer. Stir in the remaining ingredients for the sauce. Heat to boiling, reduce the heat and cook, uncovered, over low heat until very thick, about 1½ hours.

❦ Preheat the oven to 400°F (200°C). Lightly grease two 9-in (23-cm) round pans about 2 in (5 cm) deep. Divide the dough in half; roll each half into a 10½-in (27-cm) circle. Line each pan with dough and press over the bottom and slightly more than halfway up the sides.

❦ For the final assembly, sauté the sausages in an oil-rubbed skillet over medium heat until browned. Cover the skillet and cook, shaking the pan frequently, for 5 minutes. Drain the sausages and cut into slices ½ in (1 cm) thick.

❦ Place the sliced mozzarella over the bottom of each crust. Spread half the tomato sauce over the cheese in each pan. Then place half the sausages over each. Sprinkle with the shredded mozzarella and Parmesan cheeses and bake until crisp and golden, about 25 minutes. Let stand for 5 minutes before slicing.

SERVES 8

Utah

ROAST BEEF HASH

In its simplest form, hash (from the French hacher, *meaning "to chop") is nothing more than cut-up cooked meat or fish warmed in a creamy gravy or sauce. However, most American hashes include vegetables because it was traditional to throw the leftovers from the last night's meal into the pan for the next day's breakfast. The following recipe is reputed to be the handiwork of one of the many wives of Brigham Young, the great Mormon leader who brought the faithful west in 1847.*

2½ tablespoons (1½ oz/50 g) unsalted butter
1 onion, chopped
1 large garlic clove, minced
½ green bell pepper (capsicum), seeded and finely chopped
1 small celery stalk, finely chopped
2 potatoes, cut into ½-in (1-cm) cubes
2 cups (12 oz/375 g) chopped cooked roast beef
½ teaspoon dried red pepper (chili) flakes, crushed
⅓ to ½ cup (3–4 fl oz/80–125 ml) beef stock (see glossary)
½ teaspoon Worcestershire sauce
½ teaspoon salt
¼ teaspoon freshly ground pepper
pinch of ground allspice
2 teaspoons cider vinegar
chopped fresh parsley (optional)

❦ Melt the butter in a large cast-iron skillet over medium-low heat. Add the onion; cook for 1 minute. Add the garlic; cook 4 minutes longer. Add the bell pepper and celery and cook another 5 minutes.

❦ Slowly stir the potatoes and roast beef into the vegetable mixture. Add the pepper flakes, ⅓ cup (3 fl oz/80 ml) stock, Worcestershire sauce, salt, pepper and allspice. Mix well. Cook, uncovered, tossing occasionally, for 30 minutes. Add more stock if the mixture seems too dry.

❦ Preheat the oven to 325°F (165°C). Transfer the skillet to the oven and bake for 30 minutes.

CREAMED CHIPPED BEEF ON BAKED POTATOES (top) AND ROAST BEEF HASH (bottom)

🍎 Preheat the broiler (griller). Sprinkle the hash with the vinegar and place under the broiler until very crisp. Sprinkle with parsley.

SERVES 4 TO 6

Ohio

CREAMED CHIPPED BEEF ON BAKED POTATOES

Dried chipped beef is considered an oddity today, at least outside army mess halls, but was extremely popular earlier in this century. When served in the following manner, chipped beef can make the most satisfying breakfast, brunch or Sunday supper meal.

4 large baking potatoes
6 oz (185 g) dried chipped beef
¾ cup (6 fl oz/180 ml) boiling water
½ cup (4 oz/125 g) unsalted butter
2 tablespoons minced onion or shallot
¼ cup (1 oz/30 g) all-purpose (plain) flour

1 cup (8 fl oz/250 ml) hot chicken stock (see glossary)
¾ cup (6 fl oz/180 ml) cream
½ teaspoon Dijon mustard
¼ teaspoon ground ginger
dash of hot red pepper (Tabasco) sauce
2 tablespoons dry sherry
chopped fresh parsley (optional)

🍎 Preheat the oven to 400°F (200°C). Bake the potatoes until tender, about 1 hour.
🍎 Meanwhile, cover the chipped beef with boiling water; let stand for 5 minutes. Drain and coarsely chop.
🍎 Melt half of the butter in a large saucepan over medium heat. Add the onion; cook until barely golden, about 5 minutes. Stir in the flour and cook, stirring, for 2 minutes. Whisk in the hot stock; cook, stirring constantly, until the sauce begins to thicken. Stir in the beef, cream, mustard, ginger, hot pepper sauce and sherry. (The sauce should have a velvety consistency; if it is too thick, thin with a little milk.)
🍎 Cut the baked potatoes in half lengthwise. Fluff the centers with a fork and dot with the remaining butter. Spoon the creamed chipped beef onto each half. Sprinkle with chopped parsley.

SERVES 4

GLOSSARY

BEANS: The common bean (French, kidney, navy, pea, Great Northern, pinto, pink, black, snap), a native of the Americas, is extremely versatile. The immature pods of the common bean are eaten fresh in their pods as snap, string or green beans, while the mature beans are shelled and dried for easy storage. The broad or fava bean, a native of Europe, is an important crop worldwide except in the United States and Canada. It is eaten fresh or dried. Unless very young, broad beans must be peeled before they are cooked. The black-eyed pea, or cowpea, is in fact a bean native to Africa and is used throughout the southern United States, Africa, India and Southeast Asia. It is available frozen or dried in the United States. Lima beans, or butter beans, originated in Peru and are eaten fresh when young (available frozen in the United States), or dried when mature.

BUTTER: Unsalted, or "sweet," butter is recommended for use in cooking because it is inevitably fresher than the salted variety. Unsalted butter may be frozen for long-keeping.

CHEESE: America produces some top-quality blue cheeses, excellent mild to tangy goat cheeses and outstanding Cheddars, although most are to be found only in specialty shops. Monterey Jack, first produced by Spanish monks in California, is a mild melting cheese often used in southwestern cuisine. Monterey Jack is related to American (very mild) Muenster, though Muenster cheese in other countries is decidedly more pungent. Any young, mild melting cheese may be substituted. Imported Parmesan cheese from Italy is available in most towns and cities across the United States, as are most great European cheeses. If only the domestic variety of Parmesan is available, do not buy the pregrated packaged stuff.

CHILI POWDER: In the Southwest, ground dried chilies ranging from mild to hot are common. They are only recently becoming available outside that area. Most commercially packaged "chili" powders contain not only ground chilies but powdered onion, garlic, cumin, oregano, cloves and cilantro (coriander) and therefore should be used with discretion.

CHILI SAUCE: Prepared chili sauce is a mildly spicy, thick, tomato-ketchup-like sauce commercially produced in the United States. The taste can be approximated by adding sautéed onions to tomato ketchup with a splash of vinegar to cut the sweetness and a dash of chili powder and cloves or allspice to zip up the flavor.

CHORIZO: *Chorizos* are spicy cured and dried sausages used in Spanish-style dishes from New York and Florida to California. These sausages are called *chaurice* in Louisiana.

CORNMEAL: Cornmeal, ground dried yellow or white corn kernels, is processed in two ways: stone ground and enriched-degerminated. Stone ground contains more of the grains' natural richness, although both varieties are fortified to meet U.S. standards. Fine-ground cornmeal, used in some Spanish-American recipes, is available in the specialty sections of many supermarkets.

CREAM: "Cream" as called for in this book refers to cream that contains not less than 36 percent butterfat. This type of cream is marketed as "heavy" or "whipping" cream in the United States. Cream labeled "light" or "half and half" (half milk/half cream) contains anywhere between 18 and 30 percent butterfat and is referred to as "single cream" elsewhere. Many American products are overpasteurized ("ultra pasteurized") and contain stabilizers and emulsifiers as well. High-quality cream with a good butterfat content may still be found, however, at some specialty stores and dairy centers.

EGGS: The recipes in this book use "large" eggs except where noted. Since sizes vary throughout the land, 2 large eggs, as used in this book, equal about 3 fluid ounces or 100 grams.

FILÉ POWDER: Filé powder, the crushed dried leaves of the sassafras shrub, is used mainly in the South. It should be added only after a dish is completely cooked or it will turn stringy in the pot. Sassafras, used in tea and root beer, was one of America's first exports to England.

FISH

Catfish: Catfish, an important freshwater fish in the South and Midwest, has a sweet, though sometimes muddy, taste. There are many varieties in the United States, but the channel catfish is the variety most often raised on fish farms. The Wels, or sheatfish, the largest of all catfish, can be found in European rivers, notably the Danube, Elbe, Vistula and Oder. The estuary catfish lives in the estuaries and sandy bays of inshore Australian waters. The pungas catfish swims in many Asian rivers, and the silond is highly regarded along the Ganges.

Codfish: Cod has long been one of the most important food fish of the Atlantic waters both in Europe and America. It is a member of the family that includes haddock, pollock, hake and cusk.

Flounder: Flounder (petrale, rex, fluke, plaice) are a firm-fleshed flatfish family that is related to halibut, brill, lemon sole, dabs, sole, turbot, bream and sunfish (the latter two being freshwater fish found in American streams and France's Seine River).

Lake trout: Lake trout are actually chars and belong to the salmon family. They are found in deep cold-water lakes in the northern United States, Canada and Europe. The *omble chevalier* from Swiss, Italian and French lakes is considered the finest in flavor.

Pompano: The pompano is a flatfish native to the waters off Florida and the West Indies and is often prepared like any flatfish. Its taste has been described as nutty, somewhere between salmon and turbot.

Salmon: Salmon is one of the most revered of all fish and can be found in both Atlantic and Pacific waters.

Shad: Shad belongs to the herring family, and the American shad, the largest of all, is highly prized in the United States. Shad can also be found in the North Sea and Mediterranean, but only in France is shad as popular as in the States.

Smelt: Smelts, also called sparlings, are small fish related to the salmon family and are an important commercial fish crop in virtually the whole Northern Hemisphere.

Snapper: Snappers are important in Pacific regions, particularly in Australian and New Zealand waters. The red snapper of warm Atlantic waters is a firm-fleshed white fish often compared to swordfish in taste.

Swordfish: Swordfish are found in temperate waters all over the world and are most often eaten broiled or grilled in both the United States and the Mediterranean.

Trout: Members of the salmon family, trout inhabit freshwater streams the world over. The only native American trout is the rainbow trout found in western states.

Tuna: Tuna, the largest members of the mackerel family, are common to the Mediterranean, Atlantic, Pacific and Indian oceans. White-fleshed varieties such as albacore and yellowfin are preferred in the States, whereas dark-meated bluefins are popular in Asian countries.

FLOUR: Flours vary from region to region. All-purpose flour, a blend of hard and soft wheat flours, is suitable for general use in baking. Southern flours are usually soft wheat flour, known as cake flour in other parts of the country. Cake flour often contains baking powder and salt and is labeled "self-rising." Whole wheat flour (graham flour) is made from the entire wheat kernel and has a higher gluten content than all-purpose cake flour. Bread flour, sometimes called hard wheat flour, has the highest gluten content of all.

HAM: Ham is the smoked and cured upper part of a pig's hind leg, although fresh pork shoulder and butt are often sold as "fresh" ham in the United States. Small rolled processed hams are sometimes labeled "porkette." Aside from canned ham of varying quality, there are regional hams produced in parts of Vermont, Tennessee, Virginia and elsewhere that have gained worldwide attention. Since hams are sold cooked and uncooked, it is important to know which kind one is purchasing. Some salt-cured hams should be soaked overnight in water before cooking.

HERBS: Fresh dill and parsley are available year round and are best used fresh. Cilantro, it should be noted, also travels under the names fresh coriander and Chinese parsley and is used extensively in southwestern cooking. Substituting dried herbs for fresh is a matter of taste. From one-third to one-half the amount of fresh is usually more than sufficient for the dried amount, depending on freshness. To perk up dried herbs, chop them with fresh parsley.

HOMINY: Hominy is swollen corn kernels that have been hulled and degerminated; it is available canned, frozen or dried. Native Americans and early settlers used wood ash to swell the corn, but lye is most often used today. Hominy grits are dried hulled corn kernels (generally hulled these days using a steaming process rather than lye) that are ground into various degrees of smoothness. Coarsely ground hominy is sometimes called pearl hominy.

LETTUCE: Many of the lettuces available around the world are grown in America, including the Italian red lettuce *radicchio*. The main types of lettuce grown in the United States are head lettuce, including Boston, bibb, butterhead and the ubiquitous iceberg; leaf lettuce; and Romaine or Cos lettuce. Iceberg, far inferior to other lettuces in a salad bowl, is shredded as a garnish in southwestern cuisine because of its crispness.

MUSHROOMS: The common mushroom is still the most available mushroom in American supermarkets, but in large cities wild mushrooms are gaining a strong foothold in gourmet groceries. It is interesting to note that the flavorful shiitake mushroom, essential to Asian cuisines, is becoming an important commercial crop in the United States.

MUSTARD: Dijon mustard refers to the so-called Dijon-style mustard produced in the United States, as opposed to the "ball park" yellow variety. Any good imported mustard may be substituted.

OILS: Vegetable oils, made from corn and other products, are generally bland-tasting and may be used for sautéeing or baking. The relatively small amount of olive oil that California produces is generally first-rate, but most virgin and extra-virgin olive oils are imported from Italy and Spain.

OYSTER CRACKERS: These are small, puffy, round yeast crackers that are invariably served with chowders. They are sometimes called Trenton crackers in the eastern United States in honor of the New Jersey town where they were first made in 1848.

PEPPERS: A wide variety of hot peppers is available both fresh and dried; for information on them, see the chapter on the Southwest (page 138). Hot peppers are also dried and crushed and sold commercially as "red pepper flakes" and turned into hot pepper sauce, the most famous of which is Tabasco, which is available outside the United States as well.

RICE: Most rice eaten in this country is white long-grain rice. The uniquely American aromatic rices such as Popcorn, Wild Pecan, Texmati, Calmati and Wehani are all variations of Della rice, which is thought to be a strain of Indochinese and Indonesian rices grafted onto long-grain rootstocks. Soil and climate play a large role in the distinct flavors of these rices.

SALT: While finely processed, iodized salt remains popular because it is easily incorporated into foods, more and more Americans are turning to coarse salts such as kosher, crystal or sea salt. The advantage of these salts in health-conscious America is that less is needed to flavor foods. The disadvantage is that they do not contain added iodine, essential in diets that are iodine deficient.

SHALLOTS: Shallots belong to the lily family, as do onions and garlic. Shallots, larger than garlic cloves, are milder than onions and have a delicate garlicky flavor. Green (spring) onions or scallions are often erroneously called shallots in other parts of the world, notably Australia.

SHELLFISH

Abalone: A mollusk found in California, abalone is known as muttonfish in Australia, *awabi* in Japan and *loco* in South America.

Clams, Oysters, Scallops, Mussels: Clams, oysters and scallops exist in all parts of the world. Mussels are plentiful on both U.S. coasts and in Europe, where they are more popular than in America.

Crayfish: These freshwater crustaceans, resembling small lobsters, are found in all parts of the world. Called crawfish in the American South, they are equally popular in France. The spiny lobster is erroneously called crayfish in Australia and South Africa.

Lobster: European lobsters are found from Norway to the Mediterranean. American lobsters, the larger of the two, range from Labrador to Cape Hatteras. Spiny lobsters, clawless crustaceans that frequent warmer waters, are not as flavorful as true lobsters.

Shrimp: Shrimp, or prawns, are by far the favorite shellfish in America. There are hundreds of species worldwide.

SHORTENING: Solid vegetable shortenings are used mainly for baking and deep-fat frying. Lard, or hog fat, was extensively used until about 1950, when health concerns were first raised. Many cooks still prefer lard, particularly in pastry crust, but use it with somewhat more discretion.

SQUASH: In America squash are usually divided into two categories: winter and summer. Winter squash, which include the pumpkin, butternut, hubbard and acorn, are classified as pumpkins in some countries. Summer squashes include the yellow or orange crookneck, the turban, spaghetti squash, pattypan and, of course, zucchini. Summer squashes are referred to as vegetable marrow in many countries.

STEAK SAUCE: "Steak sauce" is a thick, spicy, dark brown sauce used to flavor meat dishes or served as a condiment with hamburgers and steak. The most readily available steak sauce is Brand's A.1. (of England) which includes tomato paste, vinegar, corn syrup, raisins, orange peel and spices in its ingredients list.

STOCKS: Canned broth may be substituted for stock in most recipes, but it should be used with discretion because most of these products are notoriously salty. Frozen stock, available in certain parts of the country, is far preferable. Homemade stocks, however, are easy to make and can be frozen for future use.

To make beef stock: Roast 4 lb (2 kg) raw beef bones (with some meat on them) in a 450°F (230°C) oven in a roasting pan for 30 minutes, turning once. Place the bones in a large pot or stock pot and add 3 chopped onions, 3 chopped carrots, 3 chopped celery stalks, 2 garlic cloves, 6 parsley sprigs, 1 bay leaf, 3 whole cloves, 8 black peppercorns and 1 teaspoon salt. Discard the fat from the roasting pan and deglaze the pan with 2 cups hot water. Add to the stock, along with 3 qt (3 l) water. Heat to boiling and *simmer,* partially covered, skimming the surface occasionally, for 2 hours. Add 2 tablespoons red wine vinegar and simmer about 1½ hours longer, or until reduced to about 1½ qt (1.5 l). Strain.

To make chicken stock: Place 4 lb (2 kg) chicken pieces (backs, wings, necks) in a large pot or stock pot and add 4 qt (4 l) water or more to cover chicken. Heat to boiling and boil 5 minutes, skimming the surface. Add 2 unpeeled onions, 1 chopped leek, 2 garlic cloves, 2 chopped carrots, 2 chopped celery stalks, 2 chopped turnips, 2 chopped parsnips, 8 sprigs parsley, 4 whole cloves, 8 black peppercorns, 1 teaspoon salt, 1 bay leaf, ½ teaspoon dried thyme leaves and 2 tablespoons red wine vinegar. Heat to boiling and *simmer,* partially covered, skimming the surface occasionally, about 4½ hours, or until reduced to about 1½ qt (1.5 l). Strain.

To make fish stock: Place 3 lb (1.5 kg) fish bones, including heads, in a large heavy pot or stock pot. Add 1½ qt (1.5 l) water, 2 cups dry white wine, 3 cups bottled clam juice, 2 chopped onions, 2 chopped celery stalks with leaves, 6 parsley sprigs, 1 bay leaf, 4 whole cloves, 8 black peppercorns, 1 teaspoon salt and 1 halved lemon. Heat to boiling and *simmer,* partially covered, 1½ to 2 hours, or until reduced to about 1½ qt (1.5 l). Strain.

TOMATO SAUCE: American canned tomato sauce is a smooth, bland sauce, somewhat on the thin side. Although these sauces are mildly seasoned with spices, pureed fresh tomatoes may be substituted in most recipes.

UTENSILS: American cooking requires no special equipment. Cast-iron skillets, which have been in use since colonial days, are still favored by many cooks and, more often than not, are passed down from generation to generation. Large pots or Dutch ovens should be noncorrosive for multiple use; enamel over cast iron is common in many kitchens. Stainless steel is also popular for all sizes of pots and pans. Dutch ovens were initially cast-iron kettles that the early colonists hung over smoldering embers to create an "oven" effect. These days, the name is applied to any large, heavy pot with a tight-fitting lid that can go from stovetop to oven.

ACKNOWLEDGMENTS

First and foremost I wish to thank Beverley Barnes and Jane Fraser of Weldon Owen Inc. for their support and faith. Thanks also to Virginia Croft, who had the not-so-easy task of converting American weights and measures into metrics. I am also grateful to food authority and writer Nao Hauser, whose comments on the manuscript were invaluable. I owe a large dept of gratitude to all the people around the country that I was fortunate to meet in my many travels during my long association with the late, beloved food writer and teacher Bert Greene. Without their generous bequests of family recipes that Bert and I collected and tested over the years, this book would not have been possible.

Phillip S. Schulz

The Publishers would like to thank the following people and organizations for their assistance in the preparation of this book:

Beverley Barnes, Dana Morgan, Laurie Wertz, Rosemary Wilkinson, Jacki Passmore, Katherine Stimson, Vida Merwin, Tom Morgan, Sanny Himawan, David Carriere.

Sandra Griswold; William R. Peabody, Tiffany & Co.; Williams-Sonoma Inc.; Sue Fisher King, San Francisco; Mr. & Mrs. J. Van Lott; Claire's Antique Linen & Gifts, San Francisco; Dillingham & Company, dealers in English Antiques, San Francisco; Villeroy & Boch Tableware; Fillamento, San Francisco; Willmann Antique Pine Imports, San Francisco; Judy Goldsmith; Bernie Carrasco; Cottonwood, San Francisco; Ed Hardy, San Francisco; Santa Fe, San Francisco; Upstairs Downstairs, San Francisco; The Ames Gallery of American Folk Art, Berkeley; The Bombay Company; Beaver Bros. Antiques, San Francisco; Martin & Beatrice Glenn; Nancy Glenn & Ward Finer; Deak International; Missy Hamilton; Stephanie Greenleigh; Cookin, San Francisco; Merwa Oerberst; Little Joes, San Francisco; Naomi's Antiques, San Francisco; Dan Pogrelis; J. Goldsmith Antiques, San Francisco; Eileen West at Home, San Francisco; Shawn Harris; S. B.

INDEX